T0305225

Detecting Fraud in Organizations

Founded in 1807, John Wiley & Sons is the oldest independent publishing company in the United States. With offices in North America, Europe, Asia, and Australia, Wiley is globally committed to developing and marketing print and electronic products and services for our customers' professional and personal knowledge and understanding.

The Wiley Corporate F&A series provides information, tools, and insights to corporate professionals responsible for issues affecting the profitability of their company, from accounting and finance to internal controls and performance management.

Detecting Fraud in Organizations

Techniques, Tools, and Resources

JOSEPH R. PETRUCELLI

WILEY

John Wiley & Sons, Inc.

Library of Congress Cataloging-in-Publication Data:

Petrucelli, Joseph R., 1960–
   Detecting fraud in organizations : techniques, tools, and resources / Joseph R. Petrucelli.
      p. cm. — (Wiley corporate F&A series)
   Includes bibliographical references and index.
   ISBN 978-1-118-10314-2 (cloth) — ISBN 978-1-118-22392-5 (ePDF)
   ISBN 978-1-118-26218-4 (Mobi) — ISBN 978-1-118-23735-9 (ePub)
   ISBN 978-1-118-55597-2 (O-BK)
   1. Commercial crimes—United States. 2. Corporations—
   Corrupt practices—United States. 3. Fraud investigation. I. Title.
   HV6769.P48 2013
   658.4'73—dc23

                         2012034377

Contents

Preface

I N WRITING THIS BOOK, MY goal was to keep the subject matter as simple and straightforward as possible. This book is designed to get you thinking about fraud from a new perspective, with a focus on people and proactive thinking.

When people in organizations put their own self-interest (greed) above the interests of others, it creates an atmosphere conducive to fraud. The FBI's fiscal year 2010–2011 *Financial Crimes Report to the Public* states that "corporate fraud matters involving self-dealing by corporate executives, particularly utilizing companies to perpetrate large-scale, high-yield fraud schemes, continue to be an issue of concern."* The focus of this book is the people in today's organizations and identifying how and where the value in those organizations is exposed to fraud.

I have spent more than 30 years in the accounting field in various positions. From my experiences and observations, I have learned that fraudsters ultimately give themselves away, through guilt, stupidity, or the obvious dissipation of assets. I have seen fraud perpetrated by the most unlikely person as well as by the most likely person in an organization. I have seen fraud in government, in private and public organizations, and domestically and internationally. One common theme has permeated my experiences of dealing with fraud: *people* are involved. As long as there are *people* with an *access* to something of *value*, the need to combat fraud will exist.

My mission in writing this book was to make learning about fraud both fun and easy. I express my concerns through cartoons, pictures, and humor. I reinforce the importance of developing the proper ethical tone with the people in your organization, from top to bottom. I hope the book will challenge you by continually posing questions and offering you brainstorming opportunities

---

* Federal Bureau of Investigation, "Financial Crimes Report to the Public: Fiscal Years 2010– 2011 (October 1, 2009–September 30, 2011)," http://www.fbi.gov/stats-services/publications/financial-crimes-report-2010-2011.

to solve multiple one-minute mysteries. I have included motivational quotes to help you maintain a positive attitude while getting through the sometimes grueling efforts and endless documents required to establish intent.

Remember that numbers don't lie, people do. My hope is that after reading this book, you will see beyond the numbers and learn the importance of transparent and open communication with the people involved in various organizational processes. It is important to maintain independent and ethical judgments when you are called on to deal with the often gray areas that can arise in an organizational process. I believe that an 800-pound friendly gorilla awareness of fraud can aid in detecting, deterring, and preventing it. The only way to accomplish this is through the development of ethical people in organizations in order to maintain proactive rather than reactive thinking.

Acknowledgments

WHENEVER YOU ACCOMPLISH A DREAM, it is possible only with a supporting cast. I would like to thank Mike Breon. I'm glad we had that first Jack and Diet Coke, and I appreciate all your initial input on the ideas for what would become this book.

I also want to thank Cheryl Hyder. What can I say, aside from the fact that having the same birthday makes us complement each other in all aspects of our professions. Thanks for your support and your contributions to this book.

I also want to thank James Lee for your incredible artistic contribution. Your artwork helped to shape my vision and give the book its perspective and personality.

Thank you to Brien Jones from the National Association of Certified Valuation Analysts for your continual support for this book.

Thanks to Jennifer MacDonald, Kimberly Monroe-Hill, Judith Antonelli, Judith Howarth, Brandon Dust, and John DeRemigis at John Wiley & Sons for believing in this project and for dealing with the twists and turns we encountered. Jen, I promise to "mind dump" less next time! John, I told you "I think I can" and managed to get the book done! Thanks for sticking with me and believing in me.

Thank you to my partners, Tim Piotrowski and Kevin Duffy, for your continual support and friendship and for being a big part of this book. I greatly appreciate all of your insight and input. We truly are the Three Musketeers! I want to thank our staff at PP&D Accounting: Lynn, Ian, Joey, Nicole, Matt, and Lauren. Your loyalty, integrity, and commitment to our firm have brought insight and energy into our business. I thank you for being a big part of getting this book done, too.

Thanks to all of my students at the College of Staten Island for challenging me every day and giving me the opportunity to make a difference in your lives and help you develop into professional accountants. To the Business

Department at the College of Staten Island, thank you for your support and for allowing me to help create our Forensic Accounting Introduction course. Special thanks to Loretta, for believing in me, and to Professor Thomas Tellefsen.

To Professor Patricia Galletta, I thank you for taking the time to review the copyedited manuscript and your input. I appreciate your support and perspective not only in helping with this book but also as a colleague and friend at the College of Staten Island.

To Timothy G. Little, Esq., partner at Katten Muchin Rosenman, LLP. Tim, next to my family, you are one of my oldest relationships. It has spanned from being soccer teammates in grammar school to our current adult life. You are one of the smartest individuals I know, and I appreciate your taking the time to review the copyedited manuscript and provide feedback. But what I appreciate most is our lifelong friendship and the common values we share, specifically that we both live for our families.

To Sergeant Howard "Howie" Askelson, who gives me the opportunity to relive those moments when we first started our families. The expressions of love you show your children and wife make me feel as if I am looking back in time. Your ability to be an 800-pound friendly gorilla in as calming a manner as I have ever seen is a model for my 800-pound friendly gorilla spirit. Your ability to immediately take the copyedited material and make it your own amazes me. My purpose in writing the book was to capture that exact spirit. Thanks for your insight and input, but more important, the friendship we have developed.

To Robert Morrison, CPA, Hodulik & Morrison PA, thank you for taking the time to review the copyedited manuscript and provide me valuable feedback. It is not often that professionals support each other. Thank you for the wisdom you continually share and for the friendship we enjoy. You truly are an 800-pound friendly gorilla.

Thank you to my parents who taught me that I can be whatever I want to be. Mom, I think of all those times you made me read *The Little Engine That Could* and do my homework till I got it right. You taught me that practice and persistence lead to success. Dad, thanks for always encouraging me to make the most out of my life.

To my dog, Buddy, my miracle with paws: You are greatly missed.

To my brother, this is a professional book, so I cannot call you the names I would really like to. As your older brother, I learned to protect, help, and love. Everyone needs a little brother to act as the caboose and tag along. Thanks for always looking up to me and making me *feel* like a big brother.

Thanks to Spencer Rockman, my mentor, who proved to me that everything a person does is a life lesson and that life skills can be learned through soccer. Your advice over the years has been priceless. You truly are the older brother I never had.

To Rob Karabinchak, who always seems to bring me back down to earth: Thanks for the friendship and support and making me continually believe in my abilities. Rob, the numbers don't lie with integrity like yours.

To my adopted accounting daughters, Nicole DiGeso and Lauren Komar, and my adopted son, Ian Aizenberg, thanks for the continual rereading and corrections and your youthful input to this book.

Thank you to my two sons. First, to Matt, for teaching me that it's important to follow *your* dreams and not someone else's. Thanks for all of the copying and organizational help. Second, to Joey, for being himself all the time—your genuineness is amazing. You help me to look at things from a different perspective. I could never have written this book without your help. What a great gift it is to be able to fulfill a dream with my child! I can't wait to read your first book!

Thank you to my mother-in-law and father-in-law, who not only gave me the best soul mate and partner one could ask for but who have also provided continual support and love.

And finally, thank you to my wife, Angela, for your love, affection, amazing dedication to our family and continued support. Without you, this book could never have been written. I love you!

Introduction

HAVE DRAWN INSPIRATION from the many people and experiences that have shaped my career and my life, and especially from the classic children's novel *The Little Engine That Could*. The recurrent themes in that book are persistence, determination, and positive mental attitude. I truly believe that anybody can be what he or she wants to be by following the little train's creed of "I think I can!"

I challenge you to become sufficiently self-aware by reflecting on the key events and influences that define *you* as both a professional and a person. This quest should lead to a greater insight into yourself, your ethics, and the many people who have influenced your character and who you are. Knowing yourself well and believing in yourself will inevitably assist you in learning to detect, deter, and prevent fraud.

 ## THE 800-POUND FRIENDLY GORILLA

The "800-pound gorilla" is a concept often used to describe a person or an organization so powerful that it can act without regard for the rights of others or established principles and rules.[1] In this book, we are going to adapt this

1

metaphor for a more positive concept. The 800-pound gorilla in this book is friendly and promotes the interests of the organization in a positive manner. He or she generates effective communication with all of the people in an organization in a friendly, proactive way.

The 800-pound friendly gorilla has power, but his or her job is to ensure that people in the organization follow the rules. Our gorilla uses his or her power to ensure not only that people obey the organization's principles and rules but also that the organization does not infringe on the rights of others and that it maintains open channels of communication. If someone commits fraud, for instance, the gorilla will not be happy, but he or she will try to understand why it took place and learn from it.

Throughout the book you will see that organizations need more than one 800-pound friendly gorilla to combat fraud. Organizations need to create a spirit that helps to develop a workforce full of 800-pound friendly gorillas. Whether investigating a potential fraud, or detecting, deterring, or preventing fraud, the 800-pound friendly gorilla seeks to understand the people in the organization in a calm, rational, and friendly manner. Start to think of who the potential 800-pound friendly gorillas are in your organization.

Organizations worldwide lose an estimated 5 percent of revenue to occupational fraud each year, according to the reports of the Association of Certified Fraud Examiners (ACFE). As a result of my professional experience, I believe the number is much higher because many frauds are not included in the ACFE estimate because of bankruptcy, failure to prosecute, insurance payments, and restitutions.

Clearly, we need to detect fraud in organizations by looking beyond the numbers and developing proactive thinking about the people in organizations. Starting with the device of our 800-pound friendly gorilla, we can communicate an organization's principles, ensure that an organization tells the true story about its numbers, and discover any falsification or deception. To find where in an organization the business risk of fraud exists today and in the future, we will consider the following:

- What role should current or future technology play?
- Is using futuristic technology to identify fraud the answer?
- What role should third-party risk management consultants who develop ethics and compliance policies play?

This book suggests that fraud detection is a matter of identifying the people involved in the organizational process who can commit fraud and learning from people who have committed various types of fraud in the past. We will discuss how to think like a fraudster in the organizational process. The 800-pound friendly gorilla maintains professional skepticism (a questioning of people) and understands the importance of interviewing, performing proper background checks, and getting to know the people in an organization's processes. Our gorilla also understands where the potential fraud forces (value) exist. The key to detecting fraud in today's organizations is simply to understand where people and organizational value meet, paving the way for fraud.

 ## NUMBERS DON'T LIE, PEOPLE DO

It is true that numbers don't lie. But what most people fail to realize is that even though numbers don't lie, the people reporting them often do. Numbers can be manipulated by people who want to advance their self-interest (i.e., greed). In fact, numbers can often be manipulated so well that the average person is unable to detect the misrepresentation. A statement may be considered true when enough people believe it is true and is considered false when enough people believe it is false. Statements are perceived as true or false because of judgments *made by people.* The concepts of truth and falsehood depend on there being minds to judge a situation, and we need those minds to belong to people we can trust. Still, people will think some things are demonstrably true or false no matter what. For example, people once believed the earth was flat even though this is not true and there was evidence to prove that it is round. It is accepting "truths" at a perceived acceptable level of thinking that enables fraud to exist. Organizations should develop 800-pound friendly gorillas who think beyond accepted levels and formulate questions that challenge statements and actions involving the organization to ensure that those statements and actions are not later found to be false.

What do Enron (energy), WorldCom (telecommunications), Adelphia (cable television), Tyco (manufacturing), and Bernie Madoff (financial services) all have in common? They fell victim to greed and false numbers and were eventually destroyed by frauds conceived and committed in the C-suite (i.e., by the corporation's "chiefs," or most important senior executives: chief executive officer, chief operating officer, chief information officer, and so on). These frauds brought out the familiar refrain, "Where were the auditors?"

Each gouged its own gaping wound in the soul of the global economy, further contributing to a larger economic collapse. Revisiting any of these frauds will not solve the glaring and ongoing problem of fraud overall. But at their most basic level, fraud and other financial irregularities need people to perpetrate them, or they do not happen. Therefore, without people, there is no risk of, vulnerability to, or susceptibility to fraud.

AN OVERVIEW OF FRAUD

Fraud is an incredibly dynamic phenomenon stemming from greed and self-interest. While fraud has been around as long as people, modern fraud is exacerbated by the complexities of today's business environment. You can hardly pick up a newspaper or turn on the news without hearing about fraud. This book explores fraud from the unique perspective: the people perspective.

When you employ people, they are immersed in an environment full of fraud enablers and detractors. This book will help you to understand your employees and the fraud enablers and detractors in your organization. It is easy to become distracted by the schemes themselves or the drama associated with a potential fraud. However, it is essential to recognize that *people* are the root cause of fraud, not the enablers or the schemes themselves. Most organizations focus on the *apples* on the tree rather than the tree's *roots*. Are you looking at the roots or just the apples? Remember, an organization is a group of people who come together with a common goal. Unless all the people in the organization are rowing the boat in the same direction, fraud will be a greater threat.

Understanding the concepts in this book will help you to assess where the risk of fraud is rooted in your organization and to implement strategies to prevent some of it. The book examines business processes (e.g., the collection of cash) that will help you apply the ideas to your workplace or the specific business processes within it. I believe that this book is an essential read for everyone from the business school student to the board member, since fraud puts everyone's financial well-being in jeopardy.

The only way to minimize fraud and its impact is for everyone to understand fraud and how fraud can manifest itself in what he or she does day in and day out. It is important to create the 800-pound friendly gorilla (see Exhibit I.1) in the room to establish the sense that someone is watching but in a professional, skeptical, and friendly manner.

Detecting fraud in organizations requires an Albert Einstein level of thinking. Einstein once said, "Problems cannot be solved at the same level of thinking that created them." I believe that if you want to detect fraud, you need to replicate the thinking of the fraudsters, but you also need to break away from the traditional control- and rules-oriented thinking and start approaching fraud in a more creative manner. By using your imagination and creative thinking,

EXHIBIT I.1   The 800-Pound Friendly Gorilla

Copyright © 2012 James Lee

you can make sense of the often bizarre world of fraud. Fraud detection does not depend on highly complex formulas or theories. Deterring and detecting fraud requires people who can look at things from different perspectives, moving away from the traditional paradigms.

Widespread fraud will continue to occur until there is sufficient outrage expressed by all stakeholders in the business world that will result in a restructuring of some of the fundamental institutions and processes of business, such as how an audit is conducted. This book explains how the business community, legislators, and others have actually made perpetrating fraud easier over the years while spending a tremendous amount of time and money supposedly fixing the problem. All the fraud checklists, formulas, triangles, diamonds, and pentagons in the world will not detect or deter fraud, because people commit fraud. Most fraud is discovered through tips or whistleblowers, so you need to start from a new level of thinking that is centered around people:

- Where and when did the fraudster become predisposed to commit fraud?
- Was it before becoming part of the organization or after?
- Was his or her behavior influenced by the organization's environment?

Fraud occurs where people meet value. Value takes many forms, such as cash, inventory, copyrights, patents, and customer lists. It is essential to understand how the concept of value has changed over the years. In the past it was clear: Value resided in cash, buildings, and equipment. Now the value in many organizations resides in information. This is not a traditional value. Where does the value reside in your organization? We will explore this very important concept throughout the book.

Understanding that fraud occurs where people and value come together is the crux of many strategies to stop fraud. However, many of these strategies have simply become too focused on the actual processes of implementing the strategies. High-priced consultants are often leading the charge. But fraud is not a hard thing to find if you know what to look for—and if you are in a business of any kind, you owe it to yourself and your employer to know what fraud looks like.

Fraud is everywhere, and it is a relatively easy thing to detect if you understand where the value lies in your organization and its processes. Fraudsters will always find a way to take advantage of a given situation to perpetrate fraud. Fortunately for us, even the smartest people outsmart themselves while perpetrating fraud, which usually results in their discovery. It is not practical to think that you can ever prevent all fraud from happening. However, you can do some quite simple things to deter fraud or to identify it once it happens.

Notice that I say it is relatively easy to *detect* fraud, not *prevent* it. The most important point is that no matter how good you think your people, internal controls, and auditors are, fraud is happening in your organization, so unless you take a proactive approach, fraud will continue to exist. To conduct business, you need employees, and you must be able to trust them with things of value in order to get anything done; otherwise you would be out of business very quickly. The decision of whom you trust to conduct business on your behalf is probably one of the most important decisions you will make in business.

At this point, you may be thinking:

- "My organization does not have to worry about fraud. This is something that happens to others. We only hire honest people."

■ "I know nothing about our books because I am not a numbers person, but my bookkeeper has been here for years, and I trust him or her completely."

In my years of experience in detecting fraud, I have heard all of the excuses, and it is this type of thinking that allow fraud to exist. Unfortunately, so many of the people who once thought it could not happen to them are now out of business or have suffered extreme financial loss. Had they taken a critical look at where the people they employed came into contact with value, they might have predicted to a certain extent where fraud would be likely to occur. If you are thinking that it could not happen to you, you really need to keep reading this book, because it will probably save you a lot of money and frustration.

Enablers of Fraud

Everything in your organization, beyond the understanding that fraud actually exists, is essentially an enabler of fraud. Organizations that do not think fraud can exist do not have 800-pound friendly gorillas watching and are therefore susceptible to fraud. In this book, I discuss these enablers in great detail and show how they are embedded in various layers of an organization.

Enablers help fraudsters perpetrate and conceal fraud. An enabler can be as simple as a lax supervisor who fails to understand the importance of reviewing his or her employee's time sheet or expense reports, or it can be the use of the complexities of accounting principles to mask the true results of an organization's performance. A fraudster who creates complexity has created the necessary diversion or distraction to be able to perpetrate the simplest frauds.

An enabler can also be a false sense of safety and security established through a false pretense or a misunderstanding. For instance, people often think that a financial statement audit will detect fraud. They are mistaken. In fact, auditors go out of their way to communicate the fact that they are not responsible for the detection of fraud. The auditor or accountant statement in the body of the report purports to provide reasonable assurance, which in itself means that the financial statements are not 100 percent guaranteed to be correct. Auditors are not engaged to detect fraud, and an audit conducted in accordance with all applicable professional standards could easily miss a multimillion dollar fraud in an audit of a Fortune 500 company.

The problem is that many of these communications are addressed to the organization and its management and not to the investing public. Just because an organization has an auditor or accountant does not mean it does not have fraud. Remember, fraud is happening in every organization, large and small, even those that have been audited. The only unknown variable is *how much* fraud is actually occurring. The actual value lost to fraud is something we will never know because most fraud is never reported.

But some enablers of fraud are much simpler than accounting and auditing complexities and/or shortfalls. Probably the biggest enabler is the fact that businesspeople simply do not know what fraud looks like, because they are too busy or it does not affect them—compounded by the fact that as humans we want to trust the people around us, even when we know we shouldn't. Knowing the common enablers of fraud and how to overcome them is essential for the success of your company and your future. This book explores the potential enablers in detail and how to overcome them.

Detractors of Fraud

There are ways to reduce the likelihood and impact of fraud through detractors. The 800-pound friendly gorilla, for instance, is a detractor and can help to watch what is going on in the company.

Detractors are intended to lessen the likelihood or impact of fraud. When people think about fraud prevention, they usually think about internal controls, which are indeed essential for preventing fraud. Many times, however, small-business owners will say that internal controls are expensive and that they do not have the personnel to implement them. This concern about implementing fraud prevention is referred to as the "dreaded cost-benefit analysis." It is far from the reality. Internal controls can easily be tailored to meet the size of your organization and do not have to cost anything. The challenge is to maximize the resources you already have to limit the risk of fraud.

One of the most powerful controls is simply for owners and managers to pay attention to detail and spend time with the employees, making them think that you (the 800-pound friendly gorilla) are watching them. Don't overlook the fact that this simple control has a significant influence on people. Knowing your people and what they are doing goes a long way in deterring fraud. This book covers detractors in detail and offers practical ways to implement them.

 THE ONE-MINUTE FRAUD MYSTERIES

When evaluating a person's role in fraud, we look at things like character and how it is developed. Perhaps a person's character was formed on the nights that Mom read him or her a bedtime story, or maybe it was formed by family dinners, friends, school experiences, religious services, television, or even a tragic event. All of these things and more can shape a person's character. What were your defining moments? What are your ethical and moral boundaries?

You may be asking, "What does this have to do with fraud?" People are shaped by their experiences and environments, and you should take this into consideration as you read this book and learn how to assess the people in your organization to work toward the detection and prevention of fraud.

There is nothing we do can do to stop fraud altogether, but creating a sense of outrage that normally emerges after the fact in the news media and transforming it into a preventative measure can create sustainable action in which businesspeople can understand the dynamics of fraud before it happens and can try to control it.

At the beginning of each chapter in this book, there is a "one-minute fraud mystery." Each mystery outlines a hypothetical situation. Using the objectives and ideas presented in that chapter, you should analyze the situation and try to determine where fraud may be present in the organization in the example. Specifically, focus on where the people meet the value. At the end of the chapter, I reveal my thoughts as a guide from my years of experience.

Approach the one-minute fraud mystery in each chapter with skepticism, almost like playing the game 20 questions. Develop questions for the individuals of interest or create a road map for understanding the organizational process that is taking place in as simple a perspective as you can. Be sure to ask questions of the individuals you believe to be the most ethical and the most likely to tell the truth, but be cautious; remember that as humans we like to trust.

As you work through the various one-minute fraud mysteries, develop questions beyond the examples given in the chapters. Use your imagination by first thinking divergently ("outside the box") and then thinking in a more convergent (critical) fashion. But, most important, always try to maintain independence, objectivity, and integrity.

Suggested Thought Processes and Questions

Here is a list of sample thought processes and questions you can use as you review the one-minute fraud mysteries:

- Develop an understanding of the organizational and individual ethical tones of the people involved.
- Identify the organizational business process being examined and the value (cash or cash-convertible) involved.

- Map out the organization, its people, and those who have access to its value.
- What are the people's jobs?
- How do the departments operate?
- What do you think about the problem the mystery is trying to exemplify?
- What is the process in the mystery?
- What accounts have the potential to be circumvented?
- What are the policies of the organization? Where are the distractions in the process?
- Where are the diversions in the process?
- Where is the division in the process?
- Who are the people of interest? The enablers? The detractors?
- Who are the responsible parties overseeing the business process
- controls?
- What are the potential overlapping responsibilities that require a segregation of duties with access to organizational value?
- When was the last time any person of interest took a vacation?
- What potential conflicts exist?
- What are the underlying assumptions?
- What skills are needed to employ or develop the fact-finding aspects of the case?
- What accounting principles and standards may have been violated?
- Have any laws been broken?
- What documentation is available to prove the case?
- What are the potential deceptions between the people and the organization?
- Where is there a clear division between the people and the organization?

These are just some of the questions you can keep in mind when reviewing the mystery in each chapter. Remember, whenever applying any level of thinking, you must also adhere to the American Institute of Certified Public Accountants (AICPA) General Standards rule 101 (independence) and rule 201 (professional competence, due professional care, adequate planning and supervision, and sufficient relevant data). Also make sure that when you are reviewing a possible fraud incident, your people can adequately answer the classic questions of who, what, where, when, why, and how.

This book encourages you to develop your own outline and decide what works best for you. There is no one way that fraud is committed, and as a result, there are multiple ways to detect, deter, and prevent it. Make sure that whatever approach you use is simple and to the point; the last thing you want is to be led on a wild-goose chase.

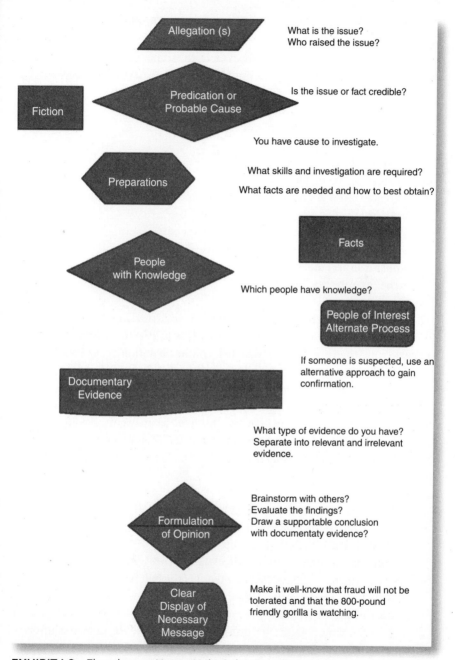

EXHIBIT I.2 Flowchart to Use to Help Solve Fraud Mysteries

Exhibit I.2 shows a flowchart you can use when formulating your findings for the mystery in each chapter.

Think of the organizational processes in the same context that the organization did when formulating its overall business plan, including the following:

- Who are the people of interest?
- What activities are being performed?
- What resources are needed?
- What are the cost centers?
- Where is the value found?
- Who are the customers? Distributors? Vendors?
- What are the potential conflicts of interest?
- What are the market segments for the business?
- What are the business's revenue streams?
- What generates the organizational goodwill (i.e., an intangible value such as the organization's good name)?

Then look at the trends and the market, industry, and macroeconomic forces in play to develop the various scenarios in the mystery. Describe the scenarios and then brainstorm them to formulate a well-documented opinion.

Basically, do not just accuse someone of fraud. Only a judge and jury can do that. As a fraud detector, you are more of a fact finder. Exhibit I.2 offers a great method for collecting the necessary ideas to solve most fraud mysteries as well as to understand where the people and the value in an organizational process meet. You need to focus on that dynamic to detect, deter, and prevent fraud.

Solving fraud can be broken down into the following simple checklist by subject:

- **Allegation.** What is the issue? Who raised it?
- **Predication.** If there is probable cause to investigate, then continue. If the allegation is only fiction, then stop.
- **Preparation.** What skills and investigation are required?
- **Facts.** What facts are needed and what is the best way to obtain them?
- **People with knowledge.** Which people have knowledge?
- **People of interest.** If someone is suspected, use an alternative approach to gain confirmation (i.e., a third-party approach so the person of interest is not clued in to the investigation).
- **Documentary evidence.** What type of evidence proves the alleged facts: documents, testimony, electronic data? Separate your evidence into two

piles: relevant and irrelevant evidence. Also maintain a chain of custody: the chronological documentation or paper trail showing the seizure, custody, control, transfer, analysis, and disposition of evidence (physical or electronic) to support your opinion and findings.

- **Formulation of an opinion.** Brainstorm with others to sort out the evidence, draw supportable conclusions, and confirm all documentary evidence.
- **Clearly display the necessary message.** Send the message that fraud will not be tolerated and that the 800-pound friendly gorilla is watching.

 ## A FEW TIPS FOR DETECTING FRAUD AS YOU BEGIN

There are a few things you should note up front to get you started in reviewing situations and events for possible fraud and in thinking differently about the who, what, when, why, and how of your business. As you delve into each chapter, you'll gain a greater understanding, but here are a few things to keep in mind.

Keep a Chain of Custody and Organized Records

A chain of custody keeps a paper trail of the documents that support a case in chronological order (i.e., as received). Maintaining a chain of custody is one of the most critical components of a fraud investigation. After the documents are put in chronological order, they should be organized by the parties they are received from (i.e., witnesses, professionals, or others).

A chain of custody helps to establish a "smoking-gun file" for easy access to the most relevant documents that support your fraud investigation findings. When you expect a large amount of documentary evidence to surface, it helps to establish an organized database early in a case. Microsoft Excel is a good program for organizing a chain of custody because it has an easy Find feature (Ctrl + F). A well-organized chain of custody allows you to provide a list of what documents you reviewed when formulating your opinion on a case.

Understand Data Analysis Queries

The steps in the following accounts payable example show the data you would analyze to detect fraud in this area of a business:

- Examine paid invoices to manually compare them with actual invoices.
- Summarize large invoices by amount, vendor, and so on.

- Identify debits to expense accounts outside the normal default accounts.
- Look for journal or correcting entries in the subsidiary or general ledgers.
- Reconcile check registers to disbursements by vendor invoice.
- Verify vendor 1099 requirements.
- Create vendor detail and summary analysis reports, which include an aging analysis to look for past-due vendor accounts, duplicate payments, and unusual or unexplained variations.
- Review recurring monthly expenses and compare to actual posted and paid invoices.
- Randomly and vendor-specifically generate reports on particular vouchers for manual audits or investigations.
- Look for conflicts of interest.
- Make sure you set up data analysis to be used in analyzing any organizational processes.

Know Whom You're Dealing With: Background Checks and Confirmations

Where permitted by law, the following checks and confirmations are useful to note when reviewing cases of fraud:

- Check the status of licensed individuals (such as certified public accountants and doctors) and entities with the appropriate boards or overseeing bodies. Remember, licenses exist to ensure that basic job requirements are met.
- Confirm addresses and Social Security numbers by using credit header searches.
- Research state and federal criminal court records and statewide criminal convictions to uncover past criminal histories.
- Obtain consumer credit reports for employee selection, retention, and promotion (making sure you get the proper authorization to pull these credit reports, of course).
- Obtain public filings such as bankruptcy filings, tax liens, and judgments to identify adverse financial matters that can serve as potential motivators for fraud.
- Check Department of Motor Vehicle driving records when a prospective or current employee drives a personally owned vehicle or an employer-owned vehicle to perform responsibilities for the employer. These types

of responsibilities may expose the employer to liability for damages if the related background information is not reviewed.

- Perform education and employment verification searches concerning employee job qualifications. Develop your own database of useful search sites for investigating fraud.

Consider Computer Fraud

Today more than ever, computers are the target of fraud. Fraud committed against computers includes computer theft, hacking or system intrusion, software piracy, and software theft. Computers can also be used to aid the fraudster in committing acts of fraud because the speed in which computers transact is so fast. Computer fraud can have extremely devastating effects on an organization. Fraud examiners should expect to commonly encounter such computer frauds as identity theft, check fraud, and counterfeiting.

Recognize Lifestyle Changes

Analyzing simple lifestyle changes can aid in the detection of fraud. For example, a person of interest has no money in the bank on January 1, but on the following December 31 he has a million dollars. We know from his job that he earned $100,000 in wages. Where did the rest of the money come from? Did he win the lottery? Did he inherit the money? Did he sell his house? What exactly is the story?

Other lifestyle changes to be on the lookout for include the following:

- Driving an expensive car
- Wearing an expensive watch or jewelry
- Going on vacations frequently
- Owning an expensive home

When a fraudster gains wealth from committing fraud, he or she will likely want to spend it, and this often leads to getting caught. Lifestyle changes are an important red flag for catching fraud.

Draw a Simple Picture

At the end of each chapter I have included a simple drawing to help you analyze each fraud mystery. These drawings can provide you with a useful approach to analyzing where fraud may be present in an organization. My cousin's daughter Lindsay provided the drawing for Chapter 1's mystery. Lindsay is a 16-year-old sophomore in high school with no experience in fraud investigation. Yet she was able to read the mystery in that chapter and express it in a simple drawing. This demonstrates how a simple drawing can make it easier to find fraud.

Because these end-of-chapter pictures are simple, they help you to figure out the whole story by bringing things back to the basics. When you are first approaching a situation in which you are reviewing a potential fraud, taking a step back to draw a simple picture of how the pieces fit together as you collect evidence can make a difference. Step back and make sure your drawing of fraud basics tells the whole story.

 ## SETUP

This book consists of eight chapters that offer you the tools and applications you need to start detecting fraud:

Chapter 1 discusses what fraud is and why it continues to happen. Understanding these topics is necessary to develop a proper foundation on which to learn how to detect, deter, and prevent fraud.

Chapter 2 questions why enhanced legislative, regulatory, and professional oversight has failed to help prevent fraud. It discusses why we need to go beyond depending on rules and develop moral and ethical spirit to combat fraud.

Chapter 3 analyzes the fraudster and discusses why people decide to commit fraud. It focuses on balancing the needs of the people in an organization with the needs of the organization itself.

Chapter 4 discusses how to think like a fraudster. It considers how a fraudster might act within an organization to perpetrate fraud. You need to think like a fraudster to catch a fraudster.

Chapter 5 analyzes the dynamics of business. It examines how everything is connected within an organizational process.

Chapter 6 talks about the accounting process. Accounting is an important topic to discuss when considering how to detect, deter, and prevent fraud.

Chapter 7 discusses cash. Following the cash in an organization is important when considering how to detect, deter, and prevent fraud.

Chapter 8 offers final thoughts that synthesize the ideas in the book. Here we introduce our POP acronym: Perspective + Occupation + Position = Fraud from the people's perspective. Remember, people commit fraud, and only people can catch fraud.

I hope you enjoy reading this book as much as I have enjoyed writing it. I think you will find it to be practical, simple, and helpful. Good luck on your journey into the world of fraud detection!

NOTE

1. "800 lb gorilla," Wikipedia, http://en.wikipedia.org/wiki/800_lb_gorilla.

CHAPTER ONE

Understanding Fraud

What Is Fraud, and Why Does It Continue to Happen?

What kind of society isn't structured on greed?
The problem of social organization is how to set
up an arrangement under which greed will do the
least harm; capitalism is that kind of a system.

—*Milton Friedman, economist*

This chapter introduces you to fraud and helps you to understand why it happens so you can develop a proper foundation on which to learn how to prevent, deter, and detect it. Fraud is first and foremost a people problem, as discussed in the Introduction. Flawed processes may support its continued existence, but processes are only part of the environment in which fraud occurs. Processes do not commit fraud, people do. This chapter does not discuss common or traditional criminological studies but instead focuses on the human element involved in analyzing fraud within an organization so we can determine what fraud is and why it continues to happen in today's organizations.

This chapter features the following:
Fraud's many definitions.
The value of informed skepticism.
How to apply critical thinking when reviewing fraud.
Discussions of confusion about responsibility and complexity.

T O BETTER UNDERSTAND THE MANY definitions of fraud, we begin our journey by learning what fraud looks like and why you need to ask many questions to gain a clear picture of the facts. You need to begin looking through a different set of eyes: not your own, but those of the fraudster.

PEOPLE ARE GREEDY—HOW GREEDY ARE YOU?

Think about the people in your organization who have access to its financial resources and the value (money or otherwise) that is at risk with informed skepticism. Make sure the facts and findings support the organization's people in trusted positions. The value of informed skepticism lies in the level of details that support your findings. This will aid you in your fraud analysis. Think divergently and develop as many potential facts as possible. Always remain objective and independent in your thinking and apply sound principles. Remember to think *people*! People are at the heart of fraud, and critical thinking should be applied to the daily organizational processes from top to bottom.

The people in the organization are the front line of fraud defense. Fraud can begin and end with them. A fraud-conscious organization should have clearly defined roles and responsibilities for all economic activities down to specific individual tasks. People in the organization cannot be allowed to create confusion about responsibility. A fraudster generally creates confusion to deflect attention from the fraud he or she is committing. People who have access to the value of an organization need to understand their trusted responsibility in order to help detect, deter, and prevent fraud. Their responsibilities must be communicated effectively by management so they understand them. The organizational process often requires various skills in order to accomplish the desired results. The lack of a full understanding of the desired results is a breeding ground for potential fraud.

To understand the complexities that exist in an organization, start with the idea that no two people think alike. This in itself requires the development of flexibility within the established principles and rules of an organization. Everything, including people, is constantly changing on a day-to-day basis. Organizations need to monitor and analyze the people in the processes on a daily basis.

This may not be practical, yet it is imperative that the organization create an environment in which its people know that monitoring and analysis is ever present. No one acknowledges the 800-pound friendly gorilla, but everyone feels its presence. The need for daily monitoring and analysis is too big a job for one person. This is why an organization needs to make sure that all of its people have the 800-pound friendly gorilla mind-set to create effective communication through a friendly rather than aggressive approach.

A successful organization needs to be firm and flexible at the same time. It is important for an organization to maintain enough strength to prevent fraud yet maintain enough flexibility to deal with its multiple complexities. The organization will need to confront the gray areas as well as conflicts that may arise on an ongoing basis by paying attention to questions such as the following:

- Has the organization set reasonable expectations and goals for the responsibilities of its people?
- Do the incentives communicated to the people in the organization maintain ethical behavior, or do they promote greed?
- Is there an opportunity for conflicts of interest to exist in the organizational process?

Management needs to maintain effective communication with its people and its processes to ensure that gray areas are addressed before they become fraud. It is important that the people in an organization understand the incentives and potential conflicts of interest in a proper context and act in accordance with the established organizational rules and principles—not their own rules and principles.

 ## ONE-MINUTE FRAUD MYSTERY: TRUST US INC.

This one-minute fraud mystery is designed to help you begin thinking divergently ("outside the box") so you learn how to develop solutions under less than ideal circumstances. Think about the situation presented here as you read the rest of the chapter.

You are the owner of Trust Us Inc. Betty Favor, one of the organization's most trusted employees, has worked there for 15 years. She socializes with you on a regular basis. Recently, you hired a young new accountant who just graduated from college with honors in accounting. This new employee, John Asset, tells Betty that the bank statement does not reflect the same bank balance as the bank reconciliation that he just prepared.[1] Previously, Betty had taken care of all banking matters and prepared the bank reconciliations. Betty comes into your office and says it appears that John does not know what he is doing because there are errors on the bank reconciliation. She states that she redid the bank reconciliation to fix the error.

Do you think Trust Us Inc. is vulnerable to fraud? If so, where is the fraud, and how was it perpetrated? What is your approach to solving this mystery?

 ## DISTINGUISHING AMONG DETERRENCE, PREVENTION, AND DETECTION

In an Associated Press article about the sentencing of former attorney Mather Kluger for insider trading, Assistant U.S. Attorney Judith Germano stated, "He had wealth, intelligence, and family support. He abused it all. Why? Because he could."[2]

Exhibit 1.1 illustrates this dynamic.

The theme of the dialogue in Exhibit 1.1 is that the strength of the 800-pound friendly gorilla in the room is not more effective than calm rationale in dealing with the club-wielding caveman. The theme of the dialogue in Exhibit 1.1 is a theme that is maintained throughout the book. The strength of the 800-pound gorilla needs to be friendly rather than imposing. The 800-pound friendly gorilla applies a relaxed, open, and transparent process, creating the necessary communication whether the fraud has already occurred or is in the process of being detected, deterred, and prevented. If the gorilla were to verbally attack the already defensive caveman, he would not get anywhere and would probably get clubbed. In this cartoon, there was no deterence and the 800-pound friendly gorilla was performing a postmortem analysis to understand the fraud. If an organization is to create 800-pound friendly gorillas, the objective is to make people feel comfortable in discussing the facts before the fraud occurs and not after the fact.

Frauds are typically simple. The role of the fraud investigator (I use fraud investigator, detector, or examiner interchangeably throughout the book) is to assist those who are determining the facts in reaching either a conclusion of fraud or no fraud. The 800-pound friendly gorilla fraud detectors can be internal auditors, external auditors, outside forensic consultants, organizational management, boards of directors, audit committees, internal or external

EXHIBIT 1.1   The 800-Pound Friendly Gorilla Interview

Gorilla: Please, Mr. Caveman, make yourself comfortable.
Caveman: Wow, you sure look strong! [*Reaches for club*].
Gorilla: That won't be necessary.
Caveman: Well, all right. [*Pulls hand back*].
Gorilla: Just want to have a conversation. I see you brought a club with you. I hope you don't intend on using it.
Caveman: Of course not.
Gorilla: So . . . how did you commit the fraud?
Caveman: I used my club.
Gorilla: So why did you commit the fraud?
Caveman: Because I could.

attorneys, or other specialzed consultants. A fraud investigator obtains sufficient and relevant information about the event or allegation to enable a judge and/or jury to reach a conclusion. The fraud investigator should not offer an opinion on whether fraud has been committed. Only a court of law may determine a person's guilt or innocence. If the fraud examiner offered an opinion that proved to be inaccurate, he or she would be vulnerable to a defamation suit.

Developing effective interview techniques is critical in creating open channels of communication in a fraud investigation. Contrary to what many may think, interviewing and interrogating are very different concepts. The mission of the 800-pound friendly gorilla is fact finding through interviewing techiques and not to make a determination of guilt. The interrogation is designed to make a deremination of guilt and is much more aggressive than our 800-pound friendly gorilla approach. What is key is to obtain the proper facts. What kind of information is necessary to understand the facts that will establish supportable findings? Think about things like what happened, where it happened, when and why it happened (although intent is difficult to determine independently), how it happened, how much was taken, who had the opportunity, who helped it to happen, and what is necessary to enable the fact finder (judge or jury) to support a final conclusion about the fraud.

An organization's goal is to make a profit. When the organization hires people, the assumption is that they will have the organization's same goals and best interests at heart. This is the start of the need for controls as the goals and best interests between organization and employee often differ.

Much has been written about what fraud is, how it occurs, what the trends are among those committing or who are trying to commit fraud, and the importance of the "tone at the top" principle when attempting to prevent the flow of fraud. Tone at the top refers to the atmosphere created by the organization's leaders in terms of ethics. If the people at the top are unethical, then the people throughout the rest of the organization are likely to be unethical as well. Antifraud programs are typically defined as deterrence, prevention, or detection tasks, but what exactly do these mean, and how are they distinguishable?

> **Fraud deterrence** refers to tasks or barriers designed to discourage those with a temptation to commit fraud from doing so. Example: the threat of imprisonment, job loss, and the fear of becoming a social outcast.
>
> **Fraud prevention** refers to methods and strategies used to prevent those not deterred from succeeding in committing a fraud. Example: requiring two signatures on checks.

Fraud detection describes the methodologies deployed to investigate allegations of fraud. It is more reactive than proactive.

The goal of a fraud investigation is to obtain sufficient and relevant information about the event or allegation to enable the fact finder (judge or jury) to arrive at a credible conclusion of whether a fraud occurred, how it occurred, and who the potential perpetrator was. Throughout the book, I emphasize that the fraud investigator's role is not to proclaim the alleged perpetrator innocent or guilty but only to develop the facts to enable a court to determine whether fraud, in fact, exists and to help the organization develop an understanding of how to prevent fraud in the future. The AICPA Code of Professional Conduct, General Standards rule 201 states that "sufficient relevant data" may be obtained "to afford a reasonable basis for conclusions or recommendations in relation to any professional services performed." This requirement is not only necessary for compliance with many organizations' professional standards, but it also establishes acceptable practices within the industry standards.

Entities that rely on reactionary postures and wait for suspicions to arise are more susceptible to fraud. Sound fraud risk policy requires that ongoing standing procedures are in place to address deterrence, prevention, and detection simultaneously with the aid of our 800-pound friendly gorilla oversight.

Unfortunately, there are no systems, procedures, policies, or other mechanisms to deploy that provide a perfect guarantee against fraud. Both good and bad economies provide motivation for the potential fraudster. As long as there are people with access to money and other items of value that belong to someone else, there will always be a risk of fraud to manage. It is the vulnerable areas within an organization that need to be exposed and understood in order to deter, prevent, and detect fraud. Proactive rather than reactive fraud management is critical in the fight against organizational fraud.

Defining Fraud

To understand the process of fraud prevention, deterrence, and detection, let's look at a sampling of relevant definitions of fraud:

■ "Deceit, trickery; *specifically*: intentional perversion of truth in order to induce another to part with something of value or to surrender a legal right. . . . An act of deceiving or misrepresenting."[3]

- "A deception deliberately practiced in order to secure unfair or unlawful gain."[4]
- "It usually consists of a misrepresentation, concealment . . . of a material fact, or at least misleading conduct. . . . It embraces all the multifarious means which human ingenuity can devise to get an advantage over another."[5]
- "Deception by misrepresentation of material facts, or silence when good faith requires expression, resulting in material damage to one who relies on it and has the right to rely on it. Simply stated, it is obtaining something of value from someone else through deceit."[6]
- "An intentional act that results in a material misstatement in financial statements that are the subject of an audit. . . . There are two types of fraud: misstatements arising from fraudulent financial reporting and misstatements arising from misappropriation of assets."[7]
- "Any intentional or deliberate act to deprive another of property or money by guile, deception or other means."[8]
- "Any illegal acts characterized by deceit, concealment or violation of trust . . . not dependent upon the application of threat of violence or of physical force . . . to obtain money, property, or services; to avoid payment or loss of services; or to secure personal or business advantage."[9]

The common theme of these definitions is that fraud occurs when there is an intentionally deceptive act that results in another party losing something of value. (The AICPA definition—the fifth one in the list—is remarkable, however, because unlike the other definitions, it is not contingent on another party's financial loss.) Intention is largely, but not exclusively, what distinguishes fraud from error. Intention needs to be aligned with motive. Fraudsters will avoid the appearance of intent by making the act appear to be an accident or a mistake. The 800-pound friendly gorilla understands the motivation driving the act.

Each of the above definitions states a necessary action to be performed. The 800-pound friendly gorilla studies the actions of the people in trusted positions in the organization to ensure proper ethical behavior. Fraud occurs when a material fact is intentionally misrepresented and a party who was known to be relying on that representation is harmed as a result. An acronym—discussed in more detail later in this chapter—that may help you to remember these elements is MIRD, which stands for *misrepresentation, intention, reliance,* and *damage.*

Fraud is instantly recognizable, yet it remains ambiguous because of the difficulty in proving intent and the underlying motive behind the action. A proactive approach to prevention and deterrence is necessary to mitigate fraud risk. Only by getting ahead of potential fraud problems will an organization maximize its shareholder value.[10] Knowing the generally accepted definitions of fraud will not stop fraud. Awareness of popular theories that attempt to explain why individuals commit fraud will do only so much to prevent or deter fraud; having our 800-pound friendly gorilla monitoring the activities and actions of the people in the organization will be effective.

The only way to manage fraud risk effectively is by identifying value within an organization and protecting that value by using a methodology or an approach specific to the organization. There is no way to definitively predict who among an organization's stakeholders (anyone with an interest in the organization, current or future) is likely to try to commit fraud, and there is no one-size-fits-all method to prevent its occurrence. Organizations are unique in terms of structure and staffing, and individuals are unique as well, so there is no uniform system that can capture each fraud before it is committed. Each organization's situation needs to be examined on its own merits, and a solution must be tailored to meet the organization's needs based on its unique characteristics and the characters involved. Einstein said, "Human beings must have action; and they will make it if they cannot find it."[11] The 800-pound friendly gorilla makes sure that people in an organization have assigned responsibilities with assigned accountability.

Classification Systems

Frauds are usually classified in terms of how they were committed. The ACFE has a model for categorizing known fraud schemes. This model is usually referred to as the "fraud tree," even though it resembles more of an organizational chart.[12] The methodology employed in Exhibit 1.2 classifies frauds primarily as involving corruption, asset misappropriation, and fraudulent statements and secondarily by the manner in which the plot is carried out.

The study of fraud—its causes and prevention—is still relatively new. ACFE's *2010 Report to the Nations* appears to be moving away from its traditional model, having refined and broadened the principal categories to include the following:

- Misrepresentation or concealment of material facts
- Bribery and extortion
- Forgery and theft (money, property, or trade secrets)
- Breaches of fiduciary duty
- Conflicts of interest
- Statutory offenses[13]

Occupational Fraud and Abuse Classification System

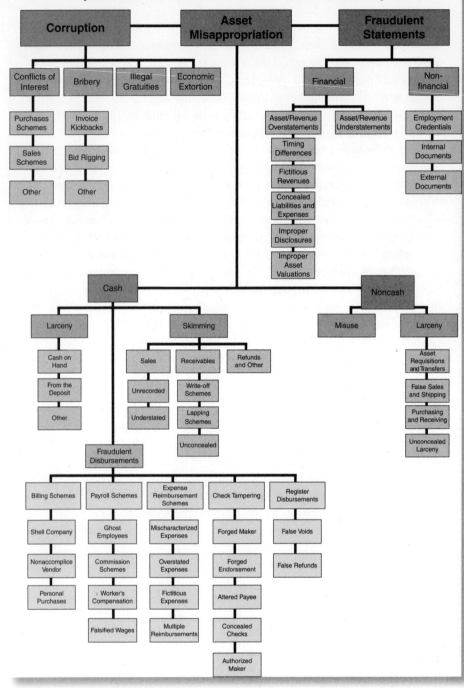

EXHIBIT 1.2 ACFE's Fraud Tree

Source: Association of Certified Fraud Examiners, *2010 Report to the Nations*

The Institute of Internal Auditors analyzes fraud by the following types of risk:

- **Financial reporting risk.** Includes not just earnings management (like overstating assets or revenues and understating liabilities or expenses) but also financial misconduct by members of the board of directors or senior management.
- **Operational risk.** Addresses obtaining revenues and assets by fraudulent means in addition to using illicit tactics to avoid incurring expenses (such as committing tax fraud to reduce tax expenses).
- **Compliance risk.** Expenditures or liabilities are incurred for improper purposes (like corrupt practices) or asset misappropriation through embezzlement of funds or other company resources.

These various types of fraud use simple stealth measures that are like a small mosquito bite, and as long as there is no interest or outrage created, they often remain undetected. Most people perceive a mosquito bite as nothing more than a nuisance, but it can spread malaria (accounting for 2 to 3 million human deaths a year) and West Nile virus with its bite. Embezzlements, unless a large dollar amount is involved, often go undetected because the organization is not watching closely enough. Often it is not until the embezzlement significantly impacts the organization that the act is brought to light, much like the effect of a mosquito bite. An organization with an 800-pound friendly gorilla has a zero-tolerance policy for fraud, so the "mosquito bites" merely remain a nuisance and do not negatively affect the organization.

Organizations will avoid fraud if they have an eye toward preventing it, rather than merely dealing with fraud when it happens. Those who do not act to prevent fraud before it happens often think that they are not likely to be victims of fraud. They ignore the possibility that fraud can happen by mistakenly relying on their auditors to find fraud, believing that their people are trustworthy, and insisting that they have insurance. But even the smallest fraud left unattended can have a devastating effect on an organization.

Why People Commit Fraud

There is no shortage of criminological studies that explain what causes individuals to choose to commit fraud. For the purposes of this book, an in-depth analysis of these theories is not necessary. Instead I offer some geometric analogies as a means of explaining fraud.

The *fraud triangle* was introduced in 1953 as part of a sociological study on embezzlement. It states that fraud is likely to occur when three elements are present:

1. **Pressure** or nonsharable need (generally financial in nature)
2. **Rationalization** (enabling an otherwise honest individual to commit a dishonest deed)
3. **Opportunity** (in terms of the skills to conduct the illicit act as well as the means or situational presence to effectuate the crime)[14]

In 2004, the *fraud diamond* expanded the triangle by maintaining the pressure and rationalization elements but separating the opportunity element into competence (or capability) and situation (weak internal controls).[15]

The *fraud pentagon* created a five-sided analysis by introducing arrogance as the fifth element of an environment at high risk for fraud. The pentagon is premised on the following:

An employee's competence or power to perform and arrogance or lack of conscience [existing alongside] the conditions generally present when fraud occurs. Competence expands on [the] element of opportunity to include an individual's ability to override internal controls and to socially control the situation to his or her advantage. Arrogance or lack of conscience is an attitude of superiority and entitlement or greed on the part of a person who believes that corporate policies and procedures simply do not personally apply.[16]

The existence of the five elements—pressure, rationalization, competence, situation, and arrogance—may lead to the commission of fraud if proper checks and balances are not in place. The main way in which an organization has direct control is by putting in place the necessary regulations and tools that the 800-pound friendly gorilla can use to detect a fraud structure. "Adept individuals with widespread access to corporate information, a mindset of entitlement, and the confidence to pull it off can compound the risk for fraud. Moreover, placing these individuals in a culturally lax environment with a poor tone at the top and weak internal controls is a recipe for disaster."[17]

These theories are by no means representative of the entire spectrum of explanations for why or how fraud occurs. They do, however, help to shape the framework for this chapter and for an analysis of the inherent vulnerabilities in business processes. From a people perspective, a *fraud tree* is more relevant

Fraud Triangle

The fraud triangle was first introduced in 1953 by Donald Cressey. The fraud triangle gave way to the fraud diamond. Notice that pressure and rationalization stay constant.

Fraud Diamond

The fraud diamond introduces the concepts of competence, (or capability) and situation. The components of capability are the position in the organization, brains, confidence, skills of coercion, and the ability to be an effective liar. Not all people are good people.

Fraud Pentagon

The fraud pentagon further expands these theories by adding another character trait, arrogance. The fraudster has to be arrogant enough to believe that he or she can go on committing frauds and be unnoticed, or simply feel that corporate policies do not apply to him or her because the person is arrogant.

The Geometric Evolution of Fraud

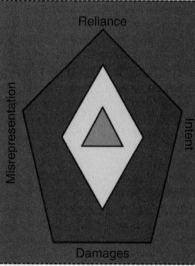

No matter how evolved our geometric fraud analogies become, the recurring theme will always remain the same. The recurring theme here is PEOPLE. Without the people factor there would be no fraud. There would be no rationalization, no opportunity, and certainly no arrogance. Anyone can be a fraudster, as we will show you. Anyone with pressure, rationalization, opportunity, or any of the other terms we have used so far have the ability to commit fraud.

EXHIBIT 1.3 The Geometric Evolution of Fraud

and useful to prevent, deter, and detect fraud than a schematic diagram that illustrates types of frauds.

Whether we use the industry-established fraud concepts listed earlier or the fraud triangle, diamond, or pentagon, there is one recurrent theme: people. Exhibit 1.3 combines the geometric theories and points toward elements that we need in order to prove fraud with supportable conclusions. The exhibit is just a guide. Each fraud is unique, and these guidelines are not intended to replace sound principles and practices acquired through experience and the continuing improvement of your skills.

Understanding what shapes the personalities of the people in your organization is a critical element in detecting, deterring, and preventing fraud. The 800-pound friendly gorilla looks at the personalities on display by the clothes people wear, the cars they drive, the jewelry they wear, and other things. Understanding the different personality traits of your people, from the board of directors to the mail clerks, will help you to shape your organization into one that is proactively addressing fraud risk. Exhibit 1.4 is an example of a fraud tree showing some of the potential perpetrators of fraud. This list is not exhaustive; anybody can be a fraudster. Exhibit 1.4 helps you think about the following questions:

- Who are the players initiating frauds?
- How are they doing it?
- What personality traits do they display?

The exhibit shows the tree's roots as the foundation (the organization) and the apples as the people creating the value through the organization's processes.

The roles and responsibilities of corporate executives should evolve with changes in the economy, technology, and the availability of information. Requiring C-suite signatures for financial statements and internal controls as a result of the Sarbanes-Oxley and Dodd-Frank legislation does not stop fraud.[18] The additional legislation and regulation typically creates more costly compliance and oversight and potential layers of distraction to the organization. The roles and interests of executives and legistors often conflict, which creates the opportuinity for fraud. Too much red tape handcuffs the organization's ability to operate and may create unethical rationalizations by the executives to meet these regulatory demands.

The money being spent on compliance with new legislation could be better invested in training the staff in an effective manner to develop and maintain fraud deterrence and prevention systems. Unfortunately, the increasing creation of external oversight acts is becoming the driving force in developing fraud risk

EXHIBIT 1.4 The People of the Fraud Tree

management programs and is replacing the development of a strong ethical and moral culture or tone within organizations. Will the next 10 or 20 years of new laws and regulations guarantee the moral character of the organization and reduce or prevent fraud? It is highly unlikely. In this book, I will continue to refer to various perspectives, such as those of legislators, CEOs, managers, and employees. Inferences must also be made. For example, say a CEO wants to avoid fraud in his organization, but what if he is the fraudster? Legislation is an effective way to set the tone in an organization, but it is not the 800-pound friendly gorilla strategy. Each organization is different, and that means its strategies will differ as well. Maybe legislation should be the motivation for top management to develop 800-pound friendly gorillas and avoid fraud at all levels, but legislation should also avoid creating too much "one-size-fits-all" red tape.

The reason legislation designed to prevent fraud fails to be effective is that it does not take into account the myriad possible organizational structures and processes where fraud could exist. A one-size-fits-all approach might satisfy the legislatures' need for a reaction to public outcry, but the resuling legislation is never a comfortable fit for all organizations. Many organizations would be better off developing an 800-pound friendly gorilla strategy for their own unique circumstances.

Think about raising kids as an example. Most parents want to raise children with proper values and to do the right thing. We teach this by developing consequences for improper behavior. As a guardian, your choice is either to tell them how to act or to actually demonstrate the proper behavior and enforce the consequences of improper behavior. This applies to organizations as well. Will the presense of laws improve an organization, or should the ethical actions of the organization mold the ethical principles of the people? We assume that the punishments are mandated by law. What are the real consequences of the laws if the situation falls in a gray area? Today's organizations need to create accountability without the reliance on laws while still ensuring that proper interests are being served.

Leading by example is more powerful than simply reciting rules. It is better to lead by example than by the "Do as I say, not as I do" approach. During the years I worked with young kids, teaching them soccer skills, my longtime mentor, Spencer Rockman, taught me that telling a six-year-old how to kick a soccer ball like an adult is not as effective as showing him or her how to kick it like a six-year-old. Successful 800-pound friendly gorillas show their people the right way to act by leading with examples they can understand. The apple does not fall far from the organizational tree. Organizational leaders (tone at the top) need to implement proper controls that limit the opportunity and situational elements that develop into fraud; they should also lead by example to help deter, detect, and prevent fraud.

THE INCREASED RISK OF FRAUD LOSS

There are common challenges in an organization that may inadvertently increase its risk of fraud loss. The hurdles an organization may face in trying to avoid fraud are innumerable, and this list is merely a starting point for dealing with such challenges, which include the following:

- The organization may not have clearly delineated markers for accountability and responsibility; therefore, it may not recognize its fiduciary obligation to reconcile line-organization responsibilities for safeguarding organizational assets with the people who have those duties.
- The organizational structure may harbor a needless complexity that fosters an environment conducive to fraud and thus creates a breeding ground for fraud.
- When facing suspicions of fraud, the organization may lack the necessary skill, education, and/or knowledge to ask the right questions and develop relevant facts in an objective manner.
- The organization may not apply divergent and critical thinking to analyze a potential fraud event when it manifests or when an allegation of fraud is presented.

Economic frauds may be committed for any number of reasons, but it always seems to come back to the individual and his or her capability and desire to commit fraud. The fraud triangle and its design speak to a perpetrator's need or ability to rationalize; however, it is not essential for fraud. Sam E. Antar, chief financial officer (CFO) of the now-defunct company Crazy Eddie Inc. and comastermind of a nearly 20-year fraud uncovered during the 1980s, openly admitted that neither he nor his coconspirators contemplated rationalizing the massive frauds that he, his uncle, and his cousin were perpetrating:

> We committed crime simply because we could. Criminologists like to analyze white collar crime in terms of the "fraud triangle"—incentive, opportunity, and rationalization. We had no rationalization. The incentive and opportunity was there, but the morality and excuses were lacking. We never had one conversation about morality during the 18 years that the fraud was going on.[19]

People are at the heart of fraud. This makes the situation more complex, because everyone is different and has different morals. There are people who are prone to doing the wrong thing because they do the right thing only when it is in their self-interest (e.g., greedy people). Changes in circumstances can cause ethical people to make poor decisions. All individuals who are facing adversity will not commit fraud, but some will.

Fraudsters like Crazy Eddie's Sam Antar demonstrate one of the key points of this book: Unless we get to know the people in an organization and understand the general how and who within the business processes, we won't be able to proactively prevent or detect fraud. The most effective fraud prevention systems are continually communicated and reinforced. An effective fraud prevention system rewards ethical behavior and has clear and undesirable consequences for those who participate in unethical behavior.

 ## DIVERGENT AND CONVERGENT THINKING

Fraud does not occur in a silo or a vacuum, and neither should its deterrence, prevention, or detection. With a divergent approach you will be able to break down an event or an allegation into its various phases and gain insight into the many aspects of fraud risk within each business process.

Divergent thinking can occur only in a spontaneous, free-flowing environment in which ideas are typically generated in a random manner. The ideas and information are then organized by applying a convergent approach (critical thinking) in which all of the spontaneous, free-flowing ideas are gathered and grouped according to similar attributes or another typology and organized in a way that enables more meaningful analysis.

This is the first step in developing a fully supportable factual position and may need to be revisited once or several times during an investigation because of the iterative nature of fraud deterrence, prevention, and detection. Sometimes fraud will not be caught on the first go-round and will require patience, persistence, and continual review. In the process you will be dealing with a lot of information. Because of this it will be useful to think divergently. We do this by continually brainstorming, keeping case notes or a journal, writing down our observations, and painting a picture (figuratively or literally).

Brainstorming

Brainstorming is a technique used to generate ideas on a particular topic or concept in an unstructured, unrestricted, and free-form manner. The goal is to generate as many ideas as possible in a short amount of time. In a successful brainstorming session, each idea stimulates other ideas. Some ideas may follow a more logical progression while others appear more random. Ground rules should be established at the outset of a brainstorming session to ensure that all of the participating members feel uninhibited in contributing to the developing ideas.

This is when you develop your initial fraud theory. All thoughts, no matter how seemingly unrelated or inarticulate, are recorded. What may seem irrelevant at the onset may later prove to be insightful. The ideas or concepts proposed during a brainstorming session are to be categorized in a logical order based on the nature of the allegations involved in order to facilitate development of the initial scope of the work.

An easy way to hone one's brainstorming skills, in this context, is to practice. Brainstorming the information at the onset of a project, possibly with management's assistance and participation, will enable you to be insightful in developing interview plans. The next time you encounter a mystery (be it in a book, a television show, or a movie), consider these questions:

- Who are the characters? What are their roles? Identify all of them no matter how insignificant they seem.
- Identify each character's motive to commit a fraud.
- Who has the most to gain?
- Which of the characters has the situational opportunity to commit the act? Who is in a position to commit the act?
- Which character has the skill set needed to commit the act?
- Based on the situation, how could each of the characters have committed the act? What could he or she know about the act?
- Based on the situation, how could each of the characters plan to conceal the act?

The point of this real-life experiment is that we are all inquisitive by nature. We observe facts (in this case, story lines and characters) and then develop theories. Because each of us has different real-life experiences that shape our perceptions, each of us will observe the same scene differently. This is why it is so important to have multiple participants in a brainstorming session and to remain open-minded to alternative explanations for how things may have occurred.

Having multiple participants in a brainstorming session, however, does not necessarily mean that the same individuals should participate in the investigation. The brainstorming session may be composed of a peer group of otherwise uninvolved professionals, and their ideas may be equally strong or even stronger precisely because of their lack of involvement in the investigation.

Keeping a Journal or Writing It Down

Record your mental impressions contemporaneously with your fact-finding investigation to track the development of your theories and findings. Carry a small memo pad at all times, since thoughts may occur to you at any time. Record your formal observations while actively analyzing the facts or conducting inquiries as well as your informal stream-of-consciousness thoughts. Written observations are more easily organized and included in a report than observations that remain intangible and unspoken. The brainstorming exercise can also be used here. While reading a mystery book or watching a mystery show or a movie, keep a sheet of paper handy and make entries as you watch.

Write down whatever comes to mind about a fraud without constraint and without stopping to worry about grammar, organization, or convention. This will ensure that a divergent mind-set is being employed. A variety of thoughts about the fraud will develop relatively quickly. The concepts developed can later be organized and critiqued to develop a logical flow and to identify and close the gaps in facts and evidence necessary to create the big picture.

A similar exercise is to write about a situation without worrying about every detail. The details are important, but they can be filled in later when you formally write up the events. This exercise develops brainstorming skills, which generally focus on the big picture. Each time there is a fact of importance, write down everything that comes to mind.

Imagine, for example, witnessing a hit-and-run accident involving a man on a motorcycle and a pedestrian fruit kiosk. Picture why someone would drive through a fruit stand—upending the cart, its produce, and the person responsible for it—and not stop. Focus on the *person*, not the mess on the street. Was he late for an appointment? Was he sick? Was he intentionally targeting the cart's handler? Was the motivation rage? Did he want to circle back and steal as much fruit as he could? Put yourself in the driver's place.

The point of the exercise is to help you develop the ability to put yourself in the shoes of the person committing the fraud and to walk through the steps he or she took to commit the fraud.

Painting a Picture

Paint the picture necessary to facilitate an understanding. Take what is in your mind about a fraud and the ideas you developed from brainstorming and visualize them to create a picture. Transfer the picture in your mind to paper so you can see the people involved. See and appreciate the relationships among the ideas, people, and events to develop an understanding of where fraud can exist in organizational processes. Start with one central idea about the fraud or fraud risk, and then draw branches from the main idea to represent different parts or aspects of the main fraud.

Now you are creating a visual image or map of the fraud that others can use to further investigate or expose the fraud or fraud risk (see Exhibit 1.5). Fraud risk represents people in the organization who deliberately use deception to gain an advantage. In either an actual fraud or the risk of fraud, you are looking at specific events or allegations that can lead to the conclusion beyond reasonable doubt of their existence.

Divergent thinking identifies issues and ideas that are later converted into relevant and provable facts through the convergent, critical thinking process. Ideas generated by divergent thinking do not commit the creator or the group to a particular position or conclusion. Divergent thinking represents a means to an end, and it is but one tool in the toolbox. Any conclusion or position requires sufficient relevant evidentiary support.

Convergent, or critical, thinking leads to documented and/or provable conclusions, in contrast to the unconstrained and free-flowing ideas generated by divergent thinking. Convergent thinking takes the investigator to a possible

EXHIBIT 1.5   Painting a Picture

conclusion and, by extension, helps him or her to identify the evidence to support that conclusion. When the evidence needed to support a fraud theory up front has been identified, an effective work plan may be developed to prove what did or did not occur. The more ideas generated, the greater the chance to resolve allegations and protect the organizational value.

An investigator cannot prove that fraud exists simply by applying divergent and convergent thinking to a situation or an allegation. The ideas generated have to be applied to the facts at hand, and a fraud theory, which is then tested, has to be developed.

Consider, for example, a hypothetical fraud that you are asked to investigate. Four of your coworkers may be involved in a potential fraud, and each of them may have several ways that he or she could have committed the fraud. Each coworker must be analyzed and asked to list related associations—such as spouses, kids, other family members, and significant others—who may have been involved. Each evaluation of a person of interest should include information about relationships and connections.

Leverage the ideas developed from brainstorming to picture the possibilities. This requires both divergent and convergent thinking. Generate as many ideas as you can in order to prevent, deter, and detect fraud in as short a time frame as possible. Did any of the four coworkers buy a new car or house recently? Did any of them go on an expensive vacation, purchase an expensive watch, or experience any life-changing events (major illness, bankruptcy, and/or divorce, etc.)? Keep your eyes open, because the signs will be there.

 ## CRITICAL THINKING REQUIRES CRITICAL QUESTIONS

What are the right critical questions? What types of questions do you think you should be asking while reading the one-minute fraud mystery and trying to work it out? The purpose of this exercise is to assist you in identifying questions to ask yourself and others as part of an antifraud project; it is not a primer on interviewing skills or even reading and interpreting body language.

There are two types of questions: general (open-ended) and specific (closed-ended). The lists below are not all-inclusive but are simply a starting point. Remember that each investigation will have different facts and require different questions. Maintaining a thinking pattern that is both divergent and convergent is necessary in developing effective questions.

General (Open-Ended) Questions

We need questions to help us develop an understanding of the players involved in a potential fraud as well as an overview of the potential fraud itself. These open-ended questions are designed to give the illusion of control to the respondent. In general, people feel more comfortable when they have the illusion of control over a situation. Therefore, a respondent who feels in control of the situation is more likely to reveal pertinent information.

The interviewer never truly releases control, however, because the inquiries that the interviewer makes will be geared to reveal specific information about a specific situation. The interviewer wants the subject of each interview to think, reflect, and give us his or her opinion. These opinions can be long, especially in response to open-ended questions. The interviewer should never interrupt. A respondent who feels comfortable will generally let his or her guard down. If there is a question about a response, or a point needs to be clarified, the interviewer should make a note and come back to it. Whether that happens immediately after the answer is provided or after all preplanned questions have been asked depends on the tone of the interview.

When possible, conduct interviews in teams of two, with one asking the questions and the other observing and recording the responses. Transcribe these notes as soon after the interview as possible to preserve the responses and memories. If the subject seems overwhelmed by having more than one interviewer, either mitigate that response in advance (i.e., explain why there are two people present) or, if the interviewer is unable to remove the discomfort, consider abandoning the team approach altogether.

In place of the team approach. you can consider using a recording device, but be sure to make the respondent aware of the fact that the interview is being recorded for reasons of accuracy, legal protection, and the avoidance of any future misinterpretations. It should be noted that in some states it is illegal to tape-record someone without his or her knowledge, so make sure you follow the applicable laws. It is important that the subject not be overwhelmed, because this can inhibit his or her responses.

The open-ended questions will often generate emotions that lead to more uninhibited information, which is the goal. This information cannot be elicited with hostile words or attitudes, so it is important that the interviewer's posture remain supportive of the subject, unbiased, and empathetic. Generally, people want to help when they are asked for help, and they may also confess to an empathetic ear when guilt sets in.

Open-ended questions have the following characteristics:

- They ask people to think and reflect.
- They often make people give their opinions and feelings.
- They hand control of the conversation over to the person being interviewed.

Open-ended questions for people with knowledge of an organization are usually asked at the onset of an investigation and include the following:

- What does the organization do?
- How does the organization treat you and your coworkers?
- Do you know why I'm here at your company talking to you?
- Do you know what's missing (e.g., cash, accounts receivable, inventory, equipment)?
- What type of problems could exist?
- Where do you think your organization is vulnerable to loss?
- Does your organization have an expectation for employee conduct? What is it?
- How do people in the organization spend their time? Are there any laggards?
- What are the employees' activities on a normal day?
- What do *you* think I should know about the organization's leaders?
- What areas of expertise are needed to perform the organizational process?
- What do *you* think I am looking for?
- What are the involved parties' hobbies?
- What are their interests?
- What bothers them?
- What do you think needs to be changed in the organization?
- What are the people in the organization's strongest beliefs, values, and philosophies?
- Who has the influence or sense of entitlement to do it? (*It* can be making changes in the company policy, committing fraud, or whatever fits into the particular situation.)
- Who do you think could have made the money or asset disappear, and why? How could he or she have done it?
- What else do you think I need to know about this problem?

Information-seeking questions are one type of open-ended question, and their purpose is self-explanatory. These are usually posed to people with information at the outset of an investigation. Here are some examples:

- What prompted you or your company to look into this?
- What are your expectations or requirements for this matter?
- What process did you go through to determine that this is necessary?
- How do you see this happening?
- What is it that you'd like to see accomplished?
- Whom have you had success with in the past?
- Whom have you had difficulties with in the past?
- Can you help me understand this situation a little better?
- What does this answer mean?
- How does the process work now?
- What challenges does the process create?
- What challenges has the process created in the past?
- What are the best things about the process?
- What other items should we discuss?

Another subset of open-ended questions is qualifying questions. These include the following:

- What do you think are the next steps?
- What is your time line for implementing the investigation?
- What other data points should we know before moving forward?
- What budget has been established for this?
- What are your thoughts?
- Who else is involved in this decision?
- What could make this no longer a priority?
- What's changed since we last talked?
- What concerns do you have?

Specific (Closed-Ended) Questions

Close-ended types of questions are used to narrow and refine the information that has been acquired through open-ended questions and other means, to form a persistent, tenacious focus.

Most interviewers prefer to develop a rapport with the subject before getting into the details with them. This portion of an interview is also used to establish credibility—both on the subject's part (why he or she is important to talk to) and the interviewer (why he or she was asked to speak to the subject). Here are some examples:

- How did you get involved in XYZ?
- What kind of challenges are you facing?
- What's the most important priority to you in this matter? Why?
- What other issues are important to you?
- What would you like to see improved?
- How do you measure that?

Closed-ended questions have the following characteristics:

- People generally find them easier to answer (yes or no).
- The interviewer controls the conversation, often utilizing a generic questionnaire.

Both open-ended and closed-ended questions are designed to yield facts. Information-seeking questions are generally open-ended, whereas confirmatory questions are usually closed-ended. Closed-ended questions are usually answered yes or no or with short answers. Interviewers typically know the answers to the questions before they ask them. Be sure to substitute the word *event* for *fraud* in all the questions.

Keep in mind that an event refers to the facts, transactions (such as source documents), and people who may be involved. Take one element at a time in the development of your supportable fact patterns and later put them together to tell the story. Additional closed-ended questions include the following:

- How would you describe the event? (This is an example of using the word *event* for *fraud*.)
- Did you see it or just hear about it?
- What are the potential causes of the event?
- What are the potential effects of the event on the organization?
- What are the most important (smoking-gun) issues about the event?
- What are the smaller issues (distractions) that caused the event?
- Has the event changed? Why are those changes important?
- What is known and unknown about the event?
- What should have been known?
- How does the event make you feel?
- What category of ideas or documents do you have about the event?
- How often do these events occur in your organization? Why?
- What suggestions or recommendations would you make about these events?

- What are the different aspects of the events that you can think of?
- Are the sales supported?
- Are there multiple bank accounts?
- Are there commission-based employees?
- Are checks ever issued to the wrong payee?
- Are there fictitious vendors (payees)?

THE PERSONALITY TRAITS OF A FRAUDSTER

Develop and identify the personality traits of potential fraudsters as you ask the questions in the preceding section. Exhibit 1.6 presents some of the personalities you may encounter as you develop your ideas to prevent, deter, and detect fraud in your organization.

A list of common traits of fraudsters with sample questions and brainstorming activities follows.

EXHIBIT 1.6 Fraud Human Traits

They are deal makers (wheeler-dealers). Do you feel like every time you speak with these people, it is like being on a game show? What is in it for the deal makers?

It's their way or the highway (dominating and controlling). Do you feel pushed or intimidated into making or supporting a bad decision? Why are the controllers so closed-minded?

They hate people reviewing their work (no oversight required!). Do you feel like you are treading on forbidden ground when you ask a relevant question about these people's work? Why are they so defensive? Are they hiding something?

Everything has to go through them (control freaks). Do you feel like these people require control over the system, or do they engage in the overrides to the controls? Why do they have a burning need to control? Are they hiding something?

Their sole desire is for personal gain (self-motivated). Do you feel like they always put themselves first at the expense of others? Is it organizational or personal gain? Are they greedy?

They are always trying to get around the system (noncompliant work-arounders). Do you sense that these people are always trying to avoid you? Whose self-interest is being served, theirs or the organization's?

They have an extended lifestyle or something else (extenders). Do you get the feeling that your colleagues who make the same salary as you have another source of income? Do they purchase a new car every year, take exotic vacations, send their kids to expensive colleges, and live in the upscale section of town? Lifestyle itself is not indicative of inappropriate conduct, but it may provide insight into someone's need for supplemental income. Legitimate explanations for the apparent excesses include inheritance, frugal lifestyle up to that point, or even generous relatives and friends. When was the last time the organization updated its background checks? Updated background checks should be performed for all employees and key contractors on a routine basis. Is this one of the most trusted employees?

They have very close relationships with customers or vendors (chummy buddies). Do you think that a particular relationship with a business associate or two is creating vulnerability for the organization? Is the relationship based on business interests, personal interests, or both? How is the value in the organization vulnerable because of such relationships? Collusion-based frauds, which involve more than one person, are likely to occur when there is a close personal relationship with vendors and clients or customers. These schemes typically include overbilling (with the refund to the inside person at the payer organization), kickbacks for influence used in obtaining business, and inventory abuse or theft.

They have close relationships with the boss (boss's pets). Do you think that these individuals have personal relationships with their immediate (or higher-level) supervisors, and do these relationship put the organization at risk? What are the relationships based on, and do they create a conflict of interest?

They can never relax or sit still (antsy). Do you think that people who cannot sit still or relax may be under undue pressure? Is it work-related or personal in nature? What is the reason?

Their work performance is off the charts (chart breakers). Do you think that there is a credible reason that these people are chronic outperformers? Is it skill based, effort based, or something else?

They are the first in and the last out (FILOs). Do you think there is a credible reason that these people are consistently the first to show and the last to go? Is it because they are overworked (and thus entitled to more), inefficient (and covering up), or conscientious? What could they be hiding?

They spend excessive time on the job (clock burners). Do you think that the jobs performed by these individuals warrant the overtime, or is there possibly an ulterior motive? Are they unsupervised, with unfettered access? Is the work product generated worth the cost?

There are frequent, dramatic changes in their behavior personalities (seesaws). Do you sense a particular trigger to these people's behavioral and personality changes (instability, substance abuse, or addictions)? Would these mood swings put the company at risk for financial loss? (Any insight derived from this line of questioning is not a substitute for consultation with a trained psychologist, when indicated.)

They appear to be completely trustworthy (trustworthy). Do you think that these people are as trustworthy outside the organization as they want you to believe they are internally? Are they too good to be believed? When was the last time you ran any background checks? As noted earlier, background checks should be performed and updated on a regular basis.

They take little or no time off (workaholics). Do you think that these people are too protective of their responsibilities (without obvious justification)? Why haven't they taken any substantial leave during their tenure? When was the last time others performed these people's duties? Many employers discover irregular activities when a "dedicated" employee is forced to take an unscheduled leave. Interdepartmental cross-training with unscheduled and periodic rotation can avoid this problem. An unavoidable consequence of that, however, is that the employees will learn extra tasks that can facilitate inappropriate conduct.

THE MORAL COMPASS

This section discusses examining your moral compass (a counterpart to the misrepresentations represented by the *M* in the MIRD acronym, which will be explained in the following section). Does your moral compass zigzag into what we call the Z pattern, or does it follow a straight line? Do you have a Z pattern in your organization? Are the people following the organization's mission and direction, or do they stray from the straight line as though forming the letter Z?

If the pattern is left unexposed, the subtle changes in people can have a significant impact on an organization. A simple example is taking home a ream of copy paper without permission. Now apply that thinking to the one-minute fraud mystery at the beginning of this chapter. Where is Betty Favor in the organizational structure? Does she have the ability to zig and zag, or does she appear to following a straight line of good moral character? Does she have control? Whom does she report to? What type of lifestyle does she have? What questions are you thinking should be asked? This is making good use of divergent thinking.

People can be slimy and are just as capable of stinging as jellyfish are (Exhibit 1.8).

THE ELEMENTS OF FRAUD: MIRD

As mentioned earlier, MIRD is a useful acronym, not just to remember the important elements of fraud's definition (*misrepresentation, intention, reliance, and damage*) but also to implement a divergent way of thinking. You can use it to understand where people and value meet in an organization and to expose the potential for fraud. Again, these are elements to help define fraud and not nessarily the ingredients needed for fraud to occur.

To analyze fraud through this acronym, start by considering what is the *misrepresentation.* How much would the facts have to be misrepresented to be

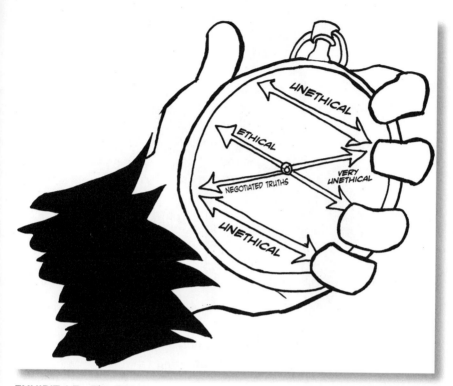

EXHIBIT 1.7 The Z Pattern

considered material?[20] The answer is clearly more qualitative than quantitative. This is not something that can be assigned a percentage of a larger item or expressed numerically. The key to materiality is the ability of a false statement about a fact to cause action or inaction on the part of an individual who is relying on the statement's accuracy to define his or her action. This does not mean that an immaterial misrepresentation is not fraud. For instance, say someone tries to steal inventory and is caught before the goods are removed. There is no dollar loss since the goods were not lost, a quantitative measure. However, when that person tried to steal the goods, he or she broke the law, a qualitative measure. The 800-pound friendly gorilla looks at the motives behind the actions rather than just at the numeric values when addressing a misrepresentation.

Next, examine the *intentions* of the people in the organization. Intention is an important concept to understand when discussing fraud; it is critical to

People can be slimy and are just
as capable of stinging
as jellyfish.

EXHIBIT 1.8　The Jellyfish Analogy

understanding someone's actions. Intent is necessary to prove fraud—either beyond a reasonable doubt (99 percent convinced), in a criminal matter, or by preponderance of the evidence (more than 50 percent belief), in a civil matter. Remember that fraud analysts serve as fact finders only and do not supplant the judge or jury in declaring guilt or innocence. Intention is a state of mind and can be very difficult to prove. The utilization of open-ended questions and other effective communication is the key to determining intention, because it is less accusatory and more proactive.

Apply some divergent thinking with the facts in our one-minute fraud mystery to develop what the intention is. What is John Asset's intent in raising the issue of the discrepancy? What is Betty Favor's intent in rebuffing him? What is the owner's intent? It may be easier to soothe ruffled feathers and overlook the fraud, but is that the best answer for the organization in the long run if the goal is to establish the correct ethical tone? Whose interests are being served? What controls are in place? What questions do you think should be asked?

Necessary or unavoidable *reliance* creates situations that are vulnerable to fraud or the exploitation of value. The world is governed by people. The same people who create the laws, regulations, and other oversight mechanisms generally provide the direct or indirect oversight of compliance with these measures. It is important not to assume that people will automatically observe or follow the same rules they create or enforce.

Furthermore, organizational leaders rely on others (employees) to be sufficiently trained and educated to perform the tasks they are hired to perform. The leaders of an organization often believe that their people are not so covetous of what is not theirs, that they would not overtly commit fraud or covertly engage in the exploitation of another's assets or value for personal gain. Leaders need to take pause and ask the following of themselves and their subordinates: Do we and our people have the necessary skills to perform the required tasks? Do we and our people know what fraud looks like?

In terms of our mystery, does Betty Favor or John Asset have the trust of the owner? Whom do you give more credibility to? Who is more qualified? Who has more to lose: John, by pointing out the discrepancy, or Betty, for telling her boss that his newest employee is incompetent? What questions do you think should be asked? We rely on people in the organizational structure, and we need to make sure that these people have good moral character and fully understand their role in the organization.

Finish your examination of the MIRD acronym by thinking of *damage* in terms of value. After all, the financial damage comes from the value taken inappropriately (directly or exploitatively) from the organization. Think about the item of value within the organization that was lost as a result of the reliance on an intentional misrepresentation. The value can be as simple as having check-signing authority, writing off uncollectible accounts, making deposits, or ordering inventory.

Apply the concept of damage to our one-minute fraud mystery. Who has access to the value: Betty Favor? John Asset? The owner? What questions should be asked?

In applying the divergent thinking process to the mystery, we have not yet asked to see any documentation, such as the bank reconciliation or the bank statements, nor have we contacted the bank. Yet a fraud theory or plot has emerged, which will be useful to draw a final conclusion about the one-minute fraud mystery by the end of the chapter.

EDUCATION ABOUT FRAUD

Educating people about what fraud looks like and where the value and people meet in an organization is the first step in preventing, deterring, and detecting fraud. Many organizations rely on the assumption that people in particular roles understand their responsibilities and have the necessary education and skill sets to competently meet their obligations. Yet there is an 80-20 rule for a typical organizational structure: 80 percent of the process is controlled by only 20 percent of the individuals.

Organizational values and beliefs play a role that transcends an obligation to follow the rules. Does the organization's culture emphasize building for the company's future or for the C-suite's retirement? The moral of Dr. Seuss's children's story *The Lorax* is that destroying the environment in the name of growth and profiteering destroys the future.[21] This is a concept that even young children can grasp, yet many corporate leaders fail to see it. An organization should maintain an environment that does not succumb to pressures that have the potential to jeopardize the company's long-term existence. Unfortunately, this is not a universal statement. When an organization believes in the maximization of shareholder value, it often can mean the sale of all or part of the organization, without any regard for the interests of the people working there. Such a situation could be rife with fraud possibilities since the employees may feel betrayed.

One way to gauge the relative moral compass of an organization is to consider whether executive salaries or staff training and education are likely to be the chosen victim of a budgetary contraction. In an economic environment where people are being asked to do more with less because of downsizing and other cost-cutting measures, training and continuous improvement may not be a top priority. The fraudster is aware of these cuts, and it allows him or her to perpetrate a fraud.

Consider the organizational impact of reducing annual training budgets. The staff members, which may or may not experience changes (up or down) in their salaries, are being asked to expand their responsibilities, perhaps into new territory where some individuals have little or no experience. Yet they may not be given the appropriate tools to do the job. How will this affect morale? Does this give the employees an incentive to work harder? Are the employees who are being asked to do more still willing to protect the organization's value?

An organizational process is only improved by the continual education and reeducation of the people involved in it. What does the education in a typical organization generally consist of? It is true that there are those who do a job and those who have a career. Continuous improvement and job training are not on the radar for all organizations or individuals. Fraud develops in organizations with leaders who believe there is no need to stay current with the trends and techniques in their chosen field.

Most antifraud professionals, if they belong to credible professional organizations, are required to constantly manage their personal knowledge base and maintain and improve their skill sets. Some are required to annually attend professional ethics training. A well-trained staff represents the front line of an organization's fraud fighters, and failing to prepare the personnel with the best tools to meet their duties in protecting their organization from loss is preparing the organization to fail. Create a "neighborhood watch" in your organization by keeping your employees trained and educated. Develop a proactive approach to fraud by having all people in the organization fully trained and ready to combat fraud.

The Public Company Accounting Oversight Board was created by the Sarbanes-Oxley Act of 2002 to provide independent and external oversight to public company financial audits in the form of informative, accurate, and independent audit reports. Its purpose was to protect investors and the public interest.[22] Senator Paul Sarbanes (D-MD) and Representative Michael Oxley (R-OH) cosponsored this legislation to establish new and enhanced oversight standards for U.S. public companies. Sarbanes is a Harvard-educated attorney, and Oxley is a lawyer from Ohio State University. Neither had formal or practical training in financial auditing, internal control, or risk assessment.[23] Their views were limited and were based on the assumption that people will follow rules. Fraud is unique and is still occurring despite these new standards.

Oscar Wilde once said, "Education is an admirable thing, but it is well to remember, from time to time, that nothing that is worth knowing can be taught."[24] Gaining knowledge is worthwhile, but nothing replaces learning from past experiences and actually applying what you have been taught. More involvement in the unique organizational processes through hands-on experience is lacking in the development of these laws. The only true way to avoid fraud is through understanding the people who are being asked to comply with these laws by analyzing their application of them.

Fraud risk evolves from the intersection of people and value, and fraud is mitigated by the introduction of appropriate education and training. Checks and balances can be, and are, circumvented when the scale of self-interest tips in the direction of unchecked greed. The mere presence of financial audits and systemic checks and balances will not alone prevent or deter fraud. The use of random data selection to screen for errors and irregularities is a flawed approach to managing fraud risk, because it is impossible to replicate or automate the human factor. There is often an assumption (which may or may not be true) that the individuals charged with the responsibility of protecting organizational value are properly trained and understand how fraud may occur.

The solution to the issue of organizational fraud is to develop people in the organization who have a shared vision of the company's goals and who are invested in the organization and its success. These people should be trained so that they can properly apply divergent and convergent thinking to identify the fulcrum where value and peope meet and whether or not fraud exists there. An organization has to have value, or it would not exist. The same people who create or maintain value can also destroy it. To protect the value in an organization, we need to understand the people who have control over it and the inherent process-based vulnerabilities of the organization.

Three things must be present to allow fraud to exist and remain undetected in your organization: distraction, deception, and divison.

Add the human element to the three Ds, and you have the formula for fraud to exist in your organization. People are easily distracted, and that distraction leads to the opportunity for deception. The great promise of increasing one's net worth and obtaining a thing of value with minimal relative effort leads some to take the risk of enduring unpleasant consequences. There is a line separating those who would be willing to take that risk from those who would not. Throughout history fraudsters have added creativity to deceptions.

In your defense against fraud, you must examine the people who distract others in the process and the means by which these distractions are formulated. Do the distractions allow the fraudster to deceive the people involved in the process so that he or she can access the value and remain undetected? By the time we get to the third D, division, these distractions and deceptions have created a division among the people in the process that exposes the value to the fraudster.

These distractions may appear to be from sources beyond the people in the organization, such as a speculation created by a negotiated truth (white lie) that creates unreasonable expectations as a result of leaked misinformation by the fraudster. The organization must train people in the process to look for the distractions that create the opportunity to camouflage the deception and create the necessary division for the fraud to exist.

We are a society of tangibles, so it is often difficult to stimulate interest in the intangibles. Value is an intangible concept. For example, a car loses significant value when it is driven off the showroom floor, yet people continue to purchase it, because the car can be touched and value can be assigned to it. The concept that its value will almost certainly decline is conveniently ignored by most people because it is something that cannot be identified by the five senses. It is important that the fraud investigator pay attention to the intangibles.

Let's examine the one-minute fraud mystery by considering the following questions:

- How do we begin our divergent thinking process?
- Where is the organization's value?
- Who has access to the cash?
- Is the organization's value exposed?
- Are the parties involved educated, and do they understand what fraud looks like?

The fraudster knows what fraud looks like. In our mystery, Betty clearly has the authority, since she has directly gone to the owner. Betty also oversees the functions concerned with banking; John went to her upon discovering the discrepancy. John is a new accountant—could he have made a mistake? Who is lying, and how do you know? Is this situation simply an error and John and Betty are both protecting their jobs, or is it there an ongoing fraud?

What questions should you continue developing to educate people on what fraud looks like? How do we balance the idea that an 800-pound friendly gorilla is watching that creates enough consequence, yet maintains open communication and rewards ethical behavior?

 ## CONFUSION ABOUT RESPONSIBILITY

Responsibility and fraud prevention, deterrence, and detection go hand in hand. Exposure to fraud risk arises when there are ambiguities related to operational and oversight responsibilities or when there is conflict between the responsible party and the benefiting party. The proverbial fox cannot be allowed to guard the henhouse. You cannot have the controlling party guarding the value in the organization without developing the proper oversight and checks and balances.

Who are the people with knowledge? Who has the most to gain (or lose)? In our one-minute fraud mystery, is it Betty, John, and/or the owner? Which people manage any part of the revenue stream or asset structure, and do they have relevant practical knowledge (no technological malarkey)? Who makes the decisions? In our mystery it appears to be Betty.

Who are the customers, investors, and bankers? Who is the organization's audience? What level of understanding can you establish? Is it simple, or can you start at an advanced level? In our mystery, we know that cash is involved, and we know the three parties involved. What documentation is available? Who is the intended user of the documents? In our mystery, it appears that we have bank statements and reconciliations. What other documents and information should we or could we expect to find?

People provide answers to questions, or they provide guidance on where the answers may be found. This is why we often find ourselves unwittingly playing the "he said, she said" game when tracking down key answers to critical questions. Your best friend in determining responsibility is often a disgruntled employee, a former spouse, a competitor, law enforcement or governmental agencies, credit collectors, and others who are often not part of the organizational culture at the time.

So how do you manage concerns about confusion of responsibility? By introducing an 800-pound friendly gorilla to the organization to develop open channels of communication.

The 800-pound friendly gorilla represents the oversight necessary to continuously monitor both systemic controls and the human factor (reliance on personnel to do the right thing for the right reasons), and it also provides the appropriate consequence systems to address ethical lapses or poor judgment. Think of the organization fraud risk management process as a movie script. Who is the cast? What is the plot? Unfortunately, these scripts do not always have happy endings when organizations are not monitored. An organization left unexamined will have fraud.

 ## COMPLEXITY

Is fraud complex or simple? Our caveman in Exhibit 1.1 states that he used a club to commit fraud, similar to the rationale offered by Willie Sutton, the infamous American bank robber of the early twentieth century. According to legend, when asked why he robbed banks, Sutton said, "Because that's where the money is." Frauds do not have to be complex, but in some instances the complexity is necessary to circumvent the controls that are in place or to discourage questions from the 800-pound friendly gorilla.

A good exercise is to think about how you would design a fraud. Which people have full control of the value, and how would you circumvent their controls? Continual exercises should develop potential fraud schemes and plans to deter, prevent, and detect fraud. The best defense is developed through past experiences, such as an analysis of prior frauds to see how they occurred and how they could have been prevented. You need to think like a fraudster to catch a fraudster.

GAAP and/or IFRS (the use of GAAP and/or IFRS depends on where the organization does business and where geographically its customers are) establish the best practices for recording the value in an organization. Proper accounting will assist in detecting fraud, but too often organizations focus only on the results of the reporting protocols to foster the comparibility of entities, and they ignore or do not understand how accounting records can serve to deter, detect, and prevent fraud. What communications about fraud risk are relied on, and where are they represented in the financial statements? Generally accepted accounting principles (GAAP) or international financial reporting standards (IFRS) are not intended to deter, detect, and prevent fraud. Intent does not matter from a financial reporting prespective since fraud is clearly a departure from these established standards.

Balance sheets are purportedly accurate for one day, although companies are not static and their performance changes constantly. Financial statements are developed by people and are easily manipulated by knowledgeable individuals. The income statement references a specific time period and, because it too is developed by people, is accurate only if the underlying records are complete and accurate. The cash-flow statements, supplemental disclosures, and notes to the financial statements are all subject to the same risks of misstatement, error, or fraud. The fraud that occurs is in the development of these documents and is subject to people and the judgments that are made. The fraudulent reports are a symptom of the disease (fraud), which is characterized by unchecked greed.

You have both corporate and individual greed to consider in your pursuit of fraud. You might like to think that all disease could be eliminated, but this is not a reality, and the same is true of fraud. Developing, maintaining, and rewarding people with the correct ethical tone is the best medicine for fighting fraud in your organization.

Fraudsters typically know how to manipulate the traditional pathways to communicate organizational results because they understand the organizational process. The methodologies are innumerable but generally include some variant on fictitious revenues, deferred or false revenues, and conspiracies with other greedy people in the organization's process. Fraudsters often know how to manipulate others. People are often implicated by association. Therefore, it is important to have 800-pound friendly gorillas that know when they are being implicated by other's actions.

Having a working knowledge of an organization's performance communication system enables the fraud to occur and in some cases continue for an extended period before being detected. Any successful fraud plan requires an understanding of the inner workings and a knowledge of what people want. Nothing will destroy an organization's value faster than a well-planned fraud. Knowing who is able to influence these communications and circumvent these processes is critical in preventing, deterring, and detecting fraud in an organization.

Typically, the board of directors and management leaders make the accounting decisions. What training and education do they have, collectively, that make them the *right* team to generate decisions? Are their decisions chained to organizational transparency by the rules, or are individual performance bonuses factored into the decisions they make? Does the organization's decision-making team consult with its independent accountants for major reporting or accounting policy decisions?

Accountants, particularly certified public accountants (CPAs), are expected to uphold the public trust. Although their fees are paid by the organization that engages them for financial statement preparation, the accountants' duties extend to those who are reasonably expected to rely on their work. It is critical that oversight include management of the gatekeepers and their responsibilities, as well as any apparent or perceived conflict of interest that may be present (e.g., an accountant's permissiveness because the client generates substantial annual revenues).

According to the economic entity assumption principle, entities are legally separate from their owners and should therefore account for their activities separate from that of their owners. This is the flip side of what is known as *piercing the corporate veil*, when a court deems that the owners of organizations are not distinguished separately from the entity because of the commingling of business transactions with personal transactions. Because of limited liability, most business owners are generally not personally liable for the debts, losses, and liabilities of the business itself. The business is considered an artificial person.

However, if the owners act in a manner that does not distinguish between themselves and the entity, a court may determine that the entity should be set aside formally, since its form of business was not respected by its owners. If this occurs, and the court decides that the business is merely an alter ego of the owners (i.e., the owners are not considered separate from the organization and are therefore subject to personal liability due to the commingling of business and personal transactions), then those owners will generally not be able to avail themselves of the protections from liability normally enjoyed by businesses. Business law and the intricacies involved in the formation of business entities are beyond the scope of this book, but most businesses are organized in such a manner that the owners are afforded protection from any liability resulting from the business.

There are many things that a court will look at in determining whether alter ego liability should be applied. Typical factors include (but are not limited to) the following: whether the company was adequately capitalized; whether the company kept its own records; whether shares (for a corporation) or units (for a limited liability company, or LLC) were actually issued; whether the owners commingled their finances with the business entity; whether there were corporate directors or LLC managers running the business; how the legal formalities were followed; and whether the owners used the business for personal purposes. It is always a case-by-case situation. An organization should take every precaution to run its business in full compliance with the legally required formalities and use the business in a proper way in order to avoid alter ego liability and remove the complexities it can cause.

Truly great leaders have learned how to leave their egos at the door and create a tone for their organization based on principles. They make sure that the right questions are asked so that when the people meet the value, the people perceive that oversight exists (regardless of the actual oversight in place). This holds true for governmental bodies, Fortune 500 companies, or a simple corner grocery store.

An organization's internal control model should maintain zero tolerance for any violations of these controls. It's the risk-reward concept at its best: the risk must always be greater than the reward. Even the 800-pound friendly gorilla cannot argue against that in preventing fraud. Yet, ironically, people often circumvent internal controls for their own benefit. Regardless of the organizational structure, if there is not a perceived consequence, then deceptive behavior will exist. Even a deterrent like death will not stop fraud from existing if the reward is perceived as being greater than the risk.

In this chapter's mystery, the owner and Betty are the two people in the organization who appear to have the power to override the control. John, as an employee, appears to be the least likely to override the control since he does not have access to the bank and is not involved in the receiving of funds. Other parties that should be considered are the bank, the independent accountant, the attorney, and other organizational personnel. Who has the greatest opportunity to commit fraud against the organization?

In this scenario, the owner does not appear to have access to the cash control. In most companies, the owners trust their employees with this. Remember that Betty has worked for the company for 15 years. Betty can speak for Trust Us Inc. and does so with apparent authority. She appears, in the eyes of a reasonable person, to have the authority to act on behalf of the organization. Her apparent authority is vested in her status as its most trusted and longest-tenured employee.

However, one would do well to remember that *apparent* authority is not the same as *actual* authority. Where are the bylaws, minutes, organizational charts, and so on that give her the authority she has assumed? One of the problems with apparent authority is that by providing the appearance of such authority to outsiders, the company may become responsible for that person's actions and be bound accordingly to any agreements.

Does your organization have a proactive approach to deterring, preventing, and detecting fraud? Is the organizational code of conduct clearly communicated? Are there needless complexities perpetuated, and do they enable or invite fraud? Consider the message being sent internally and externally. Is it okay to have an alter ego that mixes business with personal matters? Is it okay for employees to act with apparent authority? Ostrich management, in which one's head is buried in the sand, at great risk, is not workable, and it promotes a culture in which these very pitfalls arise. We can no longer be like the three monkeys that "see no evil, hear no evil, speak no evil."

"Healthy greed" is an oxymoron, since *greed* is defined by *Merriam-Webster*'s as "a selfish and excessive desire for more of something than is needed." That is, the essence of greed is *the selfishness and the excess*, not the mere desire to have more than one needs. Milton Friedman's view of greed, which was quoted at the beginning of the chapter, does not necessarily contradict the dictionary definition; it probably just accepts Ayn Rand's principle that selfishness is a virtue. Most for-profit corporations are not content with simply surviving or breaking even; they look to prosper by continuously providing a return on investment to their shareholders. This would be an example of healthy greed. Healthy greed should exist to create competitive and thriving markets, and it should not be driven merely by one's own self-interest but instead be intended for everyone involved in the process. We need more "we the people" thinking and less "what's in it for me?" mentalities. Remember, everyone is greedy, but just how greedy are they? Make sure the 800-pound friendly gorilla is ensuring that any greed present in the organization is healthy greed.

SUMMARY

Simple embezzlement can lead to significant losses in an organization. The party embezzling faces jail time and can be charged with more than embezzlement alone. Typically, wire fraud, mail fraud, and tax evasion (since embezzlement income is taxable even though illegal) can also be added. An organization can be put out of business by this type of fraud because of the cost of lawyers, the time necessary to investigate, and the missing value (if not recovered).

It's like comparing death from a mosquito bite to death from a shark attack. Everyone's much more afraid of the shark. However, your chances of being attacked by a shark are just one in 11.5 million, according to the University of Florida. Meanwhile, the mosquito bite is more dangerous, in terms of worldwide death rates, from malaria, West Nile virus, and other diseases.

Similarly, an organization often positions itself to protect against the occurrence of the big fraud (a shark attack), which is less likely to occur, and ignores the small frauds (mosquito bites), even though the mosquito bites are much more likely to occur.

An organization seldom even prosecutes embezzlement because of the way it makes the organization look. The organization figures it has insurance, prosecution is costly and time-consuming, restitution may be made, and the ethical tone is not moral and breeds more fraud. Without a fear of fraud, organizations often ignore the small frauds. Instead, an organization must follow through and publicize the behavior to send a message that it will not be tolerated. Organizations should not be reactive in their approach but should rather be

EXHIBIT 1.9 Shark Attack

proactive by creating the correct moral ethical tone and having the 800-pound friendly gorilla watching from the start.

Outrage equals interest; without it, no one is watching. Typically, if the event or transaction does not create outrage, no actions will be taken. This is one of the reasons most frauds remain unreported and continue to exist in today's organizations. A wrongdoing should not need media attention or have to be selective to cause the proper actions to be taken. In small cases of fraud, the fraudsters are often forced to quietly resign in order for the organization to avoid the lengthy and public process of prosecution. All fraud, whether outrageous or not, needs to be addressed by today's organizations to set the proper ethical tone. In Chapter 2, we discuss the fact that even when someone is watching, fraud will continue. We will see why enhanced legislative, regulatory, and professional oversight is not helping auditors in the fight to combat fraud, and how through this understanding the nonauditor can grasp the necessary organizational tone to proactively establish the fight against fraud.

Regardless of outrage, the most successful fraud defense is interest.

 ## ONE-MINUTE FRAUD MYSTERY ANALYSIS

After reading this chapter, are you able to establish where the value exists in the process at Trust Us Inc.? Can you determine which people had access to the value, and where the company was vulnerable to fraud? Remember, you are the fact finder and need to apply divergent thinking. Here are some thoughts on this chapter's mystery based on my experience in the field:

- **Allegation.** The bank reconciliation and bank statement records do not match.
- **Probable cause.** At this point, you know that something has occurred. Either Favor or Trust could have been mistaken in their reconciliation, or they could have committed fraud. If Asset had discovered fraud, then it would appear that Favor was trying to cover her trail. It is also interesting that Favor went straight to the company's owner with her findings and did not address them with Asset.
- **Action.** Further questioning is necessary. A cautious approach is necessary for this situation. While you want to treat Betty Favor as a person of interest, you need to use the 800-pound friendly gorilla approach when investigating her. You need to understand the level of socialization and relationships that exist between the parties. Make note of the 15-year

relationship between the owner and Favor. Who else may be involved (the owner)? Is the relationship between them limited to this transaction or is it ongoing? Favor clearly has an understanding of the organizational business process and may be the potential ring leader. John Asset brought the problem to his direct supervisor (Favor), which appears to be the typical process. However, remember that Asset's involvement can only be dismissed after a proper investigation is complete. Do not rule out victims or parties that bring the problem to light. Rule them out only after the proper due diligence has been completed. Examine where the greed exists that enables the fraudster to start rationalizing his or her thinking. Are there external influences? Look for lifestyle changes. Look for conflicts of interest. Know your answers before you ask critical questions by having a well-thought-out and planned approach.

- **Preparation.** Get bank records directly from the bank (third-party documents are the best source) and start within the house records. Caution should be used; you may need to get the records without Favor's knowledge. Develop open-ended questions for brainstorming. Are the books audited by independent auditors? Develop a nonaccusatory theme when asking employees questions as to avoid raising their defenses. If the preparation phase gets too involved or complicated, bring in a high-level investigator with good communication skills to help. Questions to ask include the following:
  - Are the entries in the books and records being altered?
  - Are there overdrafts?
  - What is the financial condition of the organization and the parties involved?
  - How do the canceled checks compare to the general ledger?
- **People of interest.** Betty has knowledge of the process and the ability to override control, and her background has not been checked in 15 years. She is a trusted employee and is in the right position to succeed in perpetrating a fraud.
- **People-with-knowledge interview plan.** Interview John Asset first (least likely to commit fraud; he has no signing authority and reports to Favor), Betty Favor second (owner's "pet"; everything goes through her; enjoys personal gain), and the owner last (never assume the owner is not in on the fraud). Also, is it possible for any other parties to have knowledge of the potential fraud?
- **Documentary evidence.** Collect bank statements and all supporting documentation, including bank reconciliations, tax returns, general ledgers (organized or messy?), financial statements, and loan applications.

◾ **Formulate opinion.** Embezzlement. Greed. Long-standing relationship situation, with a well-established level of trust bestowed on one individual. Owner is involved directly or indirectly, since there is a lack of 800-pound friendly gorilla oversight in Trust Us Inc. See if the company documents conflict, because there is the potential of embezzlement. The difference between larceny and embezzlement is that in the latter, employees and owners have authorized access to the funds. You need to develop proof. An example could be outstanding checks that never seemed to clear.

800-Pound Friendly Gorilla Suggestions for Trust Us Inc.

Trust Us Inc. was in need of a better control system to protect itself from fraud. It had no controls in place to deter, detect, and prevent fraud, and its systems could be overridden. The fraud was discovered inadvertently when a new employee was hired. Trust Us Inc. needs to establish a new level of thinking to protect itself from further fraud. It needs an 800-pound friendly gorilla solution. Too much trust in any one person can lead to fraud. The following actions are needed to reduce the risk of fraud in the organization, and it is a good starting point to begin by developing the 800-pound friendly gorilla protection needed to safeguard the organization and implement the following tactics to reduce the risk of fraud:

◾ Separate the authorization of the transactions from their recording.
◾ Monitor the responsibilities given to people with access to the organization's value.
◾ Require multiple signatures.
◾ Perform background checks initially and annually.
◾ Institute a policy of job rotation.
◾ Have employees bonded with the proper insurance policies (to reduce risk exposure).
◾ Institute a mandatory vacation policy.
◾ Create annual financial disclosure policies for the people in the organizational process.
◾ Define the trust levels with the appropriate checks and balances as needed.

A Simple Picture

As I mentioned earlier, I gave the facts of this chapter's one-minute fraud mystery to my cousin's daughter Lindsay, a 16-year-old sophomore in high school, and asked her to draw her perspective of what happened based on the facts at the start of this chapter. Where does the greed exist in Exhibit 1.10? Lindsay's drawing clearly indicates who has access to the money and organizational value. It also shows the reporting functions. In this one image, you can see where the organization is susceptible to fraud through the fact that Betty has direct access to the cash. In the end, we need to articulate the evidence and

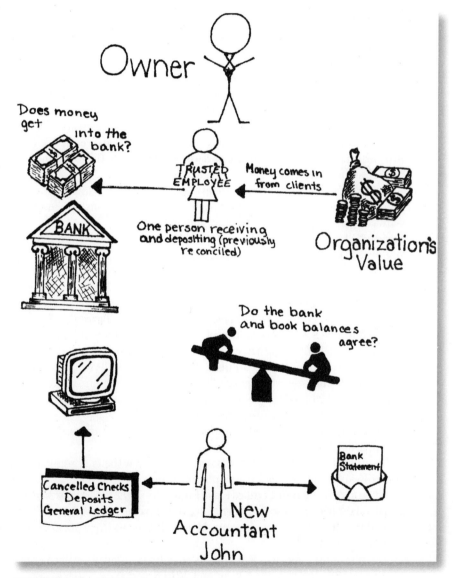

EXHIBIT 1.10 Trust Us Inc. Drawing

supports in the same simplistic manner that Lindsay has in this drawing by focusing on the relevant facts. The simpler the approach that the organization utilizes to expose where people and value meet in a process, the greater the chances are for deterring, detecting, and preventing organizational fraud.

NOTES

1. A bank reconciliation is a critical fraud review process that ensures the transactions on the books are consistent with the bank. The bank statement is a third-party source document. Third-party source documents are able to be obtained independently, which aids you in your fraud investigation since the person of interest may not know that he or she is being investigated. Third-party information is the most reliable source when obtained directly from the third party, assuming that the third party is not involved in the fraud and has not altered the document.
2. David Porter, "Ex-Lawyer Gets Longest Insider Trading Sentence Every, Associated Press, June 5, 2012, http://www.dailyfinance.com/2012/06/05/ex-lawyer-gets-longest-insider-trading-sentence-ever.
3. *Merriam-Webster's Collegiate Dictionary*, 11th ed., http://www.merriam-webster.com/dictionary/fraud?show=0&t=1322278715.
4. The Free Dictionary by Farlex. *Fraud. The American Heritage Dictionary of the English Language*, 4th ed. (Boston, MA: Houghton Mifflin, 2001), http://www.thefreedictionary.com/fraud.
5. Stephen H. Gifis, "Fraud,"*Law Dictionary* (Hauppauge, NY: Barron's, 1984).
6. Internal Revenue Service, "Definition of Fraud," *Internal Revenue Manual*, Sec. 25.1.1.2, July 18, 2008, http://www.irs.gov/irm/part25/irm_25-001-001.html.
7. American Institute of Certified Public Accountants (AICPA), Codification of Auditing Standards AU Section 316 (formerly Statement on Auditing Standards [SAS] 99). AICPA's definition neither contemplates corruption (e.g., kickbacks or bid rigging) nor requires financial injury.
8. Association of Certified Fraud Examiners, *2010 Fraud Examiners' Manual* (Austin, TX: ACFE, 2010), 2.201.
9. The Institute of Internal Auditors, *Glossary*, http://www.theiia.org/guidance/standards-and-guidance/ippf/standards/full-standards/?i=8317.
10. According to Association of Certified Fraud Examiners, *2012 Report to the Nations*, entities, on the average, lose 5 to 7 percent of their revenues to fraud annually.
11. Albert Einstein and Sonja Bargmann, *Ideas and Opinions* (New York: Crown Publishers, 1982).
12. This classification system was first introduced in Association of Certified Fraud Examiners, *1996 Report to the Nations* and *2010 Report to the Nations*.

13. Association of Certified Fraud Examiners, *2010 Fraud Examiners' Manual*, Sec. 2.201. Frauds classified as "statutory offenses" include those resulting from the violation of federal or state laws. Some of the more significant federal laws are the Sarbanes-Oxley Act, the Dodd-Frank Act, the False Claims Act (as modified), the Honest Services Fraud Act, and the Foreign Corrupt Practices Act.

14. Donald R. Cressey, *Other People's Money: A Study in the Social Psychology of Embezzlement* (New York: Free Press, 1953).

15. David T. Wolfe and Dana R. Hermanson, "The Fraud Diamond: Considering the Four Elements of Fraud," *The CPA Journal* (December 2004), http://www .nyscpa.org/printversions/cpaj/2004/1204/p38htm.

16. Jonathan Marks, "Playing Offense in a High-risk Environment," Crowe Horwath International, http://www.crowehorwath.com/folio-pdf/RISK8115_ PlayingOffenseWP_lo.pdf.

17. Ibid.

18. The Sarbanes–Oxley Act, enacted July 30, 2002, created the Public Company Accounting Oversight Board and the Investor Protection Act. It is commonly referred to as Sarbanes–Oxley, Sarbox, or SOX. The Wall Street Reform and Consumer Protection Act, commonly referred to as the Dodd–Frank Act, is a federal statute that implements financial regulatory reform; it was signed into law by President Barack Obama on July 21, 2010.

19. Herb Greenberg, "Making a Strong Case for Sarbanes-Oxley: A Former Crook Argues against Watering Down Securities Laws" *Market Watch*, October 11, 2006, http://www.marketwatch.com/story/a-reformed-crooks-view-of-sarbanes-oxley. A detailed discussion of the Crazy Eddie Inc. fraud can be found on Sam Antar's website, http://www.whitecollarfraud.com.

20. The Securities and Exchange Commission suggests a 5 percent starting point in developing a materiality threshold. Similarly, there is no absolute definition of *materiality* for Internal Revenue Service purposes. Generally, if something has the ability to influence another's actions, it is material.

21. Dr. Seuss, *The Lorax* (New York: Random House, 1971).

22. The Public Company Accounting Oversight Board's website, http://www .pcaobus.org, contains a wealth of information about the group's mission as well as the oversight it provides, including inspections and enforcement and its liaison with the Securities and Exchange Commission.

23. We presume that Senator Sarbanes and Representative Oxley had qualified personnel advising them on relevant matters. The point is that lawyers are again proposing to fix a potentially broken system by creating additional layers of oversight (which potentially divert the resources available to address the matter directly) and not by enhancing education and awareness.

24. "The Objective of Education is Learning, Not Teaching," Knowledge Wharton. University of Pennsylvania. August 20, 2008, http://knowledge.wharton .upenn.edu/article.cfm?articleid=2032.

CHAPTER TWO

2

Fraud Detection Approaches

I think greed is healthy. You can be greedy and
still feel good about yourself.

—*Ivan Frederick Boesky*

Old wisdom states, "Inch by inch it's a cinch, mile by mile it's a trial."[1] The wisdom of this simple quote can help organizations gain control in the fight against
organizational fraud. This chapter addresses the issue of expectation gap in
organizations, taking into consideration twenty-first-century capabilities and
events. Far-reaching legislative thinking cannot replace inch-by-inch analysis and
coordination of the people in an organizational process. Organizations should
encourage their people to have a self-governing, morally correct attitude. This is
far more effective than regulating moral behavior simply through the establishment of rule-based communications. Essentially, rules will not always deter fraud.
Involving the people in the process is necessary.

This chapter features a discussion of the following:
The people perspective in implementing compliance.
Whether laws create efficiency and/or a cost benefit.
Reconciling professional and client relationships.
The assumption that people will follow rules.
Balancing employee self-interest with the organization's interests.

———————————

THERE IS AN EXPECTATION GAP ISSUE in today's organizations, created by the assumption that external auditors and/or accountants are specifically engaged to find fraud, which is not the case. Auditors and/or accountants are charged with providing reasonable but *not* absolute assurance of whether the examined financial statements are fairly presented in accordance with certain prescribed rules. Therefore, there should be a basic mind-set that the information being presented is not 100 percent accurate (this is thinking divergently).

One of today's major accounting debates involves the comparison of the U.S. GAAP's rule-based approach and the IFRS principle-based approach.[2] The principle-based approach looks at the intent of the underlying concepts or principles and does not require a strict reading of a particular rule, which creates different interpretations for similar transactions based on the people making the judgments.

Let's look at the rule-based approach by thinking about Mr. Miyagi from the first *Karate Kid* movie. There are two rules of Miyagi karate. Rule number one: Use karate for defense only. Rule number two: First learn rule number one. Rules and principles are no different; proper enforcement needs to be in place. Regardless of whether one uses the rule-based approach or the principle-based approach, all transactions require a thought process that allows for second-guessing and uncertainty, leading to more extensive analysis and disclosure in the financial statements that tell the true numbers story.

 ## WHY DOESN'T ENHANCED LEGISLATIVE, REGULATORY, AND PROFESSIONAL OVERSIGHT HELP TO PREVENT FRAUD?

Fraud risk awareness regulations arose out of the Treadway Commission.[3] There have been fraud regulations in the past, such as the 1933–1934 Security Exchange Acts, the 1977 Statement on Auditing Standards No.16 Detection of

Errors or Irregularities of the Auditing Standards Board, the 1977 Foreign Corrupt Practices Act, and the 1986 Fraud Detection and Disclosure Act, all established either by the government or the accounting regulatory bodies. These and others existed before the colossal failures of Enron, Parmalat (food manufacturing), and Madoff. The frauds in these entities led to additional studies of internal controls, accounting policies, reporting, management compensation, and so on that called for monitoring and a more active role by the accountant. The outcome of these various studies was that regulators increased regulations by passing more laws, and a new accountancy oversight body for public companies was created.

The body of accounting knowledge, including financial reporting, compliance rules, and regulations, continues to be studied in the wake of these and other financial frauds and economic failures. Has the legislative approach—which at least in part encourages and leverages increased transparency while promoting accurate reporting through increased legislative and regulatory oversight—been successful in enhancing deterrence? One needs only to look to the financial market crises of 2008 and 2009 (the housing bubble, financial institution failures, and government bailouts) for that answer. Government and accounting regulatory bodies do not create moral behavior; people, with help from the 800-pound friendly gorillas in your organization, do.

The adoption of an oversight model to aid in the detection of fraud may cause a real-world gap between, on the one hand, the expectations of the users and the providers of a company's financial information and, on the other hand, the perceived context in which it is being used. People believe that these oversight models will protect the organization, but legislation can only serve as a tool. Enforcement of the current regulations often works better than creating new laws that only serve to create more red tape and complicate the process. It all comes back to the people and their motivation to either do the right thing or stray off the moral highway. This chapter explores this perspective and the responsibilities in implementing these compliance measures while looking at the established, existing principles and rules used to limit an organization's exposure to fraud.

Any practical oversight model that is being introduced to detect, deter, and prevent fraud will be met with real-world problems. There will be the typical mind-sets that present barriers to the oversight controls, such as "but this is how we do it here," working around them for efficiency, or cost-benefit concerns. The presence of external pressures, the need to reduce the workforce, and a heavier reliance on technology are making it more necessary to analyze whether laws create efficiency and/or a cost benefit. Does more red tape cause people to act more ethically and in the best interest of an organization? Or does it just increase fees and costs without creating any true value, including enhanced compliance with ethical standards?

The differences between the organizational expectations gap and the accountants' expectations gap are important. Is it possible for these gaps to be reconciled, given an established professional-client relationship? Who are the professionals advocating for: the interests of the organization (their client) or the interests of the external parties (the public) that they are regulated to protect? The external auditor is clearly in violation of General Standard Rule 1— maintain independence—as he or she is advocating on behalf of the client. This is a difficult ethical dichotomy that needs to be reconciled by the 800-pound friendly gorilla.

As an accounting professor and a partner in an accounting firm, I frequently test my students and colleagues in the industry by asking them what the basic GAAP or the general standards of the AICPA Code of Professional Conduct with which we operate under are, and very few can recite them. Hopefully after reading this book, you will be able to recite them as they make accountants answerable and preserve the integrity of the profession. I challenge today's organization to make sure that all of its people can recite the established principles and rules at all levels of the organization—even the person right out of high school who is hired as an accounts payable clerk. Otherwise, we maintain a wishful-thinking assumption that people follow rules and principles and are not willing to suffer the consequences of violating them. If everyone had admirable morals, proper principles, and a rule-based thinking, there would likely be no fraud in today's organizations.

Creating manageable expectations in alignment with an organization's strategic vision helps you to preserve the professional-client relationship. In other words, how do you balance people's self-interest with the interests of the organization to create a win-win situation?

ONE-MINUTE FRAUD MYSTERY: BIG FISH INVESTMENT INC.

Big Fish Investment Inc., an investment advisory and brokerage firm, has a sales associate named John Sales who has brought in more money for the firm than anyone else. His immediate supervisor is Charles Biggs. Biggs's oversight includes instructing Sales to push certain stocks and discourage trading in others. The firm has $110 million under management and is regulated by the Financial Industry Regulatory Authority (FINRA).[4] FINRA is overseen by the Securities and Exchange Commission (SEC).

Big Fish has specific stocks for sale that no one else has. These stocks are mostly trading under $10 a share. The firm does a terrific job marketing the initial public offerings for new companies and develops the expectation that these start-up companies could become the next Apple or Microsoft. Big Fish's chief executive officer (CEO), Gordon Walls, calls Biggs to let him know which stocks their clients and prospects should buy and which ones they should sell. Walls appears to be a market maker in these securities.

A CPA firm has been providing Big Fish with accounting services (including a financial audit) since Big Fish's inception. One of the CPA firm partners, Tom Ticker, often plays golf with Gordon Walls. The CPA firm conducts its investment activity through Traders Inc., a major clearinghouse. The CFO of Traders Inc., Hector Moneymaker, is concerned that Big Fish is heavily leveraged and could face a margin call.

One of the stocks that Big Fish holds a major position in (and is focused on selling) is Too Good to Be True Inc., which is under heavy selling pressure. This drives the price down from nearly $20 to its current market price of $2 because Big Fish's clients have refused to buy. With knowledge of the heavy selling volume, Moneymaker called Walls to ask the investment firm about its outlook for Too Good to Be True Inc. in light of the decline and unusual volume in the shares being traded. He asked about its performance and financial position, and Walls told him that he would look into it.

Immediately after this call, Walls and Biggs started shredding documents and told all sales associates to suspend trading activity in Too Good to Be True Inc. until further notice. Ticker, the CPA of Big Fish, watched Walls and Biggs shredding documents from an office at Big Fish's facility while he was performing work on the company's annual audit.

While the shredding was going on, one of John Sales's biggest clients, Omar Carton, attempted to visit the headquarters of Too Good to Be True Inc., since he was concerned about the market action and his $100,000 life savings investment. He discovered that the "headquarters" was an abandoned warehouse with no furniture or people. It only had a phone with an answering machine stating that "someone will get back to you." Carton threatened to go to the FBI with his concerns over Big Fish and its people's actions.

Carton has requested that a forensic accounting investigation of Big Fish Investment Inc. and all related parties be performed concerning the stocks it was pushing to its clients. You have been retained by Carton and other concerned investors to do the investigation. How do you go about it, and what do you look for as Carton's engaged professional?

PRINCIPLES AND RULES ALONE CANNOT ELIMINATE ALL FRAUD

Think of the exterminating fumes shown in Exhibit 2.1 as the rules of an organization and the ants as the potential fraudsters.

Ants live in colonies and work together for their collective survival; similarly, organizations are colonized by people, and often the fraudster just blends in. Principles and rules are necessary to provide structure and governance, and to ensure an organization's survival. People in an organization must communicate and work together to succeed in preventing or deterring organizational

EXHIBIT 2.1 Fraud Exterminators

fraud by evaluating and understanding the people in the process and continually adjusting to change. This is necessary to maintain the necessary ethical harmony within the organizational colony.

Ants recognize the importance of working together as a colony, and so must the people within the organization to avoid fraud. An organization needs to create the ant that always adheres to core ethical principles and follows the rules that are in the best interest of the organizational colony rather than the ant's own interests. All it takes is one rogue ant to lose its way in the colony, and the whole colony is at risk. Similarly, it takes just one lone fraudster to bring down an entire organization.

Compliance brought about by legislative action does not create a people-friendly control environment. People resist change, and forced control does not breed a self-governing type of control environment in an organization. In fact, forced control is likely to have the opposite effect and encourage fraudsters to find ways around the regulations. Lawmakers and oversight or regulatory bodies create a false sense of security by insinuating that the legislation will build integrity (the exterminator fumes). Legislation and regulation cannot replace the human element, because the people being asked (or required) to comply with these rules are not machines devoid of individual capability, thought, and emotion.

These people are like the ants in Exhibit 2.1, where just having controls (the exterminator fumes) in place was not enough to stop the ants from stealing the basket. Principles and rules are not absolute. In organizations, protections that are put into place to control often do not account for the potential human element. People interject their personal rationalizations into the decisions they make on behalf of the organization.

The rules and controls put in place by management, accountants, and external stakeholders will not by themselves be effective against what the organization perceives as a potential fraudster. People formulate their own perspectives without the development of the proper organizational (colony) principles and rules. Even when principles and rules are absent, these people could make choices that either deter or result in fraud.

In order to identify potential fraudsters, an organization needs to define its level of uncertainty regarding people doing the right thing in the organizational process. Establishing the necessary principles and rules with a well-defined implementation strategy creates an environment in which people in an organization follow the principles and rules not because they have to but because they want to. These people are moral and ethical and more likely to expose a potential fraudster.

A REAL-WORLD PERSPECTIVE

When companies create an oversight model as part of their governance, it is because they make speculative assumptions that cause real-world misunderstandings between the expectations of the users of an organization's financial information and the providers of that information. Who are the real gatekeepers: the independent accountants and auditors who provide reasonable assurance, the governing oversight bodies that create the "catch me if you can" way of thinking, or the organization that develops people with integrity?

Unfortunately, no oversight model can be designed to stop all fraud by using checks and balances without enlisting the support of multiple people. There may be one person who initiates the necessary action, but it takes more than one person to implement it, whether or not the other party is enabling the initiating fraudster. The difference between real life and what books tell you will happen is often significantly different. It is like someone saying, "Well, in theory it should have gone this way" when in reality it did not.

I like to refer to the scene in the movie *Back to School* in which Rodney Dangerfield is attending his first economics class. The professor is discussing the costs associated with creating a company in a textbook-like approach. Dangerfield's character interrupts and says to the professor, "You left a lot out when considering the building of the factory." The professor asks what he has left out, and Dangerfield asks him about bribing the local politicians, working with the unions, and so on, saying that these things are also necessary to build the building. The professor says that they are not going to build the building that way. The professor then asks where they should build the factory, and Dangerfield replies, "Fantasy land."

The point is that the red tape is created by the same rules and principles that restrict capitalism. The professor's building may take longer to build, cost more than Dangerfield's, or never get built. It is the ever-present greed factor that exists in today's capitalist society that allows fraud to exist. It is often a mixed signal created in real-world behavior that makes it difficult to maintain the established principles and rules if the organization is to survive in today's capitalist society. Unfortunately, the fate of an organization is perceived to lie in taking these risks.

The challenge lies in aligning an organization's expectations with the theoretical perception of what should happen. Unfortunately, there is no way to guarantee an outcome based on the expectation that it should work or that people will always adhere to the principles and rules. If you remember the human element, you are presented with the dilemma that there is no guarantee that oversight or inert legislation will prevent what it sets out to prevent. The challenge is establishing common realistic expectations and matching the rules and principle-based perspectives with the needs of the people by establishing expectations that preserve the correct interests. What are the correct interests? Is it a CEO seeking to increase shareholder value? Is it being responsible to the people in the organization's processes? Is it the environment? The challenge lies in managing the apparent conflicts of interests to a level that does not require fraud.

Capitalist structures require greed in order to maintain balances like competitive prices and entrepreneurial opportunity. Gordon Gecko was right in the movie *Wall Street* when he said, "Greed. . . is good"—when used with the correct morals. Unfortunately, those morals are not always maintained. Moral greed maintains transparency and openness. If an average person was asked about the action or transaction, he or she would deem it reasonable. To maintain moral greed, a person needs to advance his or her self-interests over others, while adhering to ethical principles and existing laws.

Let's look at some examples that demonstrate the effects of probability and doubt. Baseball players do not have to get a hit at every bat. In fact, if they bat .300 (which means hitting 3 out of 10 balls at bat), they make millions of dollars. In a civil lawsuit, the burden of proof falls on the plaintiff, who must show that the defendant in the case has more than a 50 percent probability of being guilty or not proving the facts. In a criminal case, the standard is beyond a reasonable doubt, but shouldn't it be without *any* doubt? Society sets the acceptable level of doubt. Again I have to revert back to "no outrage equals no interest." In an organization where employees do not have to follow the rules and principles 100 percent of the time, fraud can and will exist. In organizations where the rules are not enforced 100 percent of the time, the evidence becomes more difficult to uncover. Therefore, the burden of proof lies in the documentary evidence that you are able to obtain in support of your fact-finding conclusions.

Looking at the various definitions of forensic accounting helps to explain the difference between GAAP and IFRS auditing in a worldwide perspective. One definition of forensic accounting is the application of accounting principles, theories, and discipline to facts or a hypothesis at issue in a legal dispute. It includes every branch of accounting knowledge.[5] The term *forensic accountant* refers to an accountant who performs an orderly analysis, investigation, inquiry, test, inspection, or examination in an attempt to obtain the truth and develop an expert opinion.[6]

Yet another definition of forensic accounting applies accounting, statistical, research, and economic concepts and techniques to legal problems or potential legal problems.[7] According to the AICPA:

> While many definitions exist for the general term forensic, the AICPA's Forensic and Litigation Services Committee (FLS) believes that forensic accounting consists of two major components: litigation services that recognize the role of the CPA as an expert, consultant, or other role, and investigative services that make use of the CPA's skills that may or may not lead to courtroom testimony. Forensic Accounting may involve the application of special skills in accounting, auditing, finance, quantitative methods, certain areas of law, research, and investigative skills to collect, analyze, and evaluate evidential matter and to interpret and communicate findings.[8]

Note that the other definitions of forensic accounting apply financial techniques to all matters of law, regardless of whether they are financial matters. Another definition, by forensic CPA Darrell Dorrell, is that forensic accounting is "the art and science of applying financial techniques to matters of law."[9] Both art and science are necessary when applying methods; thus the forensic accountant's experience becomes a crucial component of the analysis and shows that the fraud requires a different level of accounting thinking. I like to think of the art as using one's reasoning without limits to develop an idea and be guided by a practical approach, whereas the science takes that reasoning from a specific context toward the development of a well-documented opinion.

This book defines forensic accounting as the study of greed through the application of art and scientific techniques to detect, deter, and prevent the risk of fraud, with an emphasis on people inside and outside an organization.

Unfortunately, fraud exists even though the auditors and accountants are performing the checks and balances. To date, the approach to organizational fraud is to use computer simulation models to randomly select data input for errors and irregularities, fill out reports, and have faith in the huge assumption that people are trained and actually understand what they are looking for when it comes to fraud.

This is why tips (think of it as "telling if people steal") are the main way that fraud is exposed. Audits catch fraud intentionally 4.2 percent of the time, accidentally 9.3 percent of the time and through tips 37.8 percent of the time.[10]

As an investigator, you need to think divergently to find the people willing to give the necessary tips to detect, deter, and prevent fraud.

 ## GETTING A HANDLE ON TRANSACTIONS

To develop effective oversight, it is necessary to gain an overall understanding of the entire set of economic transactions within the organization and the interested users or benefactors of these transactions. There are two broad categories of users of financial information:

1. Internal users (people within the organization)
2. External users (people outside the organization)

The purpose of accounting is to identify these economic transactions; record, classify, summarize, and communicate them through the preparation of financial statements or some other means of financial communication; and provide a reasonable assurance that they are correct. Understanding the following financial statement communications and the way the fraudster can create the necessary diversions to perpetrate a fraud is a critical tool:

- **Balance sheets.** By understanding these, the fraudster can defer expenses, manipulate inventory, and write off receivables to create the necessary diversion to commit fraud.
- **Income statements and/or statement of earnings.** By analyzing these, the fraudster can use improper revenue recognition techniques, simple deferral of expenses, or incorrect capitalizations to create the necessary diversion to commit fraud.
- **Statements of owners' equity.** With these, the fraudster has to increase the owners' equity by increasing the equity through the other financial statements (balance sheet, income statement, or cash flows).
- **Statements of cash flows.** With these, the fraudster misclassifies the cash flows by manipulating the balance sheet and income statement to misclassify one of three activities: operating, investing, and financing.
- **Financial projections and forecasts.** These are the fraudster's easiest manipulation. All he or she has to do is create unreasonable assumptions.
- **Note disclosures.** These are another breeding ground for fraud. All the fraudster has to do is not disclose or incorrectly disclose pertinent information.

All of these potential frauds are created by the fraudster's ability to identify the perceived speculations and expectations of the interested parties. The 800-pound friendly gorilla must identify the needs of the interested parties before the fraudster does in order to detect, deter, and prevent fraud.

People have a created expectation or belief that something will happen, and it often creates disappointment when it does not occur. Organizations run into problems when their expectations are misaligned. For instance, Wall Street may expect a specific division to have good earnings, but what happens when the division is shut down because of a hurricane? The thinking that every organization has accounted for every possible outcome creates a misaligned expectation.

Add to that the expectation of a targeted earning number without factoring in all foreseeable and possible unforeseeable events. You have created positive speculation and no longer have tangible value, because people tend to get caught up in the idea that the speculation will last forever. An organization cannot develop a futuristic outlook based on assumptions or intangible value that is not monitored. An intangible can change at a moment's notice by an inability to satisfy the perceived expectation (in the above example, the hurricane). We need to explore the various potentially overreaching expectations that have developed around organizational processes in order to prevent fraud and determine how much organizational fluff exists.

A capitalist society cannot exist without accounting. Just look at what happens anytime there is a financial scandal in an organization. The whole financial structure comes to a grinding halt, as it did with Enron, Lehman Brothers, and WorldCom. The speculative bubble is burst by fraud, and the financial goodwill of the organization is no longer evident.

The development of an oversight model must take into consideration the miscommunications that are often made in the development of the assumptions by comparing the established rules-based model of accounting to the organization's principle-based models, which often conflict. Greed has to be considered as part of any equation to determine if fraud is present. It's about the people and their choices, and the choices are more demanding in a principle-based regimen. Whereas in a rules-based environment one might say, "Nothing says I can't do it," in a principle-based environment, one looks to the spirit of the guiding literature.

If people in an organization are made to feel that they are part of the organizational culture and that they have a vested interest in its value, they are more likely to act ethically. Great leaders lead by example. If too much force is necessary to get the people in your organization to act with good moral character, then your organization has the wrong people. Management must foster the mind-set that all of their people are members of one unit, working for the greater good; even then, there are always going to be people who will manipulate and gain access to the value regardless of the organization's controls (think of all of the fraud that occurred after a national tragedy like 9/11, for instance).

Accountants and auditors cannot allow established professional industry principles to be replaced by an organization's principles if they conflict. It is important to state the principles, then, since they paint a clearer picture of the potential fraud. Let's take, for instance, the term *forensically accepted* versus *generally accepted* in reference to accounting assumptions. Here I introduce the word *forensically* to create the necessary professional skepticism regardless of the lines drawn in the sand. The intent is to avoid terms like *reasonably assured*, and substituting *forensically* for *generally* makes sense.

Before we discuss the principles, there are some terms you should keep in mind as you review them:

- An organization needs to determine if there has been the utilization of **creative** or **aggressive accounting techniques**.
- It is important to consider whether there is any **manipulation** or **managing** of an organization's earnings.
- Consider if the **financial statements** and **records** are free of **misstatements** or **omissions**.
- See whether an organization's **income** and **expenses** are free from being **manipulated** or **managed.**

THE 10 FORENSICALLY ACCEPTED GENERALLY ACCEPTED ACCOUNTING PRINCIPLE ASSUMPTIONS

The 10 forensically accepted generally accepted accounting principle assumptions (FAGAAPA) create problems unless people follow them with moral integrity. Before we enumerate the assumptions, let's make a list of 10 ways to avoid the potential problems:

1. Have only one regulator (e.g., American Institute of Certified Public Accountants (AICPA), Public Company Accounting Oversight Board

(PCAOB), various state boards of accountancy, Financial Accounting Standards Board (FASB), Auditing Standards Board (ASB), International Accounting Standards Board (IASB), Securities and Exchange Commission (SEC), Internal Revenue Service (IRS), and so on. The problem with having too many overlapping regulators is that an attempt to further clarify existing regulation can often lead to more confusion.

2. Make sure you don't find yourself following in these accounting firms' footsteps: Arthur Andersen (Bernie Ebbers, WorldCom; or Jeff Skilling, Enron) KPMG (Samuel Waksal, ImClone), Deloitte (John Riga, Adelphia), PricewaterhouseCoopers (Dennis Kozlowski, Tyco), Ernst & Young (Lehman Brothers). Learn from the past.
3. Do not use the professional regulatory standards incorrectly to save yourself or advocate your client's interest.
4. Do not hide behind engagement, management, or opinion letters with crafty wording as a result of the complexity often caused by the regulatory board's efforts to clarify the regulations.
5. Honor your shareholders and the public, even if you are the client professional.
6. Do not commit fraud.
7. Do not commingle one client with another. Keep client transactions at arm's length.
8. Do not shred and destroy documents inappropriately.
9. Cover yourself with GAAP and IFRS protection assurances.
10. Make sure that you are not acting on behalf of management but are independent and objective and hold yourself to the highest moral conduct by always applying the AICPA general standards of conduct.

Due professional care must always be maintained when making critical decisions. All processes and evaluations must have adequate planning and a supervisor with the proper oversight to support critical decisions. Critical decisions should not be made without sufficient evidence present. Treat critical decisions like write-downs, as if they are being presented in a court of law. If the parties involved in the decision do not have the professional competence, then do not allow the decision to be made. Use brainstorming and apply the concept that two heads are better than one.

All people in an organization must complete ethics training and cannot have others cover for them. Organizations must get their people to buy into the existing established controls and deterrents to ensure that the numbers tell the real story. Independence, objectivity, and integrity must be maintained by all people involved in the organizational process. Finally, the interests of all parties must be preserved over the individual's self-interest.

As we review the GAAP alongside the 10 FAGAAPA, it will become clear that either of them will give potential fraudsters an understanding of the environment required to create a hidden fraud, because the principles allow fraudsters to become master manipulators through the use of diversionary tactics. In the end, fraudsters learn the system so well that it becomes easy for them to commit fraud.

Principles and rules are defined and then interpreted by people, who are called to use their own judgment. People in an organization will have various needs, and it is important to gain an understanding of what these needs are. As an investigator, you must make sure you know which people pull the strings in the organization and understand these people's needs. The principles and rules have to focus on the needs of the organizational process and not on the needs of the individual within these processes. The successful organization that detects, deters, and prevents fraud finds a balance between the individual's and organization's needs by clearly identifying and monitoring them.

The 10 FAGAAPA are enumerated and described next.

Assumption 1: The Reliance on People Principle

GAAP's *economic entity assumption principle* formulates that business transactions are to be kept separate from the business owner's personal transactions. Individual business-entity transactions are to be kept separate from one another as well. It is important to identify people in the organization who maintain the compliance with this rule. Based on past examples, from Tulip Mania in 1637[11] to Freddie Mac in 2007,[12] it is clear that organizations are prone to unethical behavior. The need to develop compliance from today's organization is as necessary now as it was in 1637. Add to this the fact that there is a multitude of regulatory bodies of oversight that keeps growing, and you often create an environment of confusion rather than effective oversight to prevent fraud.

The first FAGAAPA, reliance on people principle, depends on the fact that people will not commingle their self-interest with the organization's interests when they believe that someone is watching and when the correct ethical tone has been established from top to bottom, both inside and outside the organization. Remember, the formula for fraud is people plus value.

Fraudsters need to see where they can convert a value into cash, and that is where the organization needs to be watching. Are the investors actually investing in the entity itself or in the entity's people whom they can relate to or trust? Know your people by having effective communication, requiring background checks, and making sure that people are well trained on an ongoing basis and subject to continually reviewed and rewritten rules and principles that the organization has established with oversight to ensure they are being followed.

It is also important that employees feel like an integral part of an organizational colony. When people believe they are part of a team, they are more likely to communicate as a team. Alienation creates miscommunication and misunderstanding. Make your employees want to be part of finding fraud as well as stopping it.

Let's start thinking like a fraudster by introducing aggressive and creative accounting practices. In accounting, business and personal transactions are supposed to be maintained separately. But what stops an organization's people from commingling transactions as well as instituting an aggressive accounting approach to serve their own self-interest? As the British historian Lord Acton said, "Absolute power corrupts absolutely."

A simple example is moving the debt from a company balance sheet to an unknown related entity. Does this not improve the position of the reporting entity's balance sheet, since the assets appear higher once the corresponding debt is no longer reflected properly? Using simple accounting manipulation, the fraudster could debit the liability account, whether or not paid, and that debit would remove the debt from the financial communication. This would increase the value of the organization.

Applying the simple accounting formula "assets minus liabilities equals equity" (in which equity is net worth, or organizational value) is helpful in understanding where fraud can exist in the organizational process. I use a forensic accounting formula that alters this formula to "assets minus people equals equity." People can create liability because they can commit fraud. Without people there is no liability, so in the new formula I have made people synonymous with liabilities. The acronym for "assets minus people equals equity" is APE, and the P is a good place for your 800-pound friendly gorillas to be positioned.

In any accounting transaction, debits must equal credits. In this type of transaction, the corresponding credit would normally be cash, when you pay for things. The fraudster will choose a revenue account so that he or she can increase the value of the organization. If the asset cash was reduced and the liability was reduced, there would be no effect on the financials, because they are both balance sheet accounts. If the accounts are shifted to an income statement or a statement of earnings account like revenue, there is an effect on the communication because the liability account went down and the revenue is eventually charged to the retained earnings in the balance sheet. In the APE formula, this situation results in an increase.

Let's put numbers into the equation, posting a transaction the correct way and then the way a fraudster would, so we can gain an understanding of how a fraud can occur.

Take the payment of an outstanding accounts payable bill in the amount of $1,000. The correct entry for that transaction would be to credit the asset cash, which would reduce it by the $1,000. Then a corresponding debit to the liability accounts payable would be made, which would reduce it by the same $1,000 and ultimately have a zero effect on the equity (since they are both balance sheet accounts). Let's plug this into the APE formula and examine Exhibit 2.2.

Exhibit 2.2 shows the effect of a credit to the asset cash, which was a reduction in the asset from a $2,000 beginning balance to a $1,000 ending balance, and a debit to the liability accounts payable, reducing its balance from a beginning balance of $2,000 to an ending balance of $1,000. Since both an asset and a liability were reduced by equal amounts, there was a zero, or no, effect on equity.

Now let's create the fraudster's account selections. The fraudster makes no entry to the asset account but makes a debit to the liability account in the amount of $1,000, which means the fraudster needs to credit $1,000 somewhere. The fraudster chooses to credit equity, because this gives the appearance of increasing the organization's value (since the asset balance was not reduced) and hides the manipulation.

EXHIBIT 2.2 Balance Sheet A

EXHIBIT 2.3 Balance Sheet B

Balance Sheet

Short-Term Loan

	Debit	Credit	
Beginning Balance		$ 2,000.00	
	Sales		
Reduced Debt	$ 1,000.00		
Ending balance		$ 1,000.00	

Asset Decreased

Accounting Formula	A	Minus	L	Minus	Equals
	$ -		$ 1,000.00		$ (1,000.00)
				Debit	Credit

Income Statement

Sales

	Debit	Credit
Beginning Balance		$ 2,000.00
		Sales
Increase Sales		$ 1,000.00
Ending balance		$ 3,000.00

Liability Decrease

Proves Out

Equals Zero (0)

As you can see, a simple changing of the accounts by a fraudster can distort the picture. Organizations need to develop an oversight model to ensure that these manipulated transactions do not exist and that credits and debits are posted properly. An example of this simple type of manipulation happened with Lehman Brothers in a case called Repo 105.[13]

A simple debit to a liability and a created sale to the income statement account allows the fraudster to use manipulation. These simple adjustments to the account selection increase the organization's value. The fraudster knows what accounts to manipulate to create these appearances. Does your organization have the 800-pound friendly gorilla making sure that transactions are properly reflected?

Ernst & Young, the auditor of Lehman Brothers at the time of its failure, raised the defense that the Repo 105 transactions in question were recorded in accordance with GAAP and that the clean audit opinion they issued was fully supported. Their probable argument was that when the Repo 105 transactions happened, the firm was not required under the accounting rules to disclose them, yet the attorney general slapped them with civil fraud charges. Whose self-interest was being preserved: the accountants' or Lehman Brothers'? What about Wall Street's? As long as there is no outrage (interest) created by the action, the rules remain subject to human judgment and the expectation gap exists.

Assumption 2: Show Me the Money Principle

GAAP's *monetary unit assumption principle* states that economic activity is measured in U.S. dollars. Only transactions that can be measured in U.S. dollars can be recorded. Organizations need to address the expectation gap issues that arise when determining monetary values. Just look at recent years' fair value standards and the accounting industry's formulation of additional and new standards.[14] There is a need to value organizational assets properly.

An organization must be mindful of inflation, because if that is not monitored properly, it can have a tremendous effect on an organization's value. When we look at inflation, we need to be mindful that we are mixing measured dollars (historical) from early years with current-year dollars that are needed to maintain an organization's value and operations (see Exhibit 2.4).[15]

Organizations have to be mindful that these types of factors can create the necessary distractions for fraud to occur. It is important to understand who can make these assumptions and underlying supports when determining whether

EXHIBIT 2.4 U.S. Inflation Calculator

Inflation Calculator		
Start	*Jan 1914	(enter year)
End	*Jan 2012	(enter year)
Cumulative inflation:		2166.65%

a current organization's fair value is correct. The fraudster understands this, so you should too.

Goodwill is the intangible value of an organization, based on its reputation or its future earnings and not its physical assets. An organization's tangible value is what is left after using the assets to satisfy all liabilities. An organization's goodwill should not only be thought of at a time of sale or purchase but reviewed and evaluated on an ongoing basis. It takes just one rumor or unexpected event to see how quickly an organization can lose its intangible goodwill value.

The requirement of maintaining multiple sets of books to comply with taxing authorities as well as financial reporting regulatory bodies is an example of conflicting legislation that creates additional costs, as well as the necessary confusion that the fraudster needs to remain undetected. Organizations maintain books and records for tax preparation (Internal Revenue Code [Federal] or state and local taxing authorities) and financial statement preparations (GAAP, IFRS, and Securities and Exchange Commission), which often report drastically different results. Perhaps there is another set of books that is not talked about (fraudster's rules?). Here, a clear expectation gap has been created simply by the fact that people want to pay less in taxes but earnings must be higher in order to increase returns. The Internal Revenue Service (IRS) regulations often conflict with GAAP for financial reporting, causing an opportunity for the fraudster in the expectation gap. Clearly, there can be two real-world differences in expectations as well as two sets of rules and principles.

For instance, can people in your organization barter? Bartering is the act of two or more parties trading goods and services without money, because of either a perceived mutual benefit or a lack of cash, it often involves transactions that are not recorded in the books. An example would be if I did accounting work for you and you fixed my car in return, and neither of us told anyone.

Similarly, may people in the organizational process use the organizational goodwill and resources to sell goods as a competitor? These various deflections are legal on the surface. However, they offer the diversion that a fraudster needs to perpetrate a fraud, and they create the various expectation gaps that exist within the system by remaining outside the recording and traditional accounting process. In both instances the fraud exists, because the cash (or cash value, in the case of bartering) never hits the books; an entry is not recorded.

Transactions that are allowed to exist outside an organization's books and records pose the most difficult challenge to fraud detectors. The only people who can expose these types of off-the-book transactions are those who are involved in the parts of the organizational process in which the value is exposed—what investigators term the "catch me if you can" approach. The solution to this lies in maintaining organizational oversight and enforcing the core principles and rules, both internally and externally, on an ongoing basis. The organization has to keep its house in order by creating the proper awareness and proactive thinking. This can be aided by establishing the presence of an 800-pound friendly gorilla to tell the people in the organization that not only is someone watching but that open communication channels exist. The same principles (rules) create the need for multiple sets of books in order to properly report the financial information that could otherwise create the potential for manipulation by fraudsters.

Remember that the fraudster needs to convert the value into cash. Organizations must watch the people who have access to the value and monitor any expectation gap issues by instituting the proper oversight modeling. This oversight modeling should be specifically designed to lead by example. Proactive rather than reactive thinking detects, deters, and prevents fraud.

The second FAGAAPA, show me the money, relies on the fact that the separation of duties does not work if the people who decide on the separation do not maintain the principles (rules). Watching one of the simplest functions within an organization, like the opening of mail, can be a tremendous deterrent and capture unexpected information. It is often not a high-level person opening the mail, yet you could be missing the opportunity to see inappropriately addressed mail, checks made to companies other than the organization in question, and other potential discrepancies. The first point of entry is by mail, whether paper or electronic, and you need to establish what I call *funnel keepers*. The funnel keepers are the first to see the information coming into the organizational process. By utilizing the 800-pound friendly gorilla as a funnel keeper, we can make sure that what comes in our organizations is handled in accordance with the organization's procedures and policies. These funnel keepers—if established properly—catch fraud before the potential fraudster has access to the organization's value or is able to continue an ongoing fraud. A simple example is the mail clerk. He or she sees an invoice addressed to an employee who is not in accounts payable. The mail clerk can raise a red flag as opposed to allowing the mail to go to that employee. Training people to be funnel keepers at certain control points will detect, deter, and prevent fraud. Ask yourself the following:

- Who is sorting and checking the initial contacts?
- Why is mail going directly to people rather than to a control point?
- Who makes the deposits in the organization?
- Is he or she aligned with the person in charge of the recording function (i.e., is there socializing between them)?
- Who reconciles the cash? Does he or she also write checks or make deposits?
- Who posts the transactions? Is this also the person who initiated the transaction or approved the transaction?
- When was the last time you rotated job functions or ran an updated credit report or background check on your organization's people (whether or not you trust them)?
- When was the last time you performed an unannounced site visit to your people to verify that controls are actually being followed?
- When was the last time you hung out at the water cooler and heard the organizational gossip?

This is type of 800-pound friendly gorilla questioning that enables organizations to find out who is not following protocol or has developed relationships that impair protocol. We often ignore the simplest control points and then wonder why fraud can exist. Put everything in the funnel and watch as it comes out. The earlier you catch something, the less impact it will have (see Exhibit 2.5).

How many directions do you allow something to go in after it has gone through your funnel control point (where people meet value) in your organization? You cannot ignore the simplest and most obvious control points in your organization if you are to be successful in deterring, detecting, and preventing fraud.

Organizations can manipulate value or transactions to manage earning peaks and valleys through the monetary measurements they choose. The potential fraudster can create a distraction by utilizing either the concept of misstatement or omission. By manipulating the timing of the transaction, the fraudster can create the necessary diversion. If you set target earnings, the organization will be expected to meet those earnings, so why are you so surprised when an organization's people are doing what they are expected to do? When you leave the organization with a simple choice, like amortizing goodwill, is it surprising when people choose the longest period (which can be

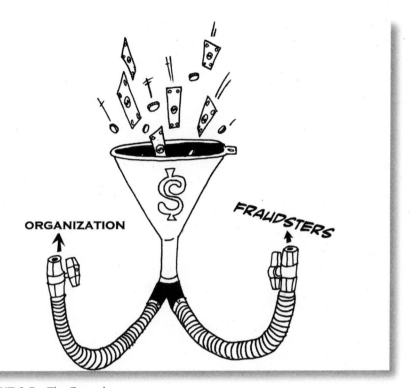

EXHIBIT 2.5 The Funnel

Copyright © 2012 James Lee

up to 40 years to reflect stronger earnings, since the amortization will be less, resulting in higher earnings)? That practiced continued until June 2001, when the Financial Accounting Standards Board (FASB) eliminated goodwill amortization by issuing statement 142, "Accounting for Goodwill and Intangible Assets," which states that goodwill and indefinitely lived intangible assets are no longer amortized but are reviewed annually for impairment. The accounting bodies make rules for accountants to follow, but when it is later determined that the rules do not work for the benefit of others, the bodies become creative and the rules are eliminated by new principles.

Not everything the people do in an organization points to fraud. What is important is that you know whether an activity is ethically proper. If you see no evil, hear no evil, and speak no evil, you cannot stop fraud. Let people in the organization perceive that the 800-pound friendly gorilla is watching through training and by creating awareness of the consequences.

It is critical for an organization to make sure that any people in key organizational positions who may be attempting to push the envelope have well-documented support for their positions and that their moral compass is pointing in the correct direction. People in the organization should feel that the 800-pound friendly gorilla is there to protect and help them. They should feel like team players.

In general, fraudsters want to tell someone about the fraud they committed and get it off their chests. Creating an atmosphere that is friendly is likely to get people to open up. Remember that the goal is to determine which people in an organization may be in the rationalization phase of deciding to commit fraud. Rationalization is often done before the actual fraud and after a need exists and an opportunity is identified. By creating an 800-pound friendly gorilla atmosphere, you may not only coax confessions but also identify potential fraudsters and their needs.

People have a natural tendency to want to trust quickly to enable them to delegate responsibility. However, there is nothing wrong with requiring the proper documentary support or evidence to ensure that people remain trustworthy. It is the rush to trust with or without a sound foundational relationship in the organizational structure that enables fraud to exist in today's organizations. If the proper documentary evidence is absent, it should raise a red flag, regardless of the relationship and the level of established trust. The same documentary evidence that provides the evidentiary proof of fraud in a court of law should be readily available and reviewed by independent people and the appropriate levels of management within the organizational structure to ensure that the transactions are proper and that your people remain trustworthy.

Assumption 3: Whatever Time Works for You Principle

GAAP's *time period assumption principle* states that financial positions and activities, even the most difficult and ongoing business activities, can be reported in relatively short periods (e.g., monthly, quarterly, semiannually, and annually). Someone who can manipulate the period can cover up fraud and create the necessary diversion.

The third FAGAAPA, whatever time works for you, is where most fraud can remain undetected. If you have the wrong people controlling this timing principle, you can utilize creative or aggressive accounting techniques to create earnings manipulations, financial statement omissions or misstatements, or income and expense manipulation by management or your people.

Ensure that the people controlling the timing of the financial reporting communications are trustworthy. Develop the factors and variables surrounding the transaction with documentary supports. The organization needs to develop an understanding of the external pressures it faces and communicate to everyone in the organization that these pressures are not to override proper reporting in accordance with the established principles (rules). The organization needs to be aware of the targets and expectations to make sure that people do not begin to justify unethical or fraudulent behavior to meet certain expectations.

The clock seems to always be ticking. Some examples of deadlines imposed on an organization's people are the IRS's April 15 federal income tax deadline, other tax (e.g., payroll, sales tax) filing deadlines, the SEC 10 K filing deadline, the due date of the earnings numbers to meet Wall Street's expectations, and something as simple as picking up the kids by four o'clock. People need adequate time to record entity transactions properly and accurately (better to be accurately slow than inaccurately fast) with the correct mental focus. People are going to make mistakes and cut corners because no one wants to lose his or her job or let an organization down by missing a deadline.

AICPA Code of Professional Conduct general standard rule 201, cited earlier, states that adequate planning and supervised people should not affect events. Rather, events affect people. People must be held accountable for timely reporting requirements, and if they can't meet these deadlines, their organizations need to understand why. Organizations must make sure that the people who are required to do the work have the adequate skills and training to meet the necessary timing to reflect organizational transactions properly and not have unrealistic expectations put on them. Organizations need to put in time clocks and require time sheets to create accountability. Timing should not be allowed to create pressures on people and create fraud opportunities within an organization.

A couple of examples that violate the time assumption principle are leaving the books open beyond the reporting period for sales recordings or deferring expenses to a subsequent period.

Time accountability is a critical element in detecting, deterring, and preventing fraud. Know what the people in your organization are doing by monitoring the time and the results associated with that time. But do not be fooled by someone who is always meeting the deadlines. Make sure that someone independent is looking closely at the finished product.

Assumption 4: Unfair Value Principle

GAAP's *historical cost principle* states that goods and services are to be recorded at their original or historical cost. When looking at this, you need to examine where there is an opportunity for invoices to be altered by the people in that process, and you need to check the financing to see whether any creative financing exists. Ongoing efforts must be in place to verify costs and ensure that the appropriate documentation exists and hasn't been altered. You must continually monitor costs to ensure that you are receiving the best price and the biggest bang for your buck. The more efficient you are in the management of costs, the more profitability the organization will enjoy.

The principle of value becomes more complex when dealing with domestic and international issues such as currency valuation, transfer pricing, stock markets, the war on terror, the Internet, the ability to disseminate information, political sanctions, and other factors that can arise.

The next issue after the ability to alter the cost is the huge assumption that you can value assets fairly. You need not look beyond the valuations utilized with collateral debt obligations, or beyond the hedge fund concepts, to see that this affords the potential fraudster with a lot of flexibility to remain undetected in an organization.

What is fair value? If you ask three people, you are likely to get three different opinions. In my opinion, if a willing buyer will buy and a willing seller will sell when neither of them is under any duress in choosing to engage in the transaction, the transaction will indicate that a fair market value or fair value exchange has taken place. An example that would not indicate market value is if a person were to physically force a buyer to purchase something for $1 million; in this case, the buyer would be under duress.

Welcome to the world of fair value accounting valuations. There is not a successful stock that does not contain speculative value. So when times are good, the investors and the executives are happy and so are the people in the organization. How is it, then, that all of a sudden we have Tycos, WorldComs, and Enrons when cash flows run out? In essence, all fraud is one big Ponzi scheme. As long as there is money (cash liquidity) there to feed the greed, fraud will remain undetected until interest and outrage are created.

The fourth FAGAAPA, unfair value, may be illustrated as follows. Items are carried on the company's books at cost, which refers to the amount spent, measurable in cash or the cash equivalent, when an item was originally acquired (whether that purchase was yesterday or 20 years ago). You now recognize that cost may not always reflect the current value of the item. A fraudster can introduce creative value techniques that may create artificial asset value and generate perceived operational cash flow. Let's call it window-dressing the financial statements to make the external users of the financial communications happy.

For instance, you buy a brand-new Mack truck for $150,000. The people in an organization give you the invoice, and the check is made out to Johnny the Mack Dealer in the amount of $155,000 to cover license, registration, and so forth. How many organizations actually verify the vehicle identification number before it is recorded in the organization's books and records to ensure that you in fact received what you paid for? What if the truck was really just a Matchbox toy car or a hunk of junk?

The organizations that successfully combat fraud maintain capital plans and well-documented maintenance records and logs. It is a bonus that the same controls to detect, deter, and prevent fraud create efficiencies and add to the operation's bottom line by creating accountability. This proactive thinking helps organizations to sustain their existence.

So how do items get valued? Are they valued utilizing an income approach, a comparable sales approach, or a cost approach? What is the difference between fair value and fair market value? *Fair value* means that your shares are valued without applying any discount considerations. Fair market value of the ownership interest applies. Let's apply these discounts to create a deception perspective and understand what fraud may look like when people do not have their priorities in line with the organization's.

To use another example, in divorce cases in New Jersey, the standard of fair value is established by *Brown v. Brown*.[16] The problem with this standard is what I call the Piscopo effect.[17] In the case of *Piscopo v. Piscopo*, the valuator was allowed to compensate comedian Joe Piscopo because of his celebrity status. In this case, a simple increase in salary compensation results in a lower benefit stream (net income), which impairs (reduces) value.

Apply the same thinking to an organizational process, and you have the ability to create the value necessary to meet whatever expectation is required to satisfy an underlying need. Is the value subject to speculative value, which can allow a fraudster to create the necessary diversion to commit fraud and remain undetected?

When applying the fraudster's perspective to the income approach, what income do you need to show to make it work, or what capitalization rate do you need to make it work? Is it the fraudster's level of thinking rather than the objective or independent thinking that should be employed? Take $100,000 and divide that by a 4 percent capitalization rate, and you have $2,500,000. This is not enough to make it 5 or 6 percent. Who is watching? Ask Crazy Eddie's Sam Antar (see Chapter 1). He committed fraud simply because he could.

So if the fraudster can find a sound rationale for the capitalization rate chosen, he or she can reflect the value necessary to satisfy the users of the financial information and gain the value necessary to get cash. The successful organization benchmark is the use of industry-independent data points. With today's technology, one can use the internet to easily make a comparison that will support a capitalization rate.

Think of what causes someone's interest cost to be higher. Utilizing this thinking in an organization will ensure a rational capitalization or discount rate. What is the company's ability to pay? You need to look at your organization's interest coverage ratio, debt service coverage ratios, and net worth to debt ratios—all typical covenants in most loan agreements. Is the organization meeting the typical loan covenants with or without effort? If it is not meeting them, a red flag should be raised.

The next issue is past credit payment history (or what the accounts payable turnover ratio is). Is accounts payable increasing? If so, is it because sales are increasing in proportion?

Then there is the collateral. How dependable is the value being utilized? It should not be the same real estate value that led to the subprime and financial meltdown.

The fraudster utilizing the comparable sales approach realizes that the selected comparables will not work. So the fraudster shows the accountant the comparables that will make the value work in the fraudster's favor. The fraudster offers to raise the appraisal fee if you manipulate the comparables, or threatens to cut the accountant's fees, all in the name of it being in everyone's interest.

The fraudster utilizing the cost approach can call up the architect and get the square foot prices raised, and if the architect needs a party from the organization to call up a contractor to get the numbers the architect needs, the fraudster will participate to inflate the proposal and justify the numbers.

Make sure that any valuations regarding the sale, acquisition, or development of cost proposals are supported in the existing documents. The existing physical assets should have unannounced inspections done by third-party independent verifiers. There are many asset verification companies that do nothing but verify and value assets.

Know that the people you are involved with in these processes are trained. Do they understand the policies and procedures? Is there a bandage approach, pressures to meet targets, and/or an incorrect ethical tone? Forensic accountants assume that their work is going to end up in litigation. Forensic accountants are fact finders for a judge and jury, but they are *not* the judge and jury, as I've said. Forensic accountants gather documentary support and physically inspect, and so should the fraud-preventing organization.

Assumption 5: Leap of Good Faith Principle

GAAP's *full disclosure principle* states that information that could affect the decisions of an investor, a lender, or another user of the financial statement, based on the presented statement, should be disclosed in the notes or other supplemental information with that financial document. The decision to make a disclosure is open to judgment. Ask yourself this question: "Is this something I would want to know if I were an investor, creditor, shareholder, or other interested party?" If not disclosing causes you to lose sleep at night, then you should disclose. The best approach for an organization is to overdisclose, since a failure to disclose can have a catastrophic effect on organizational value.

The fifth FAGAAPA, leap of good faith, reminds us that people make up the management of the organization's judgment. They can choose to disregard the necessity to disclose information about transactions if it is not in their best interest to disclose. Textbook-prescribed footnotes are made up by people with the intent of ensuring that liability is limited yet the organization disclosed fairly.

The probable determinations are made by people. Therefore, you have to establish an appropriate level of trust in the people who are determining reasonable estimable accounting standard decisions. Is it in the organization's best interest to disclose the transaction properly to preserve value?

Let's define some of the terms we just used. *Management* is the act or art of directing the conduct or supervision of something. Management requires planning, directing, and controlling. A *footnote* in the accounting world is an explanation or a comment usually placed in a separate section. *Probable* means supported by evidence strong enough to establish presumption but not proof. *Reasonable* means not extreme or excessive. *Estimable* means capable of being calculated approximately.

There is something called the "more likely than not" standard (also known as the 50–50.01 rule).[18] To apply this standard to gray-area tax positions with the IRS, for example, the position must result in the average person concluding that the tax position taken would result in a favorable outcome 50.01 percent of the time if challenged by the IRS to be allowed.

The standard also involves determining whether to disclose a contingent liability by the same type of measurement. People disclose what is best for people, and two people may have totally opposing judgments about whether their position would win more than 50.01 percent of the time if challenged by the IRS or the financial users concerning contingent liabilities. This creates a zone in which it is not required to be exact, and this is the event that creates the distraction fraudsters need.

The "more likely than not" standard is also applied in civil litigation matters and is referred to as the *preponderance of the evidence* (i.e., which way does the scale tip legally in deciding the facts?). Decisions about tax and financial determination revolve around the implied trust that people will do what is best for an organization, even though that may not always be the case.

An organization's management (people) sets the correct tone of an organization at the top by its actions when considering whether to footnote (give proper disclosure of transactions). It is always better to overdisclose than to underdisclose. Think of the last time you did not disclose something. What happened? The person you withheld the disclosure from probably became suspicious. If you're dealing with the theory of probable thinking (the 50–50.01 rule), assume it is going to take place. This is why we have the conservatism principle (this will be explained under assumption 10). Even a small mistruth can be blown out of proportion. The organization should maintain the thinking that it is better to be safe than sorry.

When dealing with contingency standards like *reasonably*, we need to consider the materiality and watch out for ethical dilemmas, since we are depending on people's judgments and the level of trust an organization has bestowed on them. One may deem immaterial what another may not. The materiality principle (see assumption 9), which allows accountants to disregard GAAP when there is no effect on the users of financial information, is not always about a percentage of the numbers in question, as people are often led to believe.

A violation of a structured transaction or regulation may have taken place that is not material in a limited period but that can affect the overall operations beyond the period in question, such as taking away a necessary license or permit to operate. It could also set a precedent for future conduct that becomes material. Financial communications are often for a specific amount of time, and that period may not capture the full effect of a transaction. The fraudster can create a lot of diversion when there is an ability to spread the fraud over a larger period. It is important to analyze not only the immediate impact of fraud but the long-term implications as well.

If you are in charge of delegating the estimating responsibility, it is important to make sure that the person estimating is qualified to do so and has the supporting evidence and the correct times for the events. Madoff is claimed to have stated that his Ponzi scheme began in the 1990s, but federal prosecutors believe it began in the 1970s. Many frauds that I have experienced have been over multiple periods.

Organizations need to encourage people to start thinking about the potential negative outcomes of transactions before they happen. Organization need to require the proper supports and documentary evidence for organizational conclusions to meet the "more likely than not" standard before the organizations are required to prove the positions taken. Make sure that the proper sign-offs have been secured and the organization remains proactive.

Organizations cannot be in an "after the fact" mode. They need to think about the deterrence of fraud and not just deal with fraud after it happens. Although you are not the judge and jury, if you are the auditor or accountant, you need to not pass the buck; you must make sure that the management of the organization understands the consequences of its actions.

When considering unrecorded and contingent liabilities, understanding Accounting Standard Codification 450, which replaced Financial Accounting Standards Board No. 5 "Accounting for Contingencies," is a useful tool for determining the best judgment based on the facts and circumstances you have been presented with.

The potential liability will continue to exist if the documentary supports do not convince the average user of the information that the actions were not improper. The fraudster always needs someone else to blame. Make sure the proper independent and transparent documents exist to support the positions taken. People disclose only what is best for themselves. A responsible organization makes sure that any of the positions taken are not at the expense of the interests of people outside the organization. Ultimately, those same positions will also not be in the interest of the organization. Make sure that any decision will not be deemed improper by a reasonable person.

Assumption 6: Going Under for Sure Principle

GAAP's *going concern principle* is that a company will continue to exist and will not have to be liquidated anytime soon (i.e., within a year). If the accountant or auditor believes that the company will not be able to continue for at least one year, then that must be disclosed.[19] At all times we must be cognizant of the working capital, which is current assets minus current liabilities. Many organizations are often only a turn away from becoming insolvent. Organizations are so busy with the historical perspective that they do not see the "forest for the trees" until it may be too late. The fraudster knows where the liquidity is in the organization.

The sixth FAGAAPA, going under for sure, is based on the thinking that every entity is a going concern because it is run by people who are under social, political, economic, and self-interest preservation influences, such as needing their jobs to pay their bills. Many times something is not disclosed because it may have a material effect that if found out could destroy an organization and uncover fraud. This makes the failure to properly disclose a self-fulfilling prophecy, resulting in devastation when withheld from the intended user. The organization that becomes proactive and properly discloses these communications will survive the inevitable concerns because it has properly trained people who can identify and address the transactions rather than ignore them because they may not be received in a favorable way. The sooner the organization or fraudster takes responsibility, the better.

An organization must know what people are steering the ship clear of the various concerns. Identify the smoking guns and make sure that people have not put blinders on toward preventing fraud. Make sure the people embrace the regulations and rules, and establish them as necessary principles rather than rules to guarantee the organization's continued existence. Make sure the people see the regulations and rules as opportunity. Setting a precedent of principle-based rule applications establishes the correct and necessary moral and ethical tone.

Organizations that are prone to social influences embrace chances to communicate effectively and bridge any differences that may be perceived. You should recognize political influences as a way of corporate life and hold the influences to the highest ethical standard to ensure your organizational existence. The organization that develops an atmosphere of self-interest preservation and a sense of entitlement that is in line with the expectations of all interested parties, both internal and external, guarantees its existence. The organization that handles economic exposure ahead of detrimental occurrences will continue to exist. Here are a few things you can do to ensure this:

- Research and keep tabs on the people steering the ship and the decisions they make. You can set up a Google alert that notifies you of anything that hits the Internet about your organization or industry. Make sure the organization is adequately insured for all potential exposures.
- Make sure the organization not only monitors but is also proactive in maintaining the necessary internal controls. Surprise people and do the

unexpected control monitoring. Putting on blinders does not excuse you. Ask Arthur Andersen, which went down, in part, because of poor internal controls and a lack of 800-pound friendly gorilla oversight.[20]

- If your organization is extremely regulated, make sure you are on the cutting edge of the regulations and changes.
- Expect and identify social influences. Make sure that organizational expectations are not misaligned with these potential influences.
- Know how political influences affect your organization. Make sure you know the political players and ensure that there is no corruption. If the political influences have a financial impact that includes proposed changes, make sure you get in front of them.
- Develop an atmosphere of self-interest preservation or a sense of entitlement with good greed, and remove bad greed. Good greed is competitive, and bad greed is deceptive or manipulative. These determinations involve the conscience, which is your intellect involved in judging what is right or wrong and are governed by the voice of truth and integrity. The goal in making the right choice with respect to good greed versus bad greed lies in making sure that your people are correctly and properly informed when making choices (see Chapter 1). Making the correct determination with respect to the level of underlying greed that may exist in your organization helps to detect, deter, and prevent fraud. These conscience decisions are not to be confused with legislation or laws that outline perimeters but rather lie in the ethical values of the people making these choices. Make sure your organization's 800-pound friendly gorillas are monitoring and maintaining the proper ethical tone with your people to preserve the organization's value.

Stay ahead of the current economics and know where your industry is heading. There is so much economic data available to make sure you engage in forward thinking and put away for a rainy day when you can, before a downturn occurs. Learn from the past and plan for the future. Provide for the worst and hope for the best. Take advantage of benchmarking data, since there is no excuse for missing the boat on economic downturns. Do not ignore the signs. Monitor this basic accounting equation: current assets minus current liabilities equals working capital. Make sure your organization is liquid enough to operate.

Often in my discussions it appears that I am talking about the difference between good and bad management more than fraud. To gain a clearer fraud picture requires you to review past examples of fraud, including fraud that is committed by management. There is often a fine line between fraud and bad management, thus the reason that we gather all the facts and leave the decision to the judge and jury to determine whether management committed fraud.

Current assets are cash, accounts receivable, inventory, and short-term investments, and they should be readily available to satisfy current liabilities, which are accounts payable, accruals like wages, and any payments expected to be made within 12 months. This is a key focus for both internal and external organizational parties in detecting, deterring, and preventing fraud. An organization's ability to meet current obligations with current funds is critical in determining its financial standing.

Assumption 7: Matching Game Principle

GAAP's *matching game principle* requires companies to use the accrual method of accounting. Expenses are matched with revenues in the period in which they are earned or incurred, regardless of whether cash has been exchanged.

Organizations must record the transactions in the correct period, or fraud can exist. The seventh FAGAAPA, matching game principle, illustrates that the entity's position is better than it actually is. The accrual or cash method allows for people to make choices that may not reflect the transactions properly. Organizations that do not match the expectations for financial communication with taxes create the necessary rationalization for a fraud to occur. If one objective of the financials (GAAP) is to show the highest income, while a contrasting objective is to report lower income and pay less tax, these differences must be well documented, since these are clearly two directly opposing objectives. The organization must match the correct revenue with the related expenses that created those revenues in the proper periods and with the proper transactions that created them.

Check the compensation levels of key employees to make sure they are in line with market expectations and competitors in the same industry. Is the salary to do the job, or is it a return on investment? This is not a shareholder investment but a self-interest distributions return for an employee. It is critical that the salary is in line with the expectation. An organization cannot be asset rich and cash-liquidity poor if it is to exist. An organization's deferral of expenses should be tested to ensure they are in line with the overall financial picture and industry standards. We need to examine acceleration revenues and determine if they are one-shot gimmicks or likely to continue. An organization must correctly capitalize its transactions so it does not mislead the users of financial communications. Organizations must closely examine all related entities or affiliations and make sure there are none that the organization is unaware of.

Pay attention to the statement of cash flows, especially the inflows and outflows within an organization. Understand the direct-method cash flows and follow the cash. Make sure a complete ratio analysis and benchmark analysis is performed and compared with other companies. Use the IRS ratios, Risk, Management, Association (RMA), and MicroBilt (Integra) ratio statistics, all of which are readily available, and use either the North American Industry Classification System or the IRS code's organizational business clarifications.

Pay attention to the required disclosure of uncertain income tax positions.[21] Test revenues and verify that expenses are recorded in the correct period. Observe unusual or unexplained growth. Match current assets with current liabilities and make sure the organization's liquidity is solid. Look for related parties and affiliations by examining unusual or infrequent transactions and/or journal entries to reflect the transactions. Look for conflicts of interest.

Assumption 8: Whatever I Need Principle

GAAP's *revenue recognition principle* is the accrual basis of accounting, which states that revenues are recognized when they are earned (i.e., when a product has been sold or a service has been performed, regardless of when the money is actually received); they are realized or realizable and the expenses are recorded when incurred (when the goods or services are received).

Alternatively, the cash basis of accounting recognizes revenues when they have been constructively received (when the cash is in hand). Expenses are recognized when the cash is actually paid. When allowing expenses to be recorded without payment, one should require an organization to disclose what portion of the revenue is attributable to those unpaid expenses. The FASB's "Statement of Cash Flows" preferred choice is the direct method, yet the indirect cashflows statement is the statement of choice among most managers and organizations.[22] The direct method shows inflows and outflows of cash, which provide for the best measurement of the financial position of an organization.

The eighth FAGAAPA, whatever I need, is often not in the interest of an organization. By understanding the impact that fees have on the financial position of an auditor, potential opportunities to manipulate are exposed. More than ever auditors need to hold to their AICPA Code of Professional Conduct general standards to ensure they maintain independence. The fact that the fee is material to the auditor may in and of itself create an appearance of a lack of independence. This will remain a constant area of scrutiny that needs to be monitored to ensure that auditors remain independent. An organization that operates within its own expectations rather than Wall Street's removes the temptation to manipulate. Organizations should communicate the proper numbers even if there are consequences. The only thing that manipulating the existing transactions does is kick the can down the street. Face and address the unrealistic expectations your organization may have rather than allowing people to succumb to them by manipulating the numbers to meet them.

Investor communications and expectations need to be in line with the organization's communications and expectations. Make sure the people in the organization are not just telling the investors what they want to hear. Has the organization determined the need to fund the lifestyles of top management and the financial impact on its operational aspects? The organization needs to gain an understanding of the people in key value opportunity positions and determine whether these people have created personal self-interest needs at the expense of the organization's values.

It is often assumed that fraudsters are bad people, but anybody can be a fraudster. Organizations need to examine their people for any gray-area political, altruistic, or socially acceptable occurrences. For instance, an employee may be giving to a charity with stolen money. Unfortunately, people's views sometimes contradict their actions.

Take a look at the histories of manipulations and the results on the organizations shown in Exhibit 2.6. These events can teach you how to detect, deter, and prevent fraud by examining and identifying whose needs were being satisfied in each situation.

Assumption 9: The Tone at the Top Principle

GAAP's *materiality* is the magnitude of an omission or misstatement of accounting information that, in light of the surrounding circumstances, makes it probable that the judgment of a reasonable person relying on the information would have been changed or influenced by the omission or misstatement. Professional judgment is needed to decide whether an amount of information is insignificant, or immaterial. Even if something is immaterial, it could violate another accounting principle (and go uncorrected).

Typically, the accountant mind-set is that if you can say something is immaterial by calculating it as a percentage of the gross dollars, it is not material and you can ignore it. Unfortunately, with fraud, the dollars may not be

EXHIBIT 2.6 Manipulation by Company

Manipulation	Company
Selling to related companies	Adelphia, Enron, and PNC
Making up the numbers	Crazy Eddie
Double-booking	Enron and Dynegy's
Maintaining continual endless growth	GE
Accelerating contracts	Paragon Construction
Smoothing revenue	Rite Aid
Channel stuffing	Sunbeam
Recognizing lease transactions in advance	Xerox
Other creative revenue recognition techniques	Waste Management

material in the context of the overall company numbers, but left unaddressed, the omission will send a bad message. If something is not material, it does not remove the responsibility to disclose it if the transaction was inappropriate. Also, keep in mind that what starts out as a minor inaccuracy can later create the need for a major lie to cover it up. An organization that maintains the correct approach with material or immaterial transactions that are not proper creates the correct environment to detect, deter, and prevent fraud in the organization.

The ninth FAGAAPA, the tone at the top, asks whether the items in question have been considered and whether the resulting outcomes are fully understood in terms of the ethical ramifications (and not just the monetary considerations). Organizations need to review the materiality decision after having brainstorming sessions, with all interested parties' interests being represented. An organization's documentary evidence must support the conclusions as though presented in a court of law.

An organization must be satisfied that the average person would consider the decision ethical. The materiality conclusion should be thought of in the context of whether it has the potential to be toxic to an organization. Is it never good practice to allow any principle to be overridden? If the self-interest of the organization is put before the interests of the shareholders, the banks, or other investors in order to alter a correct principle, the results will be toxic.

Assumption 10: Write Down, Write Off, Rip Off Principle

GAAP's *conservatism principle* directs companies to choose an alternative that will result in less net income and/or a lower asset amount. The accountant is charged with "breaking a tie" if a regulation does not direct an accountant to be conservative. Accountants are expected to be unbiased and objective. But an organization needs to ensure that the use of conservatism is not just a way to place the blame somewhere else. The use of conservatism, however, may not always lead to conservative outcomes.

The tenth FAGAAPA—write down, write off, rip off—says that timing is everything (i.e., business cycles are critical timings). When a new CEO, manager, or auditor determines that previously acquired or developed products (assets), lines of business, or business segments are not performing according to plan; that they are not profitable; or that there has been a fraud, you need to document it. These situations allow people to load costs onto someone else by write-downs. The write-down can then be charged against retained earnings or listed as an extraordinary item in an income statement simply because it is not related to the current organization's operations. It creates an opportunity to blame it on someone else, whether the accountant, a past manager, or other personnel.

The same thinking can be used in determining inventory write-down determinations. An organization needs to include all interested parties in the process of these write-downs and ensure that all relevant documentation has been made available to maintain the proper impact of these transactions. If the fraudster realizes the original reserved write-down is not as bad as was projected, it can be the necessary diversion to gain access to organizational value and blame it on someone else while remaining undetected.

A simple reading of established auditor and accounting language demonstrates the ability to hide behind the GAAP that "financial statements are the responsibility of management." Read any standard management representation letter that the auditor or accountant obtains, and you will see that the auditor or accountant takes comfort in the fact that management said it is correct—so it must be, which sounds great until the high-profile executives' names are Bernie Madoff, Bernie Ebbers, Dennis Kozlowski, or any of the other managers whose words did not prove to be accurate. While auditors do not rely solely on management representations, such representations do provide evidence of deception in cases of management fraud.

The organization that uses the tenth FAGAAPA should establish a requirement that before the allowance of factoring in economic and external forces, an analysis be performed to determine that the appropriate write-down is not temporary. An accounting basis should be formulated, and the underlying assumption that a write-off is necessary has to have been established (with the assumptions clearly spelled out and supported).

Write-downs and rip-offs should be added back when recovered. No bonuses should be given until the injured parties receive restitution. AIG and other companies should not be allowed to give bonuses after almost being bankrupt when the interests of others have not been restored. Any recovery from the write-downs should go to the people who were harmed by the write-off. No write-down should be allowed without supportable documentation. A write-down should be prepared like evidence to be presented in a court of law.

Overall record keeping must be managed in detail. The lifeblood of an organization is the sales, marketing, and financial functions, which require timely recordings of expenditures and income, as well as tax records, advertising invoices, and more. Customer management (involves the recording of all their requests), payment history, and rules violations ensure that the facilities and infrastructure are maintained. Repairs require maintenance schedules, capital plans, and proper employee and subcontractor personnel records.

Risk management revolves around the determination of risk versus reward, which is often not shared with an auditor. When a risk is identified, there are three ways an organization can address it. First, it can completely ignore it. Second, the decision can be made that it's immaterial. Third, it can be determined to be too costly to address. An organization can also employ the risk transfer concept, in which someone else takes or shares your risk: Purchase insurance and transfer the risk to the insurer.

This is no different from buying auto insurance to transfer the risk of an accident from you to the insurer. People do not start driving more aggressively because they have insurance. Similarly, in cases such as AIG, the risk transfer did little. Instead, a successful organization will plan for problems, keep excellent files and records of every activity, and continually assess the record-keeping functions to determine whether changes are necessary before a fraud occurs. The key is to be proactive and not reactive to fraud by recognizing that fraud can exist and that all organizations are prone to it in some form.

 ## SUMMARY

An organization must possess an external code of ethics that is not in conflict with its internal practices. The government's role in regulating and legislating financial reporting started with the 1933–1934 Securities Exchange Acts.

From there, we saw Statement on Auditing Standards (SAS) No. 16, "Detection of Errors or Irregularities." Then there was the 1977 Foreign Corrupt Practice Act, the 1986 Fraud Detection and Disclosure Act, the 1986–1995 Treadway Commission, and finally the creation of the Committee of Sponsoring Organizations (COSO). Next, was SAS No. 78, "Consideration of Internal Controls in a Financial Audit" and the 2002 Sarbanes-Oxley Act.

In addition, we have SAS No. 82, "Consideration of Fraud," and, most recently, SAS No. 99, "Consideration of Fraud in a Financial Statement Audit." The Wall Street Reform and Consumer Protection Act of 2010 (the Dodd-Frank Act) is the most recent regulation from either the government or an accounting regulator.

While I applaud all of these efforts, preventing fraud really just comes down to people and the trust they are given. An organization knows that there is a fine balance between controlling by a ruler (a dictator) and controlling by the people's consensus if it is to successfully detect, deter, and prevent fraud. You cannot entirely legislate moral behavior by people, and the level of trust often given to people by an organization is probably better off being monitored by the 800-pound friendly gorilla. Far-reaching legislative thinking cannot replace inch-by-inch communication in an organization. Developing self-governing people with the correct attitudes, from top to bottom in your organization, is the best, proactive approach.

Legislation can be useful when it sets a moral tone for organizations, but it cannot foresee all the potential vulnerabilities to fraud that organizations have. One-size legislation does not fit all. Only the organization itself can develop the most effective strategies to detect, deter, and prevent fraud in its unique environment and structure. This is why organizations need 800-pound friendly gorillas.

Fraud exists, and because of the expectation gaps discussed in this chapter, it will continue to exist until people align the expectations of organizations with the expectations of the people involved with them. All of the principles and rules in the world will continue to be disregarded by those who are determined to commit fraud. Until we get people to accept and buy into accepted standards of conduct, including accounting pronouncements, fraud will exist. Greed exists in us all. The key is to manage greed into an ethical and moral organizational structure with the correct ethical tone set from top to bottom.

Follow the COSO internal control framework cube (see Exhibit 2.7) and keep it intact. Recognize the places in the organizational process where people can twist, turn, and jumble up the cube (see Exhibit 2.8).

An organization has to continually watch the people and the level of trust they have been assigned (inch by inch through the process), including whom

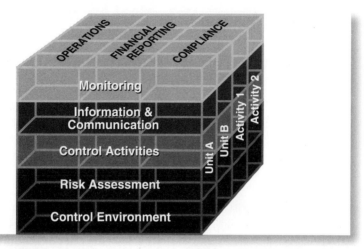

EXHIBIT 2.7   COSO Cube

Source: The Committee of Sponsoring Organizations of the Treadway Commission. From "An Update of COSO's Internal Control—Integrate Framework" presentation (May 2012), http://www.coso.org/documents/cosoicifoutreachdeck_05%2018%2012.pdf

they interact with, both inside and outside the company, especially whenever an organizational value is exposed (see Exhibit 2.9).

 ## ONE-MINUTE FRAUD MYSTERY ANALYSIS

Where does opportunity meet value in our chapter mystery? Who are the people involved? Remember that you are the fact finder and need to use divergent thinking. Here are some thoughts on this chapter's mystery, based on my experience in the field:

- **Allegation.** Carton threatens to go to the FBI after seeing that Too Good to Be True Inc. was an abandoned warehouse.
- **Probable cause.** Determine whether the intent level is civil or criminal. Note that regulated security transactions are a potential pump-and-dump scheme (an attempt to boost the price of a stock through recommendations based on false, misleading, or greatly exaggerated statements). Consider that the building that houses Too Good to Be True was abandoned and there are no people answering the phones. Note the document shredding

**Darn COSO cube never lines
up when I need it to!**

EXHIBIT 2.8 COSO Jumble

after the Moneymaker call and also that Walls and Biggs suspended trading of Too Good to be True after the Moneymaker call. This raises a red flag.

■ **Action.** Further questioning is necessary. A cautious approach should be taken. While you want to treat Wall, Biggs, and Sales as people of interest, you need to use the 800-pound friendly gorilla approach when investigating them. You need to understand the level of socialization and relationships that exist among the parties. Who has a clear understanding

**Everyone is happy and loving
when people follow the rules.**

EXHIBIT 2.9   In Line with Your People

of the organizational business process? Who has the potential to be the ring leader? Who else may be involved (Moneymaker)? Is the relationship among them limited to this transaction, or is it ongoing? Omar brought the problem to you; is he credible? Look into his background. Do not rule out victims or parties who bring the problem to light. Rule them out by doing proper due diligence. Examine where the greed exists that enables the fraudster to start justifying the rationalization to commit fraud. Are there external influences? Look for lifestyle changes. Look for conflicts of interest. Know your answers before you ask critical questions by having a well-thought-out and planned approach. Who recommended the trading?

Who maintained the required documents for trade recommendations? Who oversaw the trade recommendations?

- **Preparation.** Get records directly from Carton and see what documentary support and public information records exist about Too Good to Be True, such as location and corporate regulations, if any, electronic data gathering, analysis, and retrieval system (EDGAR), or registration-type public information are available.[23] This information does not raise a red flag to those being investigated, since most of the information is available without involving the suspect. Brainstorm and develop nonaccusatory, open-ended questions for the parties of interest. Ask whether the books are audited by independent auditors or available through the regulatory body in question. Seek legal counsel and make determination whether to involve FINRA, the SEC, and the Federal Bureau of Investigation (FBI).

- **People of interest.** Omar Carton, Gordon Walls, John Sales, Charles Biggs, Tom Ticker, and Hector Moneymaker.

- **People-with-knowledge interview plan.** Start at the top with CEO Walls and expect the finger-pointing to start. Discuss signature authority and internal reporting.

- Biggs should be next, but he is likely to point the finger elsewhere, since he seems to be the likely fraud facilitator (enabler).

- Sales is likely to expose the plot if put under a little pressure, since he seems to be executing what management tells him to do. He is the least likely to be able to commit fraud because he has no signature authority or reporting responsibilities.

- Ticker, the CPA, may be the last to know, because most CPAs are not likely to jeopardize their license. That said, refer to the general standard. Did the CPA have the competence to perform the accounting work? Was due professional care exercised? What did the CPA advocate for: the client or the public interest? Was the work adequately supervised and planned? Did the CPA gather the sufficient data to draw an objective and independent opinion?

- Moneymaker sounds least likely, since he appears to be the clearinghouse for the trades. But if Big Fish does a lot of business with Traders Inc., further consideration should be given to Moneymaker.

- See if the facts developed from the other interviews support Carton's story. Do not rely on testimony without supporting documentation. Always ensure that your opinion is supported by factual documentation and physical evidence.

- Note that everything has to go through Biggs; Walls is not likely to have his hands directly in the transactions. Is there a potential for the existence of any other parties with knowledge?

- **Documentary evidence.** Trade slips confirmations, the prospectus, marketing material, tax returns, general ledgers, and bank records.
- **Formulate opinion.** This is a pump-and-dump scheme. It involves artificially inflating the price of an owned stock through false and misleading positive statements in order to sell the cheaply purchased stock at a higher price. Once the operators of the scheme dump their overvalued shares, the price falls and the investors lose their money. Stocks that are the subject of pump-and-dump schemes are sometimes called "chop stocks."

The 800-Pound Friendly Gorilla Suggestions for Big Fish Investment Inc.

Before proceeding, we need to determine who was in need of the 800-pound friendly gorilla. Big Fish seems to be perpetrating the fraud and housing the potential fraudsters. The investors and the CPA firm need strategies to avoid fraud because they want to protect their investment; the CPA firm also does not want to be complicit in the fraud.

Whenever you have a stock manipulation, you need to protect your interest by making sure the organization that created the investment's value is not a shell. With the Internet and other resources available, it is easy to check an organization's underlying value if it promises a rate of return on an investment that is too good to be true. The 800-pound friendly gorilla level of thinking would dictate to investigate further and implement the following to reduce the risk of fraud:

- Identify the greed (where people meet the value).
- Monitor the responsibilities given to people with access to the value.
- Verify the underlying asset of the stock being traded.
- Determine if the financial statements and communications have been audited by a reputable accounting firm that has investment adviser accounting experience following the correct standard.
- Decide if it is too good to be true and think twice about your choice of investment.
- Check the float (the total number of shares publicly owned and available for trading) of the stock and see if it is prone to large swings in volume and price.[24]
- Examine who owns the stock.
- Perform a simple horizontal and vertical ratio analysis of the entity being invested in and see if it is in line with the industry averages.
- Match the company return (earning per share) with similar companies.[25] Understand why the company's earnings are exceeding expectations. Most

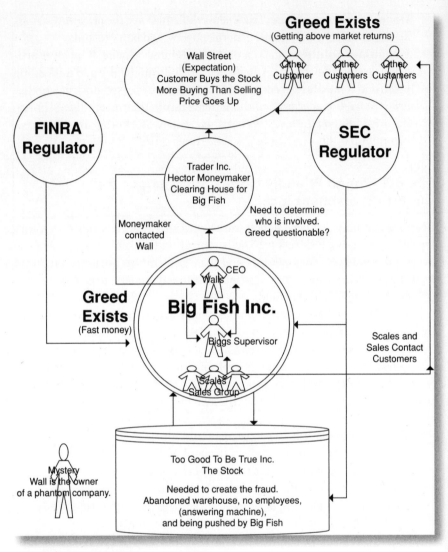

EXHIBIT 2.10   Big Fish Inc. Drawing

stocks rise on speculation, and as long as that is the case, you will understand why the price and the returns are outperforming others in the market.

A Simple Picture

Where does the greed exist in Exhibit 2.10?

If you take a look at Exhibit 2.10, you can clearly see how fraud can be created by the pursuit of returns that are too good to be true. Try to sketch a similar picture of your take on the other organizations we have discussed in the one-minute mystery in this chapter. How does it compare to Exhibit 2.10?

This exhibit shows, in a simplified way, the greed that can exist at the investor and organization levels. The presence of greed increases the risk of fraud. Draw a simple picture of your organization to determine whether it is the next Big Fish Inc.— making demands and expectations it cannot fulfill. Make sure that your organization is not sacrificing its ethics to meet expectations.

 NOTES

1. Based on a quote popularized by author, pastor, and motivational speaker Robert H. Schuller.
2. GAAP research tends to be more focused on the literature, whereas the IFRS review the fact patterns more thoroughly and focus on the professional judgment. The Securities and Exchange Commission (SEC) is trying to find the right balance between the educated professional judgment that is acceptable and the questionable professional judgment.
3. The Treadway Commission was also known as the National Commission on Fraudulent Financial Reporting. A special committee was formed in 1985 to investigate the underlying causes of fraudulent financial reporting. The commission was named after its chairman, former SEC commissioner James Treadway. The commission's report, published in 1987, stressed the need for strong and independent audit committees for public companies. The Committee of Sponsoring Organizations of the Treadway Commission is the oversight body for the internal control framework.
4. The Financial Investor Regulatory Agency is the largest independent securities regulator in the United States. Its chief role is to protect investors by maintaining the fairness of the U.S. capital markets. See http://www.finra.org.
5. American Institute of Certified Public Accountants, *Providing Litigation Services: Technical Consulting, Consulting Services Practice Aid 93-4* (New York: AICPA, 1993), 70/100–2.05.
6. American College of Forensic Examiners, "Role of Forensic Accountant," *Forensic Examiner* 10, nos. 5–6 (May–June 2001): 9.
7. American Institute of Certified Public Accountants, *Forensic Accounting and Financial Fraud* (New York: AICPA, 1995), 2.
8. AICPA's Forensic and Litigation Services Committee, July 30, 2004, http://www.aicpa.org/members/div/mcs/exec_summ_forensic_svcs.htm.

9. Darrel Dorrell, "How Do You Define Forensic Accounting?" *Financial Forensics Newsletter,* September 1993.

10. The ACFE's *2010 Report to the Nations* on occupational fraud and abuse is based on data compiled from a study of 1,843 cases of occupational fraud that occurred worldwide between January 2008 and December 2009.

11. Tulip Mania in 1637 was created by the sale of a single tulip and the consequent demand created by the desire of people to own tulips. It involved extraordinarily high contract prices for tulip bulbs that then suddenly collapsed. This is viewed as the first speculative bubble.

12. A four-year lapse in proper accounting treatment resulted in $50 million in fines for Freddie Mac in 2007. To maintain the expectations on Wall Street, this mortgage financing giant misstated $5 billion in earnings.

13. Repo 105 is a repurchase agreement that resulted in an accounting maneuver in which a short-term loan was classified as a sale. The cash obtained through the "sale" was then used to pay down debt, allowing the company to appear to reduce its liabilities for just a long enough period to publish a stronger balance sheet.

14. Financial Accounting Standards Board, No. 157, "Fair Value Measurements," http://www.fasb.org/summary/stsum157.shtml.

15. Cumulative Inflation Calculator, InflationData.com, http://inflationdata.com/ Inflation/Inflation_Calculators/Cumulative_Inflation_Calculator.aspx.

16. *Brown v. Brown,* 348 N.J. Super. 466 (App. Div. 2002).

17. *Piscopo v. Piscopo,* 231 N.J. Super. 576 (Ch. Div. 1988) was a New Jersey divorce case concerning intangible value attributable to celebrity status.

18. This was established by the FIN 48 (codified at ASC 740-10), an official interpretation of the U.S. accounting rules that require businesses to analyze and disclose income tax risks; these rules became effective in 2007. The FASB Accounting Standards Codification 450 (ASC 450) addresses contingencies for gains and losses that may be incurred now or in the future.

19. Statement on Auditing Standards No. 34, "The Auditor's Considerations," March 1981. This standard addressed when a question arose about an entity's ability to continue to exist. It was superseded in April 1988 by statement No. 59, "The Auditor's Consideration of an Entity's Ability to Continue as a Going Concern."

20. *United States of America v. Arthur Andersen,* U.S. District Court Southern District of Texas, LLP Indictment Cr. No. (T.18.U.S.C. 1512(b)(2) and 3551 et.seq.), related to Enron. The case ultimately led to the fall of the accounting firm.

21. FIN 48 (codified at ASC 740-10).

22. Financial Accounting Standards Board No. 95, "Statement of Cash Flows," November 1987.

23. All public, foreign, and domestic organizations are required to file registration statements, periodic reports, and other forms electronically through EDGAR

(which can be accessed for free). You can find links to a complete list of filings available through EDGAR in Chapter 8 under "Useful Links."

24. The float is calculated by subtracting restricted shares from outstanding shares. See http://www.investopedia.com/terms/f/float.asp#ixzz1py9i9eGF.

25. Earnings per share serves as an indicator of a company's profitability by allocating the earnings of the organization to each share of common stock minus any preferred dividends, if applicable. The calculation is net income minus dividends on preferred stock (if applicable) divided by average common stock share outstanding. If the company earned $100,000 and had no preferred dividends and the average common shares outstanding were 100,000, the earnings per share would be $1 per share—$100,000 net income (earnings) divided by the average outstanding common shares of 100,000.

CHAPTER THREE

Deciding to Commit Fraud

What Is the "Something" That Coerces People to Cross the Line?

Anyone who has never made a mistake has never tried anything new.

—*Albert Einstein*

People are the most valuable and indispensable asset in an organizational fraud strategy. We need to view people as an investment with risk and rewards that can make a significant difference in an organization's ability to prevent fraud as well as increase organizational value.

We live in a global society, bringing with it new advantages and responsibilities. A successful organizational structure creates a harmonic balance while maintaining correct ethics and treating its people as its most precious commodity.

In this chapter we discuss how external stakeholders influence today's organizations through expectations and how organizations need to adjust for the variants among the cultures of all of the corporate members, whether the chairman of the board or an employee, all while protecting the value created within the organization. The challenge in terms of fraud, therefore, is to align the competing cultural values with the corporate culture to create an environment in which organizational value thrives, yet not at the expense of moral integrity.

This chapter features the following:
Perspectives on responsibility and reward and how they vary by generation.
Methods for aligning the control environment with internal and external expectations.
Ways to develop and communicate decision-making models for protecting an organization's value.
A checklist for what not to do.

F YOU MAKE SURE YOU HAVE trustworthy individuals in your organization, you will have a better chance of deterring and preventing fraud. Perspectives on responsibility and rewards can vary by generation, as we'll discuss in this chapter. Imagine that you're in a room full of people with different expressions, views, and beliefs who all believe they have the organization's best interests at heart (or not). The challenge is to examine these often varying interests to ensure that they are in alignment with the organizational objectives.

"'Integrity,' to me," wrote William H. Swanson, the 57-year-old CEO of Raytheon, "is having the fortitude to do what is right when no one is watching."[1] This concept is useful when trying to understand how organizational fraud may occur and, consequently, how it can be deterred and prevented. No one can be watching 100 percent of the time, but creating the perception that there is an 800-pound friendly gorilla in the room can be a strong fraud deterrent. This approach could involve things like putting in cameras at the cash register. A person under watch is less likely to commit fraud.

Identifying how the people in your organization interact with other people, both internally and externally, when assets have been exposed helps to deter and prevent fraud. Contextualism, the idea that things are best understood within their context, generally means looking at a situation or a fact pattern through a particular lens. Antifraud professionals need to be aware that there are two types of contextual settings: moral relativism and situational ethics. Moral relativism holds that there is no absolute morality, that people decide (and disagree about) what is moral. Situational ethics holds that what is ethical depends on the situation; one ethical principle must be cast aside when it conflicts with another ethical principle in a given situation. Here is a simple example of each:

- **Moral relativism:** A store clerk gives an extra $10 in change to a customer. One person would return it, believing that that's the right thing to do. Another person wouldn't return it, believing that it's just his or her lucky day.
- **Situational ethics:** Your mother is sick and in need of money for an operation, so you perpetrate a fraud to get the money she needs. You cast aside your normal ethical belief that stealing is wrong because the situation, your mother's life, depends on it.

Organizations must emphasize that their people are required to be morally correct regardless of the situation and the potential consequences.

A good way to develop and communicate the correct models for employee behavior is to create a checklist for what not to do, to ensure that all people in the organization understand the consequences of fraud and that it will not be tolerated. The IRS, for example, uses what it calls "badges of fraud" to determine whether there was an intent to evade paying taxes.[2] Here is a sample checklist:

- Understatement of income (e.g., omissions of specific items or entire sources of income, failure to report substantial amounts of income received)
- Fictitious or improper deductions (e.g., overstatement of deductions, personal items deducted as business expenses)
- Accounting irregularities (e.g., two sets of books, false entries on documents)
- Acts of the taxpayer indicating an intent to evade taxes (e.g., false statements, destruction of records, transfer of assets)
- A consistent pattern over several years of underreporting taxable income
- Implausible or inconsistent explanations of behavior
- Failure to cooperate with examiners
- Concealment of assets
- Engaging in illegal activities (e.g., drug dealing) or attempting to conceal illegal activities
- Inadequate records
- Dealing in cash
- Failure to file returns

ONE-MINUTE FRAUD MYSTERY: THE HOUSE OF WORSHIP

Art Creed, a tax expert, belonged to a congregation called The House of Worship (THW). THW needed to raise funds for a new building wing and asked Creed to help organize an art auction as a fundraising event. THW was located in an affluent area.

Tony Thanks, a fellow congregant, referred Creed to an art dealer specializing in this sort of fundraiser. Creed was assured by Thanks that his contact from Art for Charity Deduction (ACD), Tina Seller, would raise a significant amount of money on THW's behalf.

The design of the auction was simple. THW would provide the venue, market the event to members and others, and receive 10 percent of the proceeds from the sale in the form of a donation from ACD. Before the auction, ACD provided certified appraisals of the fair market value of the art to be offered at the auction, and it also handled all of the other aspects of the auction.

Many people who purchased art at the auction thought it was a great deal, since they were able to purchase pieces at around 50 percent of the appraised value stated on the certificates. Seller told them they could write off the full fair market value as well, even if they paid less than the appraised amounts, because the appraisals were conservative, and if they held the piece, it would appreciate. The auction was a tremendous success and raised $100,000 for the building addition.

THW's bookkeeper calls you and asks how to record a receipt for the $100,000 raised at the fundraiser. In addition, she asks you to come to the office to review IRS audit notices given to her by Creed regarding some of the buyers of the art.

Have any inappropriate activities taken place? What are the proper recordings? Was ACD legitimate? Could THW have exposed its reputation by doing business with a company that might have used the church's goodwill to perpetrate fraud?

DO YOU REALLY KNOW WHAT THE PEOPLE IN YOUR ORGANIZATION ARE THINKING?

The hypothetical situation in Exhibit 3.1 illustrates that even when you think you know what the key individuals in your organization are thinking, you might not.

EXHIBIT 3.1 The Meeting

CEO Gorilla: I'd like to discuss your collective understanding of the Organizational Creed.
Young Gorilla 1: Dude, I cannot be bothered. I got to finish reading this book.
Young Gorilla 2: Is he kidding? I have a nail appointment! How long is this going to take?
Middle-aged Gorilla: I wonder what the kids are doing.
Old Gorilla: I can't wait until two more weeks, when I retire and my creed becomes "go fish."
CFO Gorilla: This guy comes up with great ideas without considering the consequences to the organization's cash flows, profitability, or value. Not to mention the impact on morale.

Looking into people's minds can be as dangerous as sticking your head in a crocodile's mouth.

EXHIBIT 3.2 The Crocodile's Mouth

Copyright © 2012 James Lee

Are they considering what is in the organization's best interest, or are their concerns for their own benefit? Organizations, and the personnel who are primarily charged with protecting organizational value, need to be aware of the forces affecting the key gatekeepers, both outside and inside the organization, since an employee's self-interest may be in direct conflict with an organization's.

As a fraud investigator (or a corporate executive charged with fraud prevention, deterrence, and detection), you are analyzing what people are thinking. This can be a dangerous thing if you make too many assumptions. Don't assume that fraud is always the result; instead, be aware of the traits and situations that may be indicative of fraud. Essentially, don't make snap judgments. It can be as dangerous as sticking your head in a crocodile's mouth (see Exhibit 3.2).

It is important to understand the needs of the people in your organization. In 1934, the psychologist Abraham Maslow developed the hierarchy of needs shown in Exhibit 3.3. When you look at the exhibit, can you tell where your organization's people might fall with regard to honesty and ethics?

Exhibit 3.4 shows the results of a 2008 poll in which people were asked to rate various professions on their (perceived) level of honesty and ethics.

It is important to know where the people in your organizational process fall with respect to honesty and ethics (see Exhibit 3.5). Exhibit 3.5 is a basic sample of people you will see in an organizational structure. Designing a similar

EXHIBIT 3.3   Maslow's Hierarchy of Needs[3]

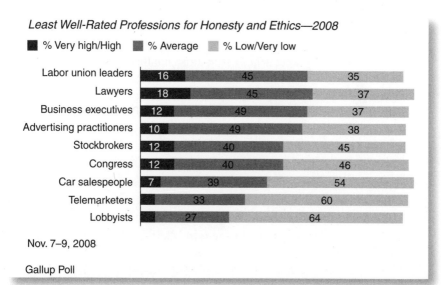

Least Well-Rated Professions for Honesty and Ethics—2008

■ % Very high/High   ■ % Average   ■ % Low/Very low

Nov. 7–9, 2008

Gallup Poll

EXHIBIT 3.4   Professions Poll[4]

EXHIBIT 3.5 Where People Fall with Respect to Honesty and Ethics?

Where Do People in Your Organization Fall with Respect to Honesty and Ethics?			
Board of Directors	Very High	Average	Low
CEO			
CFO			
Sales			
Accounting			
Manufacturing			
Warehouse			

Source: Josephson Institute

chart that is representative of your organization is helpful in determining the existing ethical tone, since understanding the people within the structure is necessary. Using the findings of a 2009 Josephson Institute Center for Business Ethics report helps us to gain a perspective on the behavior of people in today's organizations.

Here are some things to think about from the report:

■ The percentage of those who believe that one has to lie or cheat at least occasionally in order to succeed is (by age): 51 percent (17 and under) b; 36 percent (18–24); 18 percent (25–40); 11 percent (41–50); and 10 percent (over 50).

Teens are nearly five times more likely, and young adults (18–24) are more than three times more likely than those over 40 to hold the cynical belief that lying and cheating is sometimes necessary to succeed. This belief is one of the most significant and reliable predictors of dishonest behavior in the adult world.

■ The percentage who concealed or distorted information on a significant matter when communicating with their bosses in the past year is (by age): 31 percent (17 and under); 19 percent (18–24); 17 percent (25–40); 11 percent (41–50); and 8 percent (over 50). A favorite saying of television personality Judge Judy is, "How can you tell that a teenager is lying? Their lips are moving."

Teens 17 and under are nearly four times more likely than those over 50 to deceive their bosses.

- The percentage who used the Internet for personal reasons for at least 15 minutes during work time in the past year is (by age): 53 percent (18–24); 77 percent (25–40); 69 percent (41–50); and 58 percent (over 50).[5]

It is important to understand the individual perspectives and experiences of the people in your organization when analyzing fraud risk. This includes executives and board members as well as line managers and rank-and-file employees. Analyzing the personnel according to generation in order to create a snapshot of the ideology of the workforce in your organization is essential, because doing research on an individual basis is usually cost-prohibitive for many organizations.

In organizations, the goal is often to make a profit. The people in an organization will have various experiences, skills, and beliefs that lead them to the goal. People in organizations generally work best with people they feel most comfortable with, and these tend to be people who have had similar experiences. Therefore, it is best to first align people based on their respective skills and experience.

The 800-pound friendly gorilla's challenge is to take micro differences within an organization's employee pool and blend them into one successful macro process. In general, the design of an organization is to try and maintain groups aligned in one direction by utilizing their various skills in order to better detect, deter, and prevent fraud.

Considering that individuals generally believe that their own views and opinions are the best in any given situation or circumstance, this presents you with the most difficult part of the organizational structure: creating the proper hierarchy of command with the properly aligned trust assignments. Most people do not like to be wrong. However, organizations need to develop the thinking that being wrong is okay as long as you learn from it and that advancing the wrong self-interest was not done intentionally. Any time there is a struggle in the organization between doing what is right and what is wrong, you need to make sure that egos are not the driving force behind the judgments being made.

There is an old Chinese proverb: "One who asks a question is a fool for five minutes. One who does not ask a question remains a fool forever." Here are some things to ask when you're trying to understand the different aspects of the generations in today's organizations:

- What are the employees' perspectives?
- What are their needs? Their expectations?

- What type of organization do they work for (for-profit, nonprofit)?
- Are there societal pressures within the organization?
- Are there medical issues within the organization?
- Are there family or marital issues in the organization?
- Is there good communication? What is the talk around the water cooler?
- What is being said outside the organization?
- Are employee roles clearly defined in the organization?
- Are people self-directing within the organization?
- What's the tone of the organization?
- Are there organizational stresses?
- Is the organization political?
- Does the organization have global views?
- Is the organization maintaining its competency levels?
- Is the organization adaptable?
- Is the organization maintaining its goodwill?
- Are there power plays (ego struggles) within the organization?
- Is the organization complete (with teams or individuals)?
- Are there addictions in the organization?
- Is the organization made up of risk takers?
- Does the organization have an environment of entitlement?

 ## THE FOUR GENERATIONS AND MOTIVATION

Organizations need to recognize that for the first time in our history, there are four different generations in the workforce. I have assigned them the following names:

1. The foundational generation (aka the silent generation; born 1922–1945)
2. The social-change generation (aka baby boomers; born 1946–1964)
3. The on-your-own generation (aka generation X; born 1965–1980)
4. The texting generation (aka generation Y; born 1980–1994)

Understanding the egos in an organization is critical in effectively detecting, deterring, and preventing fraud. The 800-pound friendly gorilla works toward getting people to leave their egos at the door in order to create a commonality. Each of the four generations has its own perspectives and beliefs about value and the work ethic it will employ. Organizations need to classify members into these four groups to tackle the challenge of uniting them toward a common goal.

The number one driving force for people in an organization, regardless of generation, is **motivation**. My equation for reviewing motivation is the following:

Motivation = Opportunity + Planning + Attitude + Rewards + Beliefs

Following are some examples of each of these motivating factors:

- People need to feel that they have **opportunity** within an organization. It is interesting to note that these opportunities are the same ones that can wind up in the dreaded fraud triangle if put in the wrong individual's hands.
- An organization needs a clear **plan** with objectives to properly motivate its people. This plan cannot be developed by only one person with full control. There should be proper checks and balances in place.
- An organization needs to engender the proper **attitude** in the people who are implementing the plan. For instance, if an unethical attitude is established, then fraud can occur.
- An organization should set up a system of **rewards,** taking into account that an improper setup can lead to fraud (e.g., bonus incentives causing people to act a certain way because they are given the incentive to do so, consciously or unconsciously).
- An organization should make sure that its people do the right thing (or at least **believe** they can).

When reading about each of the generations, think about motivation in the context of these five drivers.

The Foundational Generation

People today need to remain in the workforce because increases in the cost of living delay the ability to retire. Because of this, we need to examine the various competitions that may exist and the dilemma of uniting all the different types of members of the organization's workforce.[6] What motivates the different groups of people associated with your organization?

The foundational generation, sometimes referred to as the silent generation, includes people born from 1922 through 1945. Keeping in mind the previous list of questions, examine the factors that contributed to this generation's thinking. What were the foundational generation's experiences, and how do they influence how its members act in today's organizational structure?

Unfortunately, because this generation has been around the longest, its members may have the most opportunity to commit fraud. For instance, a board of directors might consist of a member from the foundational generation. This member is now in a position to set the ethical tone in the organization and be responsible for the strategic direction.

The foundational generation is responsible for developing today's space program and creating vaccines for many diseases, including polio, tuberculosis, tetanus, and whooping cough. These individuals moved their families from farms and cities to a new kind of community and established the suburbs. They also were the first generation to explore equal rights through the civil rights movement. The foundational generation holds approximately three-quarters of the nation's wealth, and its members are the executive leaders of some of the most established and influential companies in the United States.

Because the major events of their early lives were the Depression and World War II, it is easy to understand the members of the foundational generation. World War II created a sense of patriotism, and the Depression taught them how to work with what they have, to rely on people and the concept of teamwork. This generation, for the most part, had respect for authority, loved its country, and followed the rules. But despite these core values, rules are still broken in today's organizations—because of greed. People who start with nothing and create wealth do not want to let go of their wealth and will likely crave more.

Let's look at some recent foundational fraud perpetrators: Bernie Madoff (born in 1938), Bernie Ebbers of WorldCom (born in 1941), and Ken Lay of Enron (born in 1942). These examples show there are always exceptions to the rule. The key is to know your people, despite their backgrounds, because they set the tone of the overall organization.

The Social-Change Generation

The social-change generation is most commonly referred to as the baby boomers, with birthdays from 1946 through 1964. Some key events experienced by this generation were the invention of television and the Xerox machine, the civil rights movement, the assassinations of the Kennedy brothers and Martin Luther King Jr., the sexual revolution, the Vietnam War, the Watergate scandal, the women's movement, and, as married adults, an increase in the divorce rate. This generation, growing up long before the Internet and social media, spent a lot of time with family and friends in "real time" (face-to-face). Today's organization operates in terms of the political and social changes that resulted from the activism of this generation—specifically, racial and sexual equality.

Because of this, in the last 20 years there has been a shift from an organization's rights to an individual's rights, with a continued emphasis on developing assistance programs for work stress, family issues, assessment for depression and anxiety, and grief and loss counseling. In addition, legal, financial, and work-life services on a variety of topics have shifted the focus to benefit the individual rather than the organization. The organization is now challenged to develop controls around these evolved rights without encroaching on people's needs.

It may become cumbersome to manage this balance, and in the wrong environment, a fraudster's rights can often prevent an organization from detecting fraud. Organizations need to have well-documented communications with their people in order to avoid the liability concerns that can arise during the development of a fraud program. Some examples of social-change generation fraudsters are Sam Waksal of ImClone (born in 1947), Richard Scrushy of Health South (born in 1952), and Sanjay Kumar of Computer Associates (born in 1962).

The On-Your-Own Generation

The on-your-own generation is usually referred to as generation X, born between 1965 and 1980. This generation grew up with the emergence of technology and with an eye toward judging unacceptable political and institutional behavior. This generation's surrounding events included the Three Mile Island nuclear meltdown, the murder of John Lennon, the attempted assassination of President Ronald Reagan, the space shuttle *Challenger* disaster, the 1979 energy crisis, the black Monday stock market crash, the Iranian hostage crisis, the Iran-Contra scandal, and the emergence of AIDS. Fax machines were introduced, heavy adding machines were replaced with handheld calculators, and the personal computer replaced the typewriter.

Divorce was common for this generation as children. The on-your-own generation is autonomous and self-reliant, which contributes to the distancing among the generations in today's organizations. Michael J. Saylor (born in 1965) of Micro Strategy agreed to pay $350,000 in penalties and to pay a total of $1.7 million to shareholders to settle SEC allegations that he had committed fraud by using improper early revenue recognition by reporting profits when the company was actually losing money.[7] Robert Tappan Morris (born in 1965) was the inventor of the Morris Worm (the first Internet worm) for which he was the first person convicted under the Computer Fraud and Abuse Act. Reomel Ramores (born in 1975) and Onel De Guzman (born in 1976) were investigated in connection with the worldwide spread of a virus called "I Love You." Within 10 days the virus infected 50 million computers, causing $5.5 billion in damages. During the investigations, De Guzman stated that he may have unwittingly released the worm.[8]

The Texting Generation

The final generation is the texting generation, also referred to as generation Y, born between 1980 and 1994. This generation grew up in an era of rapid technological advances. Cable television, cellular phones, pagers, answering machines, laptop computers, videocassette and DVD recorders, video games, and the replacement of vinyl records with compact discs are just some of the types of technology that developed during this generation's childhood. Unprecedented technological advancements in real-time media and communications fuel this generation's expectation for instant gratification.

The Columbine High School shootings and the attacks on September 11, 2001, were events that affected this generation as youths. Ostensibly, the members of this generation has had their every emotional, educational, and physical need and want provided to them by the generations before, and the result is young workers with high expectations of recognition and reward in the workplace.

The texting generation seeks its parents' advice and approval, creating the expectation that its managers and supervisors may also provide the same guidance. This generation often job-hops as a way to meet its immediate wants, needs, and goals instead of focusing on doing a job with patience, focus, and persistence. Short-term results sometimes create an environment of self-entitlement. In this type of environment, fraud can be used as a means of gaining instant gratification.

Fraudsters in this generation include Adrian Lamo (born in 1981) who was a Colombian-American threat analyst and "gray hat" hacker. He first gained media attention for breaking into several high-profile computers at the *New York Times*, Yahoo!, and Microsoft.[9] Another young fraudster is Jonathan Joseph James (born in 1983), the first juvenile, at 16 years of age, incarcerated in the United States for cybercrime.[10]

An Eye toward the Future

It is important to understand both the current and anticipated future demographics of a company's people as part of efforts to deter, detect, and prevent fraud within an organization.

The U.S. Department of Labor has reported that the workforce will contract from 2000 to 2010, compared to the baby boom years.[11] A snapshot of the changing labor market shows there will be a 31 percent drop in 35- to 45-year-olds and a 2 percent drop in 24- to 34-year-olds. The Labor Department anticipates an increased diversity in the workforce, with the largest gains by Asians and Hispanics. The department also anticipates almost 15 percent more women in the workforce, with more professional service skills. Organizations must provide for these shifts in the workforce by making sure that the perspectives of the people always stay in line with those of the organization.

 ## PINPOINTING THE FRAUDSTER

In the world of fraud, once the algorithm (the systematic means by which the organizational process creates value) is understood, the fraudster can simply move about the different levels of thinking in a multigenerational organization. Once the fraudster learns how to win at a game, he or she understands the needs and wants to establish the necessary signature moves to perpetrate the fraud again.

The world of organizational fraud is not static. Where the social-change generation sees video games as diversions or toys, the on-your-own and texting generations take them much more seriously. The texting generation, for instance, is coming into the workforce with a complete dependence on networking, multitasking, and a global-mindedness that their elders never could have imagined. Instead of affecting one person with a single act, these individuals have been empowered to affect a whole process at the flick of a button, enhanced by the instant-gratification mentality.

These new, younger employees present new challenges to fraud fighters in today's organizations. They may be keen on winning and eager to experiment and work as a team to solve problems, but they are not inclined to follow leaders just because they are the leaders. The 800-pound friendly gorilla cannot allow the desire for instant gratification to conflict with the organization's direction.

 ## THE THREE MOST PREVALENT TYPES OF FRAUD

Although people generally become more conservative as they age, based on my experience, I believe that core generational values change very little. No matter what the generation, however, a fraudster plays the odds when deciding to commit fraud. The opening sequence to an American detective television series from the late 1970s called *Baretta* contained the signature line "Don't do the crime if you can't do the time."[12] White-collar or occupational fraud is generally categorized as falling into one of three categories: asset misappropriation (i.e., theft), false statements (including fraudulent financial statements), and corruption (when a third party is introduced).

Asset misappropriation includes any scheme that involves the misuse of an organization's assets. False statement statutes criminalize one who "knowingly and willfully falsifies, conceals, or covers up any trick, scheme, device, or material fact; makes any materially false, fictitious, or fraudulent statement or representation; or makes or uses any false writing or document knowing the same to contain any material false, fictitious, or fraudulent statement or entry."[13] Corruption consists of the payment or acceptance of a bribe, a kickback, or the use of anything of value to retain or gain an improper business advantage.

There are more law enforcement agencies interested in fraud than coordinated efforts to prevent and detect it. There are many federal, state, and local agencies involved in the enforcement of white-collar crime investigation and prosecution.

Historically, the problem has been that these agencies lacked a coordinated approach to addressing specific frauds. This trend is changing, however, and as interagency cooperation continues to increase, so will the number of frauds uncovered and their successful prosecution. For instance, in hindsight, had the various agencies charged with the oversight of various elements of the mortgage servicing industry been communicating, it's possible that the 2008 economic crisis could have been averted, because assorted fraud schemes would have been detected sooner. The collateral debt obligation (CDO) industry's hunger for more paper and lax lending programs allowed fraud at the mortgage initiation level and helped to fuel the collapse of the financial market. Was the risk model for the different tranches of the CDO industry flawed because this level of thinking was not sophisticated enough to develop the proper risk model, or was the industry sophisticated and it chose to look the other way? A corollary theory is that had the investment oversight bodies been sharing knowledge and concerns, a good portion of the Madoff fraud could have been avoided (or at least stopped earlier).

Perpetrators of fraud know that law enforcement and many private detection organizations are in a reactionary rather than a proactive position. Do law enforcement and private detection organizations conduct financial investigations before an indication of fraud becomes overwhelmingly obvious? I would submit that the actual answer is yes, but the success stories are lost in a sea of financial losses. For every small business that is alerted to an ongoing fraud, there are many others that are not. The sheer volume of potential fraud vulnerabilities creates a resource gap that is nearly insurmountable.

So, should the good guys close the books and concede defeat? No. Focusing on taking away the fraudsters' head start is key. Close some of the control gaps, strengthen the corporate belief system to one of zero tolerance for misbehavior, demand transparency from the top down, and implement and apply proactive measures. Fraudsters are also buoyed by the realization that if they are caught, the victim may be disinclined to press charges out of a fear of negative publicity. Without criminal charges, however, restitution is uncertain, the crime goes unreported, and the criminal remains free to fleece the next unsuspecting victim because there is no public record of the previous bad behavior.[14]

If charges are actually filed, the time and effort required to see a prosecution through may result in the fraud not being prosecuted (this is very disheartening). The fraudster may be able to avoid financial penalty by filing for bankruptcy, by transferring assets to a nonconforming or noncooperating foreign country, or by other means. Finally, keep in mind that even though the case may appear as solid, all it takes is doubt, and the (alleged) perpetrator goes home free.

AN ACCOUNTING CREED

Behavioral expectations should be consistent with an enterprise's overall operating philosophy—not just to ensure appropriate accounting reports or protection from fraud loss, but to meet external stakeholders' expectations about value, social responsibility, and other issues. Consider whether a particular company encourages integrity and transparency at every step or whether it operates on a need-to-know basis. Does the senior leadership team derive its power base from its secrets or from its ability to lead a team in a particular direction?

An organization should formulate an overall organizational creed. In addition, a successful organization will have its people develop their own creed that incorporates the overall organization creed principles and rules by identifying them with the responsibilities and efforts they each employ in the organizational process. Here is an example of an accounting creed I created from the foundational accounting principles discussed throughout this book:

My Accounting Creed

- In order to establish a foundation of **integrity** and **objectivity**, I will maintain my **independence**. I am committed to maintaining my **professional competence** and exercising **due professional care** as I develop **adequate planning** and **supervision** in connection with gathering the necessary **sufficient and relevant data** related to the services I will perform.
- I will make reporting assumptions for the correct **period** in which a **monetary unit** of measurement can be recorded for the **economic entity** transactions and events that occur.
- I will do this by following principles that always give **full disclosure** of transactions on the **accrual basis** of accounting. I will apply the correct **revenue recognition** and **matching** of all **costs** related to those revenues so that a **going concern** status can be maintained.
- I will understand the past, present, and future outlook for the services I am being asked to provide. I will fully understand the **relevance** of the communication so that a **reliability** and **consistency** is established that makes the information useful to the intended user.
- I will not depart from my principles unless a transaction is not **material** enough to change a reasonable person's thinking (had the principle been applied). I will look at the **cost-benefit analysis** associated with the information developed by GAAP. I will examine **industry practices**. I will always err on the side of **conservatism** in the formulation of opinions and conclusions. I will always maintain my integrity and objectivity when deciding on any potential GAAP departure.
- I will always remain a principle-based accountant who does not need exact rules and restrictive oversight to maintain moral integrity.

To develop an effective creed, it is important to utilize the core organizational principles and rules that establish the proper ethical tone. Have your employees put those principles and rules into their own words (adding their own input as well). You should also have them sign this personal creed, frame it, and own it. The people in an organization will not follow an overall creed or mission statement unless it is aligned with the organization's principles and rules and they accept the responsibility of following it.

Organizations must articulate and visualize the misaligned priorities that arise from conflicts between staff members, the potential for fraud events, and the ways that the organization mitigates risk. Different expectations are stratified by age, but companies are stodgy and expect people to adapt to them no matter what. Even though there are multiple generations of people in today's organizations, no effort is made to bridge generational differences in thinking.

An organization often allows an older person to hold on to what he or she knows best (tradition) while the younger employee is allowed to get things done by using technology rather than working directly with people. How can a balance be created? One way would be to define the external consequences of one's actions so they are easily understood, regardless of age.

Many people believe that a little wrong is acceptable. For example, someone in an organization thinks, "I took a little extra auto expense; no one will notice." But a little wrong can spin out of control and cause big problems. In an organization, wrong has to be wrong. A small spark can start a fire and become an out-of-control inferno. To this end, self-discipline is important when one has access to a lot of value. Someone who has control of an organization's value needs to have self-control and a creed to live by that is aligned with the organization's goals. Integrity is what you do when nobody is looking.

 ## THE CONSEQUENCES OF FRAUD

Multiple nationalities exist in a global economy and interact despite any cultural differences that may be present. Successful organizations operate in collaborative, team-like environments.

Today people are looking for ease, convenience, and the ability to live beyond their means; they simply desire more. There is a sense of self-entitlement: "I deserve it. I don't want to miss out." This attitude, coupled with a lack of consequence or enforcement, opens the door to fraud in an organization's process. The 800-pound friendly gorilla educates employees about the consequences of breaking the organization's rules, making people think twice before they commit fraud.

Give people the facts they can weigh before deciding to commit fraud. Emphasize the jail time they could face, never mind the legal and restitution costs. I have been involved with many ethics courses, and there is usually only a brief mention of the consequences faced by people who commit fraud, beyond the high-profile names like Bernie Madoff and Ken Lay. Where do the other fraudsters ultimately wind up?

Today's organization must use these valuable lessons from the past and learn from them. If fraudsters are rationalizing a potential fraud, give them the long-term negative side to their actions, since they may only be looking at the short-term benefit. Consider Madoff as an example. U.S. district court judge Denny Chin cited the unprecedented nature of the multibillion-dollar fraud as he sentenced Madoff to the maximum of 150 years in prison—a sentence comparable only to sentences given in the past to terrorists, traitors, and the most violent criminals.

After you have an understanding of the criminal aspects of fraud, there are also the civil penalties and lawsuits to understand, which have a much lower proof level (preponderance of the evidence). The "greater than 50 percent" standard, which is similar to the "more likely than not standard," is all that needs to be met to satisfy preponderance of the evidence. So now the risks to the fraudster are jail time, fines, and possible civil judgments and damages. Knowing this, you can give fraudsters the information they need to do their risk-reward analysis. Giving them this information can ensure that they understand all the facts when deciding whether to commit fraud in the organizational process.

Let's examine all available judicial remedies and procedures to enforce the tax laws. These actions include criminal prosecutions, civil injunction actions, summons enforcement actions, collection actions, and the defense of civil suits. The government may take these actions simultaneously or sequentially. Unfortunately for the fraudster, this course of action does not just involve tax laws; it also includes mail fraud, wire fraud, and whatever else leads to satisfying the outrage created by a fraudster's actions. Remember Bernie Madoff's 150-year sentence.

Your evidence of a fraud should lay out the behavior that needs to be proven in order to prosecute. If you give fraudsters this information, they know what they are looking at if caught. Communicate the consequences to the people in your organizational process. Formulate the appropriate memos or add the information to your company handbook (and require a sign-off of the handbook).

The Sarbanes-Oxley Act of 2002 mandated the separation of auditing and consulting businesses in an attempt to restore public confidence in the investment market. The act creates a number of new federal crimes (i.e., document destruction and tampering, securities fraud, certification of false financial statements, and attempt and conspiracy), many of which apply to both public and private companies and their directors, officers, and employees. The Sarbanes-Oxley Act also significantly enhances the penalties for a host of existing white-collar crimes.

As mentioned earlier, a number of federal, state, and local agencies participate in the enforcement of white-collar crime legislation. The federal ones include the FBI, the IRS, the Secret Service, the U.S. Postal Inspection Service, U.S. Customs, the Environmental Protection Agency, and the Securities and Exchange Commission.

Acts and agencies are important parts of the fraud detection process, and people in an organization need to understand the consequences of their actions and that they are not immune to prosecution. People should also keep in mind that just because they did not actually perpetrate the fraud, that does not mean they are not going to be implicated. People are often guilty by association or even accessories after the fact (knowing about the fraud, even though not participating in it). If you create the thinking that everyone in an organizational process is held accountable, the fraud prevention plan of an organization will be more successful. If the fraud ultimately brings down the organization, everyone will be unemployed, not to mention that their vested future benefits may be lost (stock plans, pension plans, and so on). It is therefore in everyone's best interest to detect, deter, and prevent fraud.

Unfortunately, most organizations segregate duties and hold one person accountable for each duty. The fraudster thrives in this kind of structure. Ideally the one who is actually responsible *and* the ones who are making sure the duty is performed all have to be held responsible. Segregation works only if the system is self-governing by holding all the people in the process accountable for a potential violation.

How do people know whom or what the IRS will audit? During the course of an office or desk audit, something tells the revenue officer to probe further. During the ensuing field audit, something tells the revenue officer to refer the file for criminal inquiry proceedings. That "something" is published in the IRS manual and its *Fraud Handbook*, part 25, chapter 1; this is commonly referred to as the "badges of fraud," mentioned earlier in this chapter. The IRS clearly articulates the distinction between indications of fraud and more concrete actions that affirm fraud.

These IRS articulated actions are only to be probed further and not used to accuse someone of fraud. Even with proof, only the finders of fact (basically, the judge and jury) can formally find a perpetrator guilty of fraud.

Further information on what agents consider in determining whether to make a referral can be found in the abovementioned *Fraud Handbook* chapter at http://www.irs.gov.

Circumstantial Evidence and Reasonable Inference

Since direct proof of fraudulent intent is rarely available, fraud must be proven by circumstantial evidence and reasonable inference to determine the motive behind the intent. Fraud will generally involve one or more of the following elements:

- Deceptive behavior
- Misrepresentation of material facts

- False or altered documents
- Evasion (i.e., diversion or omission)

Earlier in the book, fraud criteria were presented for determining civil versus criminal liability. These consisted of a material misrepresentation that was intentionally made regarding relied-on information and that caused damage (MIRD). Intention determines whether something is raised to the level of criminal versus civil prosecution.

However, it's important to note that the limited resources of various agencies, the reality of audit lottery (that there is a small audit selection), and a lack of outrage (no one blowing the whistle) can lead to the fraudster not being prosecuted. Keep in mind that the organization that does not prosecute sends a message that encourages fraud.

Badge Determination

In tax cases, the courts focus on key "badges" of fraud in determining whether there was an intent to evade taxation. One of the common badges of fraud is the understatement of income (e.g., the omission of specific items or the failure to report entire sources of income).

Is the reason that people understate income is so they can get a big refund or pay fewer taxes? Do people really want to pay more taxes? If people cheat on their taxes or have unexplainable tax issues, this should be investigated further. Most tax liens are public record. Does your organization examine the aggressive tax positions it has taken? Uncertain tax positions are required to be disclosed by regulation. When was the last time you required copies of tax returns as a condition of employment? The 800-pound friendly gorilla requires this.

Check the documentation. It can easily be verified with form 4506T (the transcript) and 4506 (the forms). Tax returns are the most honest source of verification of an individual's current income and asset profile. It also most likely represents a conservative view, since nobody wants to pay more taxes than he or she has to.

Then there's the "I reported my fair share of income" line of thinking versus the "I reported none of the income" rationalization. Which way of thinking reflects that of your people? Do they report all of their income or what they feel is their fair share rather than what the law requires?

Other things to review include the following:

- Fictitious or improper deductions (e.g., overstatement of deductions or personal items deducted as business expenses)

■ Accounting irregularities (e.g., two sets of books or false entries on documents)

Who is the gatekeeper preventing bad behavior? Do the actions leading to fraud happen in order for the process in your organization to achieve results and preset expectations? Do people not understand the true consequences and risks they face for their actions? Are they simply in positions of trust and think they have the right to commit fraud? If so, these actions clearly indicate intent and will likely result in criminal charges, and if the IRS's Criminal Investigation Division investigates, you're getting convicted. It has an extremely high conviction rate.

Consult the proper legal counsel and make sure that you create what is known as a Koval privilege with your accountants or tax preparers.[15] Since accountants do not have attorney-client privilege in their communications, as lawyers do, have your accountant or tax preparer be retained by your legal counsel; he or she will then have attorney-client privilege as long as he or she is reporting to your attorney. When that is set in place, the information will not be discoverable. It also prevents the tax professional from having to testify against your organization. This does not mean that the accountant or tax preparer—or the attorney, for that matter—can aid and abet the cover-up of tax evasion. The IRS will have all the necessary facts to prosecute the case, which puts you in a mitigating role.

Explaining the risks involved with being an accountant or a tax preparer in connection with fraud makes people more ethical accountants. Most believe it will never happen to an organization, let alone themselves, and they are more focused on the greedy results than the consequences. Professionals and an organization's 800-pound friendly gorilla need to make sure they are retaining the proper ethical people in connection with the organization's tax filings by assigning the proper levels of trust.

The following list displays greed in the world of the IRS; apply it to the fraudster in the fraud mysteries in this and other chapters, and you will see that they all display similar facts and circumstances:

■ Acts of the taxpayer evidencing an intent to evade tax (e.g., false statements, destruction of records, transfer of assets)
■ A consistent pattern (goes to intent) over several years of underreporting taxable income
■ Implausible or inconsistent explanations of behavior
■ Failure to cooperate with the examiner (e.g., lying)
■ Concealment of assets

- Engaging in illegal activities (e.g., drug dealing), or attempting to conceal illegal activities
- Inadequate records

These are immediate signals that you cannot support the representations that have been made. The 800-pound friendly gorilla needs to address these issues immediately to be effective in deterring, detecting, and preventing fraud in your organization. Make sure your organizational process has the necessary proofs to support tax positions or any position. If you suspect tax fraud activity or unsupported tax positions, use IRS form 3949A Informational Referral to voluntarily disclose, avoid criminal prosecution, and mitigate the potential consequences of the act before the IRS contacts you.[16]

Fortunately, fraudsters believe that these records cannot be reconstructed but they can be. The IRS can subpoena bank records, casino spending, credit card information, motor vehicle registrations, and a host of other types of spending. In today's environment, cash is being replaced with debit card or electronic transactions, all of which are traceable. People get caught because they spend the cash. My favorite example is one that a colleague of mine, Special Agent Robert Glantz, a public information officer from the Newark, New Jersey, field office of the IRS's Criminal Investigation Division, uses with my students at the College of Staten Island when he appears as a guest speaker. It is from the movie *Goodfellas* and involves the Lufthansa heist, a robbery at John F. Kennedy International Airport in Queens, New York, on December 11, 1978. A guy walks into a bar and shows Robert De Niro's character a brand-new Cadillac. De Niro goes crazy, saying it will bring attention to the group. The man who bought the Cadillac says to not worry about it, because the car is in his mom's name.

Special Agent Glantz tells the class that the IRS checks the relatives of perpetrators. People in an organization may try to deflect attention from themselves to their family members, so there is a need to be conscious of the potential perpetrator's relationships. Another scene in the movie shows a guy coming into a bar with his girlfriend, for whom he just bought a fur coat. De Niro takes it off the girlfriend and tells the guy to take it back.

Special Agent Glantz shares these types of examples and experiences with students early in their career development to help shape their morals. Giving students the necessary understanding that there are consequences for their actions, and for the actions of others, is critical to their success. The hope is to continually develop a proactive thinking approach about developing proper ethics and greed avoidance with the next generation of workers. It is this level of thinking that needs to be instilled in today's organizational environment.

Dealing in Cash

People eventually spend cash. Watching the lifestyle of the people in an organization is important in detecting, deterring, and preventing fraud. A lot of wisdom is in the phrase, coined from the movie *Jerry Maguire*, "Show me the money." Following the money trail means reviewing the potential fraudster's relationships, family background, filed tax returns (or the failure to file tax returns), educational background, and overall work experience.

An organization needs to use the IRS badges of fraud in its control models to ensure that people will file tax returns properly. Ironically, illegal income is taxable and must be filed along with the expenses incurred in generating that revenue. Most investigators do not expect people with illegal income to file, but if these people are caught, they will wish they had. Al Capone, the infamous gangster during the Prohibition crime era, was convicted of *tax evasion*, not his other illicit activities. In addition, properly filed tax returns will provide the 800-pound friendly gorilla with income information such as interest, dividend, capital gains, rental, and other entity incomes (sole proprietorship schedule Cs, partnerships, S corporations, and possibly trusts) in the search to determine lifestyle changes.

The IRS has years and years of statistical data available that includes income levels and geographical data for all types of entities.[17] Where do your people fall in the benchmarking with their peers with respect to filing returns? You need to find ways to benchmark your people. The IRS has been formulating measurers for compliance for years, so why not institute established procedures like an audit lottery in your organization? Audit the people in your organization as the IRS does and create a proactive approach.

The facts section of a penalty write-up should include a detailed description of all applicable badges of fraud. In addition, the examiner should include other items of deception or instances when the taxpayer might have misled or misrepresented facts to the government. The same thinking should be employed when examining people in an organization. Why are the people in an organization able to mislead and misrepresent, creating the necessary deflections and distractions?

The fraudster may not be concerned with paying taxes, since the sentencing risk (going to jail) is worth it, especially if the benefit outweighs the tax risks, but statute 18 U.S.C. §1341, "Elements of Mail Fraud," may cause them to reconsider. People who devise a scheme to defraud and then use the mail to attempt to execute it are subject to a fine, imprisonment, or both. If the violation occurs in the context of a presidentially declared major disaster or emergency or affects a financial institution, the penalty can be as much as $1 million, 30 years in prison, or both.

Think about who opens the mail in your organization and what controls exist over its inflow and outflow. Is your organization aiding and abetting mail fraud? You send out invoices, legal documents, loans, and other transactions. When was the last time you let the people in the organizational process know that any mail fraud is subject to the punishments just mentioned? Prosecutors love to add this count onto the other charges, hoping you will plead to lesser charges. Make sure your people know that this is a consequence, because most organizational transactions involve the mail.

The fraudster's favorite con is using an organization for his or her own benefit. The consequences for this are under 18 U.S.C. §1342, "Fictitious Name or Address." This applies to people who "conduct, promote, or carry on by means of the Postal Service, any scheme mentioned in previous section 1341 or any other unlawful business, uses or assumes, or requests to be addressed by, any fictitious, false, or assumed title, name, or address or name other than his own proper name, or takes or receives from any post office or authorized depository of mail matter, any letter, postal card, package, or other mail matter addressed to any such fictitious, false, or assumed title, name, or address, or name other than his own proper name." Under this statute, the fraudster will be fined, imprisoned (up to five years), or both.

Make sure you do background checks and update them to ensure that people are not doing business as your organization without your knowledge and approval. These searches can be done by individual name, and they enable an organization to see if the individual owns any separate entities that are in competition or that afford him or her the ability to commit fraud.

Here is yet another consequence. Statute 18 U.S.C. §1343, "Fraud by Wire, Radio, or Television," may cause people in the organization to reconsider their decision to commit fraud. The elements of wire fraud under this statute are the same as those in the mail fraud statute, but they require the use of an interstate telephone call or an electronic communication made in furtherance of the scheme. A person who devises "a scheme to defraud, obtaining money or property by means of false or fraudulent pretenses, representations, or promises, transmits or causes to be transmitted by means of wire, radio, or television communication in interstate or foreign commerce, any writings, signs, signals, pictures, or sounds for the purpose of executing such scheme or artifice, shall be fined under this title or imprisoned not more than 20 years, or both." If the violation occurs in a presidentially declared major disaster or emergency or affects a financial institution, the person can be fined up to $1 million, imprisoned up to 30 years, or both.

As with mail fraud, prosecutors love to add this charge onto the others, hoping you will plead to lesser charges. Make sure your people know this if you do any transactions by wire, radio, TV, or the Internet.

In the movie *The Firm*, Mitch McDeere (played by Tom Cruise) brings down his law firm using mail and wire fraud charges relating to the overbilling of time to clients of the law firm. The FBI had been looking into more exciting crime convictions, like murder, organized crime, kickbacks, and bribes, but McDeere used these fraud statutes to expose the guilty parties in the end. The successful organization knows which people are in positions to expose the organization to this very serious punishment. The same people can also serve in deterring, detecting, and preventing fraud.

An organization needs to educate its people to recognize unethical behavior and the risks with respect to punishment. Where do the people in your organization fall on the scale, if they were to perpetrate a fraud? Have you communicated the consequences effectively? Exhibit 3.6 illustrates class offenses in the United States.

Other areas of exposure that organizations face as a result of being involved in a global business are those detailed by the Foreign Corrupt Practices Act of 1977. This is a federal law known primarily for two of its main provisions: It addresses accounting transparency requirements under the Securities Exchange Act of 1934, and it concerns the bribery of foreign officials.

The penalties for individuals under its antibribery provisions are as follows:

- Civil penalty up to $10,000.
- Criminal fine up to $250,000 and or imprisonment up to five years.
- Under the Alternative Fines Act, the fine may be increased to twice the gross financial gain or loss resulting from the corrupt payment.
- A criminal fine imposed on an individual cannot be paid directly or indirectly by the company on whose behalf the person acted.

The penalties for organizations are as follows:

- Civil penalty up to $10,000.
- Criminal fine up to $2 million.
- Under the Alternative Fines Act, the fine may be increased to twice the gross financial gain or loss resulting from the corrupt payment.

EXHIBIT 3.6 Class Offenses in the United States

Type	Class	Maximum Prison Term	Maximum Fine	Probation Term	Maximum Supervised Release Term	Maximum Prison Term Upon Supervised Release Revocation	Special Assessment
Felony	A	Life imprisonment (or death)	$250,000	1–5 years	5 years	5 years	$100
	B	25 years or more	$250,000		5 years	3 years	$100
	C	Less than 25 years but 10 or more years	$250,000		3 years	2 years	$100
	D	Less than 10 years but 5 or more years	$250,000		3 years	2 years	$100
	E	Less than 5 years but more than 1 year	$250,000		1 year	1 year	$100
Misdemeanor	A	1 year or less but more than 6 months	$100,000	0–5 years	1 year	1 year	$ 25
	B	6 months or less but more than 30 days	$ 5,000		1 year	1 year	10
	C	30 days or less but more than 5 days	$ 5,000		1 year	1 year	5
Infraction		5 days or less	$ 5,000	0–1 years	N/A	N/A	N/A

The penalties for individuals under the law's accounting provisions are as follows:

- Civil penalty up to $100,000.
- Criminal fine up to $5 million or twice the gain or loss caused by the violation, and or imprisonment up to 20 years.
- The fines cannot be paid directly or indirectly by the company on whose behalf the person acted.

The penalties for organizations are as follows:

- Civil penalty up to $500,000.
- Criminal fine up to $25 million or twice the gain or loss caused by the violation.

After examining these potential punishments, you may have felt an 800-pound friendly gorilla effect, one that you may wish to share with your employees, educating them on the potential consequences of fraud. Although it does not always stop fraud, it certainly makes people think twice. Give them the facts they can weigh prior to deciding to commit the fraud. Say something like, "This is the jail time you face, never mind the legal and restitution cost. Because I have had extensive ethics training, it is really important for me to clearly communicate to you that the people in the process and all of their final outcomes are subject to fraud charges, not just the one key individual and his or her consequences."

An organization needs to make sure its people are aware of the consequences before they complete their rationalization to commit fraud. By communicating the long-term negative consequences of their actions, you will have made them think about the short-term benefit and determine if it is worthwhile to commit the fraud. Creating the right training in thinking is an ongoing process.

Larceny versus Embezzlement

Many organizations are subject to common types of criminal charges. Larceny and embezzlement are common, but they are often not reported because either an organization is insured or it does not want to be embarrassed, and restitution has been made.

It is important to understand the main differences between embezzlement and larceny. First, embezzlement involves communication. Second, the person performing the embezzlement has to have access to and control of the assets in question in order to be able to convert the assets for an unintended or unauthorized use. I experienced a situation during an investigation in which a person used forged business checks for personal use and recorded them in a check register as a business expense. This person was entrusted with the checks and was also authorized to post the transactions. Embezzlement does not have to take the form of actual theft or stealing (taking something that does not belong to you). Embezzlement is the taking of entrusted assets by deceitful means.

When a case takes the form of actual theft, embezzlement and larceny can be difficult to determine. When dealing with the misappropriation of property by employees, it is even more difficult. To prove employee embezzlement, you must show that the employee had possession of the goods, had the authority to exercise substantial control over the goods, and was able to convert the goods for his or her benefit. The courts will look at the following in determining control: job title, job description, and the particular employment practices.

Can you distinguish embezzlement from larceny? Here is an example involving an employee. The manager of an electronics department at a store would most likely have sufficient control over the electronic items, and if he chose, he could convert the goods for his own use (embezzlement). On the other hand, if the same manager were to walk up to the auto parts counter and take items, the crime would be larceny.

Larceny is the wrongful and fraudulent taking from another with a felonious intent and then converting what was taken to your own use without the consent of the owner. It is basically outright theft. Here is another example to help you distinguish between embezzlement and larceny. If a bank customer gives some money to a bank teller for deposit in the bank, the bank teller has possession of the property, and her conversion of the property for her own use would be embezzlement rather than larceny. But if the teller deposited the money in the bank and placed the money in a drawer, the subsequent taking of the money by the teller would be larceny rather than embezzlement, because the money was no longer technically in her possession (it was in the bank's possession). However, if it was the teller's intention to steal the money all along, and she placed the money in the drawer temporarily without making a deposit, then the distinction does not apply.

Now that we have an understanding of the criminal aspects of fraud, there are civil penalties and lawsuits to consider, which have a much lower standard of proof.

In discussing the penalties (jail time, fines, and possible civil judgments and damages) with the people in our organizations, we create an atmosphere in which fraudsters consider the risk-reward analysis of fraud. Giving them this information ensures that they understand all the facts in deciding whether to commit fraud in an organization's process.

SUMMARY

Fraudsters can have a huge and negative impact on an organization. Their influence and destruction can cause others in an organization to lose out. Sometimes these fraudsters remain under the radar even though they are causing large amounts of destruction. Is there a fraudster in your organization who is the potential elephant in the room? See Exhibit 3.7.

An organization needs to ensure that everyone has common motivations and goals that allow everyone to work together in the most productive and efficient manner for the preservation of the organization. It is important to balance

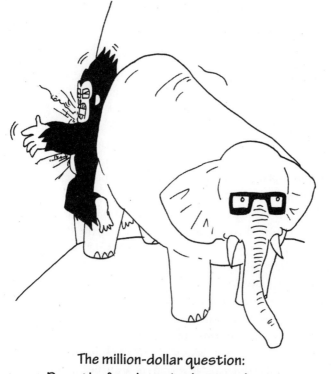

The million-dollar question:
Does the fraudster in the room leave
enough room for anyone else?

EXHIBIT 3.7   Is There an Elephant in the Room?

the four generations, addressing each generation's unique characteristics by applying the proper motivating technique to each situation and circumstance using the motivation equation. If the people in the process are not handled properly, an imbalance poses the greatest risk to your organization's value. By looking at the people in an organization and their motivations, an organization can proactively monitor and provide the best training to maintain open channels of communication, therefore deterring fraud.

 ## ONE-MINUTE FRAUD MYSTERY ANALYSIS

Where does the value exist in this chapter's fraud mystery? Remember, you are the fact finder and need to think divergently. Here are my thoughts on this chapter's mystery, based on my experience in the field:

- **Allegation.** The clients are buying limited edition art prints for thousands of dollars for charity. They are being provided independent art appraisals showing the fair market value of the prints, which is often significantly higher than the real value applied by the seller of the art. Purchasers are being advised to deduct the appraised value. This may not conform to applicable income tax regulations and statutes, though, since the appraisals have been determined to be overstated, and the individual taxpayers will owe additional tax in addition to penalty and interest charges on the outstanding tax.
- **Probable cause.** This scenario is likely a tax-sheltering scheme, but it warrants further investigation to decide whether it is reputable and in compliance with applicable laws. Although sophisticated donors were led to believe the program was legitimate, the inflated value of the donated items gives the buyer unwarranted tax benefits.
- **Action.** Further questioning is necessary. The approach you should take is a cautious one. While you want to treat Tina Seller and Tony Thanks as people of interest, you need to use the 800-pound friendly gorilla approach when investigating them. You need to understand the level of socialization and relationships that exist between these parties. Who has a clear understanding of the organizational business process? Who is the potential ring leader? Who else may be involved (Art Creed)? Is the relationship between them limited to this art sale, or is it ongoing? The bookkeeper brought the problem to light. Is she credible? Look into her background. Do not assume that the victims are not involved. Rule them out by using proper

due diligence. Examine where the greed exists that enables the fraudster to start justifying his or her rationalization to commit fraud. Are there external influences? Look for lifestyle changes. Look for conflicts of interest. Know your answers before you ask critical questions by having a well-thought-out and planned approach.

- **Preparation.** Consider the owner an interested party and collect supports, starting with the charity's records. Use caution when getting the records so as not to raise visibility for the allegations. If the IRS is already involved, allow it to investigate, since that is less costly. Find out if ACD is a registered charity. When reviewing this scenario, brainstorm and develop a list of nonaccusatory, open-ended questions. Also find out whether the charity books are audited by an independent auditor.
- **People of interest.** Most people in this chain are persons of interest, including Art Creed, Tony Thanks, Tina Seller, and the THW bookkeeper.
- **People-with-knowledge interview plan.** Interview THW's bookkeeper to determine the understanding of the transaction for accounting purposes. Also, interview Creed, Thanks, Seller, and the owner of ACD.
- **Documentary evidence.** Establish the cost basis by reviewing the actual art invoices from ACD. Review the art valuations appraisals and the tax returns of the individuals involved and of ACD and THW, if you can obtain them. Look at the general ledgers. Are the underlying records messy or organized? Also look at any canceled checks, deposit tickets, and bank statements.
- **Formulate opinion.** This is most likely a scam of overvalued art, including tax avoidance (legal use of the tax regulations to one's advantage to reduce the amount of tax due) or tax evasion (illegal use of the same). To support the opinion, see if the applicable documents determine a potential tax fraud. Specifically, it would be good to find documents that link Seller to the funds (proving she received the monies). Finding the appraisal link to Seller would help. Deflection by a person of interest is involved, and the IRS goes after the buyer, making it so that he or she has to recover on his or her own any loss from ACD. Make sure to verify the nonprofits through reputable databases and look to the state you operate in to verify them, making sure they maintain their 501(c)(3) status so the deduction remains tax-deductible.[18] In addition, since ACD is providing the paintings and the appraisals, ACD could be possibly running a counterfeit painting scheme. It could be providing counterfeit paintings and false appraisal to substantiate the inflated value. The successful forensic professional looks beyond the existing facts to make sure he or she has developed the full picture.

The 800-Pound Friendly Gorilla Suggestions for The House of Worship Inc.

The House of Worship relies on its good standing and reputation in the community. Being tied to a fraudulent scandal could be devastating. It is crucial that THW has an 800-pound friendly gorilla protecting its interest. People associated with THW, whether they are employees, vendors, or associates, need to pass scrutiny and ensure the safekeeping of THW's reputation as a pillar of society. In addition to setting the bar high for all transactions, in this case, this is what THW should have done to reduce the risk of fraud:

- Use state agencies to verify and validate the companies involved.
- Monitor the responsibilities given to people with access to the value.
- Review the values involved in the art transactions by having an independent entity revalue things.
- Find the documentation on the companies to ensure they are current and registered.
- Is the art able to be resold readily or back to ACD?

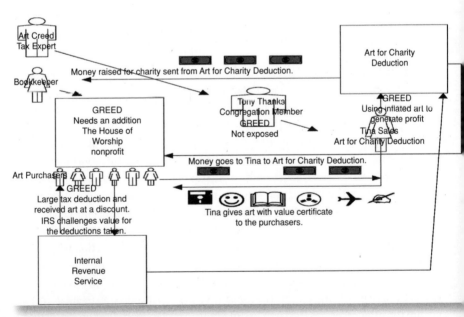

EXHIBIT 3.8   House of Worship Inc. Drawing

- Find and interview other people who have done business with the companies in the past.
- Examine Tony Thanks's relation to ACD and to Tina Seller.

A Simple Picture

Where does the greed exist in Exhibit 3.8?

When drawing a simple picture, you will probably come to the conclusion that Tina Seller is the point person. Tony Thanks may be involved, but you would need to find evidence of funds being transferred between him and Seller, which is not an easy task if cash is involved. Remember, though, whenever cash is involved, it is difficult to prove connections and often requires catching people in the act.

The fail-safe in this scenario is that the IRS did not accept the values stated. If it had, the scheme would have continued to spread through these companies' dealings with other entities. In general, if the price looks too good to be true, it probably is. Look for the greed in the process and find the proper support documentation to determine where the fraud originates. Continually examine the people behind the proofs. See Exhibit 3.8.

 NOTES

1. William H. Swanson, "Swanson's Unwritten Rules of Management," *New York Times*, May 3, 2006, http://www.nytimes.com/2006/05/03/business/media/03leonhardt.html.
2. IRS, Part 25: Special Topics, Chapter 1: Fraud Handbook, Section 6: Civil Fraud, http://www.irs.gov/irm/part25/irm_25-001-006.html.
3. A. H. Maslow, "A Theory of Human Motivation," *Psychological Review* 50(4): 370–396, 1943.
4. Lydia Saad, "Nurses Shine, Bankers, Slump in Ethics Rating," Gallup, November 24, 2008, http://www.gallup.com/poll/112264/nurses-shine-while-bankers-slump-ethics-ratings.aspx.
5. Josephson Institute Center for Business Ethics, "Character Study Reveals Predictors of Lying and Cheating," press release, October 9, 2009, http://josephsoninstitute.org/surveys/.
6. "The Traditional Generation (Born 1922–1945), Value Options, http://www.valueoptions.com/spotlight_YIW/traditional.htm.
7. Floyd Norris, "MicroStrategy Chairman Accused of Fraud by S.E.C.," *New York Times*, December 15, 2000, http://www.nytimes.com/2000/12/15/business/microstrategy-chairman-accused-of-fraud-by-sec.html.

8. Wikipedia, "ILOVEYOU," http://en.wikipedia.org/wiki/ILOVEYOU.

9. Wikipedia, "Adrian Lamo," http://en.wikipedia.org/wiki/Adrian_Lamo.

10. Wikipedia, "Jonathan James," http://en.wikipedia.org/wiki/Jonathan_James.

11. "Employment Projections: 2010–2020, Summary," Economic News Release, Bureau of Labor Statistics, February 1, 2012, http://bls.gov/news.release/ecopro.nr0.htm.

12. *Baretta* ran on ABC from 1975 to 1978 and starred Robert Blake as Tony Baretta.

13. United States of America criminal and penal code of the federal government. Title 18, "Crimes and Criminal Procedures," Part 1, Chapter 47, 1001(a).

14. Background reports provide information gleaned from publicly available information, which includes reports of indictment, arrest, and/or incarceration for fraud charges. So if charges are not pressed, a typical background check will not reveal anything, and the thief can continue to steal. A full background investigation, in which field operatives conduct live interviews with people of knowledge, would be more productive, assuming that the interviewees are forthcoming about the subject's past behavior. The interviewer needs to be sensitive to the interviewees' concerns about being accused of slandering the subject.

15. *United States of America v. Louis Kovel*, 296 F.2d 918; 96 A.L.R.2d 116; 62-1 U.S. Tax Case. (CCH) P9111; 9 A.F.T.R.2d (P-H) 366 (2dn Cir. 1961).

16. Internal Revenue Service, "How Do You Report Suspected Tax Fraud Activity?" August 1, 2012, http://www.irs.gov/individuals/article/0,,id=106778,00.html.

17. For more information, visit the North American Industry Classification System website at http://www.naics.com/search.htm.

18. "Exemption Requirements—Section 501(c)(3) Organizations, IRD, http://www.irs.gov/charities/charitable/article/0,,id=96099,00.html.

CHAPTER FOUR

How to Act Like a Fraudster

To Catch a Fraudster, You Need to Think Like One

One way to remember who you are is to remember who your heroes are.

—Steve Jobs

How would a fraudster have to act to get away with fraud in your organization? It is through an analysis of people's actions that we can develop fraud awareness and expose fraudster behavior.

Developing a trustworthy, fraud-fighting workforce is key to this chapter's methods because it helps your organization spot potential fraudsters while working alongside the 800-pound friendly gorilla to detect, deter, and prevent fraud.

Fortunately, most people inside and outside an organization give themselves away, in a number of ways (including leaving an extensive paper trail by accident or from guilt) the fact that they committed fraud. But regardless of how they give themselves away, identifying the fraud after the fact is *reactive* thinking. We want to be *proactive* in preventing and deterring fraud rather than handling it after it has taken place.

The fraudster often commits affinity fraud, which is fraud targeted at a specific group of people, by preying on members of the group, such as the elderly, a particular religious or ethnic community, a language minority, or a professional group. The group is focused, scripted, and predictable, which helps the fraudster to blend in. For example, the Madoff scam, which targeted a specific group of investors and created the facade that only certain people were eligible to participate in the investments, was affinity fraud.

The fraudster begins to understand how to act in an organization as early as his or her job interview. First impressions are formed in 7 to 17 seconds of meeting someone.[1] Many times, the fraudster takes advantage of this by dressing the part and talking a good game to get on the inside of an organization to take advantage of an exposed value.

Personalizing marketing materials or addressing potential customers by name has been found to increase the likelihood that they will respond by 36 percent. People love to hear their names, and fraudsters need to know all the people in an organizational process to find out which ones they need to help them deflect attention and avoid getting caught. Being on time to work and leaving later than others in the group is also one of the fraudster's best tools. You can be sure that the fraudster is also paying attention to what is going on in an organization in order to take advantage of it. The key to preventing and deterring fraud is to get an organization's most trustworthy people to pay attention just as hard as the fraudster does.

This chapter looks at how the incentives of an organization provide a script that helps the fraudster learn how to act to get a bonus or reward. To keep fraudsters from taking advantage of incentive plans, organizations need to clearly align their incentives with correct ethical behaviors as well as checks and balances.

Fraudsters are good at avoiding conflicts of interest, and the 800-pound friendly gorilla must clearly communicate what constitutes such a conflict to the people in an organizational process, since conflicts of interest may not actually indicate any legal wrongdoing. In my experience, I have noticed that there is often a presumption that people are getting a kickback when they are not. In other words, just because conflicts of interest appear to exist does not mean that they are taken advantage of to commit fraud.

Overall, this chapter aims to help you along with the other people in your organization and its 800-pound friendly gorillas, work together to deter, detect, and prevent fraud before it's too late by being aware of how fraudsters think. Understanding people's intentions is essential in developing the necessary proactive actions against fraud. A motivated staff that cares about an organization can be a great fraud deterrent.

This chapter features the following:
  Why fraudsters get caught (when they get greedy)
  How fraudsters blend in and avoid attention
  How fraudsters build trust to gain access to an organization's value

Details of the fraudsters' most important deceptions, such as pretending to adopt the values of an organization
How communication is the key to preventing, deterring, and detecting fraud
The importance of building reliable relationships in an organization

---

THE FRAUDSTER LEARNS HOW COMMUNICATION works within an organization so that he or she can gain access to its real value. Defining the greed in an organization and knowing where it exists can be a very difficult task, since fraudsters try hard to stay under the radar. Organizations that have not identified the greed that exists with the people in their processes allow fraudsters to blend in and keep from getting caught. Organizations are built on trust, and the fraudster learns how to gain people's trust and discover their needs and wants.

Therefore, one solution to preventing, deterring, and detecting fraud is to lead and monitor an organization's teams to make sure everyone is involved in a process of transparency and ethical behavior. The 800-pound friendly gorilla in your organization must make sure that everyone is trained properly and aware of his or her group's ethics and mission. If you make sure everyone is watching, then everyone is accountable, communicating, and independently monitoring the organization.

ONE-MINUTE FRAUD MYSTERY: CATCH ME IF YOU CAN INC.

Jim Dipper was hired by Catch Me If You Can Inc. to operate its engineering department, which constructs bridges. Dipper produced his engineering license, his college diploma from the California Institute of Technology, and references from the engineering company he previously worked for, Pan Am Engineering. The CEO of Pan Am Engineering is Chuck Finley, indicated as a reference on Dipper's rèsumè, and is well respected in the industry. John Ripley, the CEO of Catch Me if You Can, Inc., assumed that Human Resources checked Dipper's credentials and was happy to have him on board.

Catch Me If You Can Inc. was working on a new bridge project for State Bridges, Inc., the general contractor (general contractors oversee projects for clients). State Bridges, Inc.'s client, Brooklyn Bridge, Inc., was working on the project in Brooklyn, New York. It was a very technical engineering project, and Ripley was convinced that Dipper was the man for the job. In addition to their engineering credentials, a common achievement was shared by Ripley and Dipper: Both had attained Eagle Scout status. Both were also foundational generation members.

A few months had gone by, and Ripley was convinced that the Brooklyn Bridge project was making the company significant profit, since Dipper was getting an abundance of change orders and the cash was rolling in from the general contractor, State of Bridges. Dipper was working with Tim Two-Timer, the project manager for State of Bridges, Inc.

One day Ripley's secretary received a call from Anthony Oversight, the CEO of State of Bridges, Inc., asking why the project was behind schedule based on a call he received from his client Brooklyn Bridges, Inc. Ripley called Dipper, who was on vacation with Two-Timer in the Bahamas. Ripley calls you, the forensic accountant, to look over the billing and the budgets to determine what the status of the project is and respond to Oversight's call.

THE SIX Ps OF SUCCESSFUL FRAUDSTERS

It is important to watch the relationships and behavior inside and outside an organization (see Exhibit 4.1).

These relationships and behaviors often indicate whether an employee's self-interest is ultimately appropriate or inappropriate. Self-interest exists in every organization, and self-interested employees advance themselves like soldiers in a war, throwing grenades to advance upon the enemy. However, organizations cannot allow their people to pull the pins at their expense. Each time one greed grenade is allowed to explode, others will follow. Keep the pins in your employees' greed grenades by maintaining a proactive approach, knowing your people and making sure they make the correct ethical decisions to advance your organization's specific interests and needs.

There are six traits a fraudster must display to remain in the organizational process undetected (see Exhibit 4.2).

The Six Ps are passion, philosophy, planning, persistence, patience, and prison. Details on each follow. These six Ps are traits that are often attributable to success, but here we are applying them to the fraudster to show how he or she acts in order to persist in a fraud and remain undetected.

Passion

A growing company, from start-up to success, will require a ton of time and effort to maintain its overall objective, which is to make a profit and remain in

EXHIBIT 4.1 Watch the Relationships and Behaviors

Gorilla 1: Look! They threw another "self-interest greed" grenade.
Gorilla 2: It's a good thing they didn't pull the pins!
Gorilla 1: Do you think they will ever realize that it is not about them?
Gorilla 2: I don't know, but can you imagine what the organizational world would be like if everyone was only out for himself and didn't care about the interests of the organization?

existence. Therefore, when working in the organizational process, the fraudster must maintain a passion—an outward appearance of enthusiasm about the organization—with people inside and outside the organization to convince them that everything is working as planned. That means the appearance of having the organization's interests at heart.

Passion is an emotion that the fraudster maintains to divert attention and remain undetected. Without an 800-pound friendly gorilla continually checking on fraudsters, they will get by until someone questions their actions. Acting with passion allows fraudsters to be perceived as going beyond the call of duty to find ways to improve and innovate. Their actions then appear to be

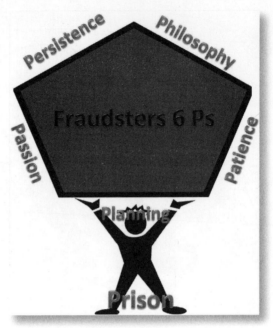

EXHIBIT 4.2 A Successful Fraudster's Six *P*s

benefiting both themselves and their organization. Passion is the driving force that is necessary for fraudsters to remain undetected.

Philosophy

A fraudster conceives a clear concept of a fraud and then works to achieve it. Early in the organizational process, he or she must instill a philosophy about how the organization, or his or her role in it, will operate in its industry and with its customers, especially to avert detection.

When an organization builds a solid culture around honest business practices, from the way its products are made and delivered to the way it treats its employees and customers, it is building a strong foundation for success, which the fraudster has to try hard to maintain in order to remain undetected.

Planning

Planning in the fraudster mind-set is not a "do it and forget it" matter. The fraudster needs a clear fraud plan for the organization that satisfies his or her perceived needs. Moreover, the fraudster's planning has to include being ready for the unexpected, which can be anything from a change in the organization's procedures (added or new controls) to unforeseen market conditions (ask Bernie Madoff what happened to his Ponzi scheme when the market crashed).

The fraudster needs the flexibility to change midstream or take a fraud plan in a whole new direction to avoid detection.

Persistence

Persistence is a key element in any fraudster's success. All organizations face challenges, regardless of their size and their industry. In my many years of helping small organizations, I have seen them all develop; not one of them is still the same company now that it was when the organization was first started. Like these businesses, fraudsters also change with the times. They innovate to overcome new challenges or simply reinvent themselves to better target their victims.

Patience

Fraudsters know the reward they are working toward. They might not achieve it as fast as they want or in the exact form they expect—but they will achieve it. Fraudsters work diligently to gain access to an organization's value. Day after day, month after month, the fraudster patiently makes the organization perceive that all of the rules and guidance are being followed, so he or she can remain undetected. The fraudster always wants to give the appearance that he or she advances the organization's needs while keeping his or her greed unexposed.

Prison

A successful fraudster must be willing to risk going to prison and accept other consequences of his or her actions. A determined fraudster convinces himself or herself that the rewards of the fraud outweigh the risks and thus rationalizes the fraud. In addition, the fraudster may simply ignore the consequences, being of the mind-set that he is invincible, that he will never be caught, or that he is too smart to get caught.

 THE CHARACTERISTICS OF A FRAUDSTER

The common underlying motivation in committing fraud is greed. The fraudster manipulates organizational attitudes as necessary to remain undetected in the overall process. The fraudster creates the appearance that processes are running as designed and that there is no need to worry, because everything is in tip-top shape. The fraudster always needs to be conscious of the others involved in the processes because everyone has the ability to expose the fraudster's actions.

We are products of our environment. An organization that does not create an honest atmosphere will fall victim to fraud.

People who commit fraud need to maintain the necessary personal attributes to work within the organizational process and remain undetected. Therefore, one attribute of the fraudster is creativity.

Typically fraudsters in an organization are creative with accounting, excuses, illusions, rationalizations, and negotiated truths (or "white lies"). A creative person knows how to get around legal or conventional organizational processes and devises plans to conceal acts. The organization needs to be as creative as the fraudster.

Throughout our lives we learn to strive to be better than others; this is normal competition. We know that no organization can be built by one person, yet society and the media want a hero. A simple example is that the generals get credit for the war, yet they are never directly involved in the hands-on combat to win the war.

Creating an organization that makes all people accountable is the greatest fraud deterrent. Developing a self-governing system of checks and balances is key. Fraudsters are often in leadership roles. Society usually focuses on a leader's achievements, and the fraudster always appears to be a team player, whether or not he or she really is. At lower levels, fraudsters thrive in organizations with idealistic figureheads and positive role models. They also love to create a fall guy.

As mentioned in an earlier chapter, tips ("telling if people steal") is the number one means of deterring, detecting, and preventing fraud in an organization.[2] People often cannot stand the guilt and feel the need to tell someone what they have done. This is why we emphasize interviewing skills. It is important to be able to ask the right questions.

People have lives beyond the organization. There will often be signs in a fraudster's life outside the organization that explain or expose their inappropriate actions in the organization. It is important to have good investigative skills while also considering privacy. An employee who is proactive in the workplace or an investigator who is on the trail of a potential fraud does not want to invade people's privacy based on unfounded accusations or be susceptible to charges of conducting a witch hunt.

A good way to get the ball rolling so that every member of an organization feels at ease in keeping his or her eyes and ears open is for the organization to consider having a tip line. If one already exists, it should be continually evolving. Tips often come from people who may have witnessed fraud incidents firsthand or who have the proof of intention which is often very difficult to document. Whistleblower programs at large corporations need to be monitored well to continually evolve. I can tell you from firsthand experience as a business owner that tips can lead to the discovery of improprieties. Well-run TIPS programs do work. The only drawback of a TIPS program is that it is not proactive; people are reporting frauds that have already taken place. A proactive organization analyzes its people and their actions before tips come in. TIPS programs remain a valuable fraud detection tool rather than prevention because they identify the intersecting points of organizational control weaknesses and greed opportunities. Unfortunately, the tip comes after the fraud has occurred.

Organizational improvement lines (or OIL, for short) allow employees to make recommendations about an organization, inherently telling the boss what may be going wrong in a department, group, or organization overall. People who make successful suggestions should get proper recognition. Because of its proactive nature, OIL is like the 800-pound friendly gorilla.

When creating a fraud-fighting workforce, it is important to consider that people's learning abilities vary. Organizations that assume that all fraudsters learn the same way are not developing a comprehensive and proactive approach to managing fraud risk. Not all frauds are perpetrated in the same way, and some require higher levels of thinking to be exposed. We need to develop the fraud risk intelligence of the people in our organizations in the context of their learning abilities.

A Master in Attention to External Cues

The boxer Mike Tyson said it best when he stated, "Everyone has a plan till they get punched in the face." Fraudsters often rehearse for unpredictable situations. The 800-pound friendly gorilla needs to make sure that the people in an organizational process address the potential uncertainties and formulate an understanding of the outcomes associated with taking risks.

Fortunately for the fraud examiner, many fraudsters are not likely to have thought through all of the potential consequences of their actions or performed a full risk analysis of the potential flags that could get them caught. The organization needs to utilize the different learning abilities of its staff to develop an

800-pound friendly gorilla "fraud force" that can identify all of the various fraud risks and exposures caused by uncertainties.

Let's examine the clues that fraudsters see in an organizational process that enable them to gain access to organizational value and commit fraud. The fraudster typically needs quiet time to study the organizational process and develop the proper way to act. The skills fraudsters need to maintain appearances ensure that they do not make any spelling errors and that they have a strong enough vocabulary to communicate effectively and not attract attention to their fraud work. A simple misspelled word can lead to the fraudster getting caught. The IRS auditor pays specific attention to people who make mistakes because they call attention to themselves. It takes fraudsters awhile to gain an understanding of an organizational process so that they can commit acts of fraud but avoid suspicion.

Fraudsters often use their organizations' charts and tables to their advantage when committing fraud. Organizational charts and tables are typically used to outline, develop, and run the organizational process. Fraudsters can take advantage of these charts and tables because they help the fraudsters to see where value is exposed and where they can remain undetected. Fraudsters rely on the fact that most people in the organizational process do not pay attention to the small details of the charts or tables. Fraudsters exploit the details that no one else pays attention to.

Everyone should be involved in the development of the charts and pictures that outline the organizational process. It is important to have checks and balances performed by someone outside the design process to ensure that fraud is not taking place. A strong organization requires all of the people in a process to understand visual aids and be involved in their development. Further examination needs to be performed to ensure that the visual aids are being implemented as designed and not circumvented. Having only one person designing and overseeing the visual aids subjects the organization to fraud risk.

In fact, having one person overseeing any single entire process is a bad idea. For instance, if you have an accounts receivable clerk who receives the customer's payment, records the transaction, makes the bank deposit, and reconciles the bank statement, then that person has the ability to override the process.

Fraudsters often make outlines, whether in their minds or on paper, of all the acts they need to perform to conceal their fraud from potential detectors. The fraudster copies whatever information he or she needs to ensure that the outline is complete and that no one can detect the fraud. The fraudster often uses others to help diagram the information and buy into the plan. In many instances, you can be sure that the fraudster's actions are based on sound, well-researched information.

The people in the organization who have the best communication skills gain the trust of the organization and have the greatest access to the organizational value. The people who always seem to have the right answer at their fingertips will often have direct access to that value. We need to monitor the level of trust we assign to people. Knowing the trusted people who are included in the design of the visual presentation determines the credibility of the process and not just of the visual aids themselves.

The difficulty lies in developing trusted people to act in the best interests of the organization and not their own self-interest. The people who often gain confidence in trusted positions can also pose the greatest threat to an organization's value. Creating a proper ethical tone as well as the feeling that someone is watching helps to deter, prevent, and detect fraud. Engaging your people to always be thinking of where the value is in your organization's process and highlighting where people have access to that value is essential. Evaluating the people and value points consistently is a good method of fraud prevention.

Clues can also be auditory. The fraudster learns how to act by hearing things; for instance, listening at the water cooler and learning information important for committing a fraud. The fraudster will also be there listening after a fraud is perpetrated to determine if anyone is onto him or her. When was the last time upper management hung out at the water cooler?

Two personality traits that may expose fraudsters' acts are a willingness to speak up whenever there is an opportunity and an ability to talk their way out of anything. Fraudsters are likely to make their colleagues think that a certain part of a process is an ongoing negotiation. They need to remember what was said in situations in order to maintain the necessary diversions and remain undetected. Fraudsters need to know the desired outcome and the necessary acts to perform and commit fraud.

Therefore, one of the most important things an organization can do is to throw curve balls when people are expecting fast balls. When fraudsters have an organizational process down pat, they are less likely to be exposed. Fraudsters tend to hang out wherever company gossip exists or wherever they can find out information that will keep them from getting caught.

An organization should take an active role in making sure that its people do not present opportunities to potential fraudsters. For example, a person with access to key proprietary information should not be disclosing it at the water cooler. An organization should monitor the people inside and outside its walls and processes so they do not expose organizational value. Watching people's interactions often brings to light conflicts of interest that can affect the organization's goodwill if that is extended to the wrong person. The 800-pound friendly gorilla watches whom your people disclose sensitive information to and requires its people to act properly while performing their responsibilities by ensuring that different types of documentary evidence support their actions.

Through repetition, fraudsters master the process of discovering every flaw and potential opportunity they can use to gain access to an organization's value. Fraudsters learn how to commit fraud by obtaining knowledge through visual cues, auditory cues, and other signs that they observe. To deter, detect, and prevent fraud, an organization needs to be paying attention to these cues and signs.

Paying attention to the clues an organization gets from the interactions of its people, as well as from the results of frauds already perpetrated, will help the organization to develop the necessary proof of intent down the road. Understanding and devising training and learning programs for the various clues an organization can note and monitor is critical.

Interpersonal Traits

In addition to monitoring the external cues, an organization should also make note of and understand the interpersonal traits of a fraudster.

People need interpersonal skills to communicate and perform within a process. Fraudsters need to have strong interpersonal skills to gain the necessary trust for getting access to the organization's value. Even one bad relationship with a colleague can lead to the dreaded tip that makes the fraudster get caught.

If they are to remain undetected, fraudsters must convince their colleagues that their actions are proper. They also need to act the way in which a specific fraud they are committing requires them to act. If a fraud requires a fraudster to keep up a happy appearance, then the fraudster will act happy. If a fraud requires a fraudster to be sneaky, then the fraudster will be sneaky. Fraudsters never want to create complicated scams or draw unnecessary attention to the process they are circumventing. They will try to have answers before questions are asked. The more difficult the fraud, the harder it is for a fraudster to have all the answers and remain undetected.

Some different types of basic interpersonal traits of fraudsters are detailed in the following paragraphs.

Superficial Interactions

One interpersonal trait you may encounter in a fraudster is the ability to act glib and superficial. The glib and superficial fraudster is smooth, engaging, charming, and slick and makes everything seem verbally simplistic. Glib and superficial fraudsters can talk their way out of anything. They know how to negotiate and put on an air of having everything under control.

Egocentric Self-Aggrandizement

Another interpersonal trait you can expect to encounter in fraudsters is the egocentric use of and grandiose actions to elevate their sense of worth and importance among their colleagues. It is not always money that motivates people to commit fraud. Many times, people who are overlooked for promotions or employees who feel unappreciated commit fraud to satisfy their egos. In relating to others, they create a sense of entitlement that fulfills their self-interest. They act overconfident so that no one questions them. Their perceived worth among their staff and in the larger group can then elevate them to the level of trust they need to gain access to an organization's value.

Lack of Guilt versus Confessing

Another interpersonal trait of fraudsters is a lack of remorse or guilt. Someone is usually being hurt by a fraud, so fraudsters have to learn to act without feelings or concern for the loss, pain, and suffering they inflict on the people and the organization.

Yet even though feelings of guilt are often not present while the fraud is being perpetrated, if a fraudster is close to being caught, guilt is often the emotion that leads him or her to confess. The level of thinking a fraudster has to enact in this regard should be an organization's focus.

It is human nature that most people cannot live with guilt and embarrassment; their consciences get the best of them and lead them to tell someone. That someone may then call the tips line, which is the main way fraudsters get caught.

Once a fraudster is caught, the typical defense attorney will instruct the accused not to discuss information with anyone. The 800-pound friendly gorilla needs to establish communication with the person of interest who has been caught by creating a relaxed and comfortable approach so the fraudster does not become defensive and uncooperative. Remember, you are not a judge or a jury, only the gatherer of facts and information.

An article examining the alternative of pleading guilty rather than going to trial states the following:

> By pleading guilty, a defendant receives an automatic sentence reduction of at least two levels, and sometimes three. In some federal cases, that means a 35 percent reduction in prison time before anything else is even considered—like cooperating with the government or other mitigating circumstances.[3]

This is why some fraudsters rationalize the risk because they believe that if they get caught, they can simply plead guilty and receive leniency. The organization needs to make it very clear that no fraud will go unpunished. An organization should reward ethical behavior by encouraging people to come forward and report fraud.

Deceptiveness

Fraudsters learn to be deceitful. They become good liars and learn to make the necessary empty promises. If an employee gives you a lot of "I'll get it to you next week" comments, finger-points, or acts in other questionable ways, make sure you investigate. It is better to be safe than sorry. The fraudster will create delay, cause confusion, or develop manipulating responses when called to explain his or her questionable actions. An organization needs to have the correct level of management (the 800-pound friendly gorilla) along with properly trained people to handle the investigation of these actions.

Behaviors

Let's now look beyond interpersonal traits and develop an understanding of the behavioral signs of fraudsters.

The first type of fraudster behavior that you may recognize is impulsivity, the tendency to act quickly without thinking about the consequences of the actions. Fraudsters often act without having thought through the consequences. Fraudsters' hasty decisions can lead an organization into trouble. Organizations should not allow people to act on their feelings in the moment rather than making a long-term plan. Short-term fixes can lead to bigger problems if not corrected. Just ask Lehman Brothers.

Fraudsters may also need to create excitement to distract from the organizational process flaws created by their actions. Fraudsters try to show management that they have no problem meeting or exceeding management's expectations, when that is not the case.

The fraudster also has to act in what appears to be a responsible manner in the eyes of the people in the organization when he or she is actually irresponsible. Creating this misperception allows the fraudster to remain undetected.

Character Traits

Let's also examine some personal character traits.[4] The typical positive and negative character traits associated with achieving goals or performing tasks are shown in Exhibit 4.3. Understanding these traits will help us to better understand the people in our organizations, which in turn will enhance the overall communication in the organization.

In today's organizations, the auditor, accountant, and fraud examiner need to all develop soft skills. Soft skills are personal attributes that enhance one's ability to perform a job. Some examples of soft skills include professionalism, work ethic, oral and written communication skills, and so on.[5] Building an awareness of soft skills is necessary to deter, detect, and prevent fraud. In order for an accountant, an auditor, and a fraud examiner to assist an organization successfully, they need to have an effective understanding of how fraudsters act. It is important to first accept that it is possible for fraud to happen in your organization and get into the mind-set of the fraudster.

For instance, when was the last time the CEO of your organization asked someone to do something inappropriate as a way of testing the moral character of that employee? This type of test will define the people in key positions. Law enforcement personnel set up stings all the time. It takes a fraudster to catch a

EXHIBIT 4.3 Traits Associated with Goals and Tasks

Attitude		
Challenge	**Positive Trait**	**Negative Trait**
Danger	Courageous	Cowardly
Importance	Conscientious	Careless
Difficulty	Determined	Discouraged
Ability	Confident	Unsure
Effort	Hardworking	Lazy

Source: http://www.school-for-champions.com/character/personal_traits.htm

fraudster. What better way to determine the weakness in an organization than by attempting a mock fraud and seeing the results?

All of an organization's processes are connected, because all of the people interact. They come together at the company picnic, at a holiday party, or through a customer who links different departments (e.g., by bringing the accounts receivable clerk together with a sales team member over a collection issue). How often are people coming together, and why? You should closely watch the interpersonal connections to control the potential for fraud.

The fraudster is always building rapport within an organization in order to monitor whether anyone is watching, and most people in the organization are too busy to notice. How often, after someone commits a fraud, do we hear "but he was so nice," or "I just cannot believe that she was capable of doing that"? This surprised reaction happens because illicit behaviors are never tested before it's too late. A creative organization can create a mock fraud and test the people within a process to see if the proper ethical tone is present and being maintained.

Organizations are often required to provide ethics training for their people nowadays because of regulations. Even CPA ethics is a four-hour training course taken once every three years. This training offers guidelines on what to do and what not to do, but it should actually ask the trainees, "Could you do this?" and "Could you do that?" in reference to potential fraud in their organizational responsibilities. It should also ask them, "How would you do it?" Asking key people in a process to describe how they would commit fraud if they wanted to gives a clearer picture of how these acts are committed and how a fraudster might think in a fraud situation.

FRAUDSTERS AND THEIR ORGANIZATIONS

Today's organizations have computers that analyze data and trends, but do organizations study the results from a horizontal analysis (comparing two or more years' financial data) or a vertical analysis (comparing one item in percentage form and dollar form)? Who is doing the review? If the people analyzing the numbers have no moral character, then the analyses mean nothing. An organization can compare its financial performance (past and present) to that of other organizations, but when was the last time you compared your organization's people to the people in a competing organization?

A successful organization combats fraud by hiring the most ethical and well-trained people it can find in its industry and then compares them to the employees of other organizations. There have been many documented frauds, especially in recent years, that you can learn from, so take the time to study them. Learn from other cases before similar ones happen to you.

Organizations should not lead their auditors, accountants, and fraud examiners. The organization that maintains independence has the necessary objectivity to establish credibility in its financial communications. These communications should never create an alarmist reaction. If there are disputes over facts, then a level-headed and controlled approach is extremely important. This can be accomplished only by keeping a close eye on the details.

Keep in mind, however, that to remain undetected, a fraudster needs to be even more accurate than a person not committing fraud. A fraudster who makes mistakes will get caught.

Fraudsters are usually well organized and convey very clear messages with the necessary supports. Whether the supports are correct is another question. Organizations that are successful at combating fraud will test the supports.

Fraudsters' reports that are not timely or that contain typing errors will call attention to the fraud plan. If everything is not buttoned up, fraudsters may be in over their heads or unconsciously want to get caught. In any event, if there are mistakes that point out inconsistencies, an organization should investigate these red flags as soon as possible.

Red Flags Warranting Further Investigation

Red flags in processes and communications that warrant further investigation include the following:

- **Excessive pressure on employees.** When there is excessive pressure being exerted on senior managers and employees to achieve unusually tough profit targets and organizational goals, there is motivation for fraud. Know why these expectations are being created and for whom. Increased annual net income and operating profits that do not lead to increased cash flow, for instance, should be investigated. A discrepancy like that can cause an organization to be the next WorldCom or Dynegy. If you have income from operating profits, know where it is reflected in the organization records and whether the accounting is proper.
- **Doing markedly better than your competitors.** When an organization is thriving while its competitors are struggling with declining sales and profits, there is an indicator for potential fraud. If your organization is thriving, know why it is doing well compared to similar organizations.

- **Nontraditional or unusual payment methods or agreements.** When there are nontraditional or unusual payment methods and agreements occurring between an organization and certain suppliers or customers, there is a potential for fraud. Any payment that is not by check, wire, or other standard means should be called to the attention of the proper authority in your organization.
- **Multiple bank accounts or arrangements.** When an organization has multiple banking accounts or arrangements, there is a potential for fraud. Make sure that every account is legitimate, has a purpose, and has adequate controls.
- **Creative accounting.** When an organization consistently pushes the envelope on matters of financial judgment or accounting, there is a potential for fraud. Creative accounting leads to manipulation and misinformation.
- **Withholding information about processes, operations, or results.** When an organization creates secrecy around its processes, operations, and/or financial results, there is a potential for fraud. Withholding answers and supporting information from internal and external inquiries is unacceptable. Transparency is essential for today's organizations. Failure to maintain an open-book policy is a cause for concern. An organization must be willing to expose itself to public scrutiny and regulatory scrutiny without concern.

Traits to Investigate

Employees who are unreliable, prone to making mistakes, and poor performers have a tendency to take shortcuts or bend the rules if ignored. They easily shift blame and responsibility for their errors onto others.

Fraudsters who are unhappy and under apparent stress or pressure often bully and intimidate other people in an organization. Make sure your personnel have open channels to communicate abuse, either through a whistleblower hotline or through access to other levels of management. Keep multiple levels of checks and balances, and be sure there are appropriate consequences when the levels of management and authority are not preserved. This is the key to maintaining your personnel's integrity.

Fraudsters may manipulate personal pay and established reward and bonus systems. Some cannot resist the urge to flash their money around with cars, entertainment, and all of the latest gadgets, often representing a lifestyle that seems excessive for their income. Others need the cash to feed their vices and addictions. When the behavior of a fraudster is out of the norm, rumors might develop and spread. This is when it could pay off to know what is being talked about around the watercooler. There are often important signs and red flags here.

Fraudsters like to surround themselves with recently hired employees who do not have the honed skills to perform an organization's responsibilities. They also tend to hire people who have limited experience on their resumes. Organizations can make sure to require independent background checks and analyses for new employees. Technology and social media sites like Facebook, LinkedIn, and Twitter are great resources to see what people are doing outside an organization, before and after they are hired, provided access is not prevented by law.

In general, fraudsters love to surround themselves with people who do not challenge them. They tend to micromanage some employees while keeping others who might expose them at arm's length. Therefore, it is good to remember to monitor relationships both inside and outside the organizational process.

Fraudsters also tend to develop preferred vendors and suppliers who, when contacted, will only deal with them. They often receive and accept generous gifts that are excessive and contrary to corporate rules. Box tickets to a major league game, tickets to a Broadway play, or an invitation to dinner with expensive wine and champagne often become the criteria to do business with them. These behaviors should raise ethical issues for an organization and be investigated.

Finally, a fraudster is likely to become volatile, melodramatic, arrogant, confrontational, threatening, or aggressive when challenged. Always consider bringing in the appropriate people from inside and outside the organization when you confront a potential fraudster based on any of the red flags.

How Fraudsters Avoid Detection

Fraudsters need to create various distractions to perpetrate fraud. The following questions will help organizations to formulate the proper awareness of fraudster behaviors:

- **Are working capital needs sufficient?** Remember that current assets minus current liabilities equals working capital. Fraudsters need to maintain working capital. Is there enough working capital to pay the current bills?
- **Is debt increasing?** Keep in mind that debt to net worth equals total liabilities divided by net worth. This equation is a simple way to measure

risk. Fraudsters need to make sure that their actions are not causing an organization to incur debt for the wrong reasons, thereby exposing it to greater risk.

- **Is the organization easily acquiring credit in a difficult economy?** A fraudster will have everyone convinced that acquiring credit is not a problem and will get it, usually through deceptive means.

- **Does the organization have restrictive covenants associated with its loan agreements?** A loan covenant is made up of conditions associated with commercial loan financing or bond issuances that require the organization to fulfill certain conditions or else not undertake certain actions or activities. A fraudster knows that these covenants must be met at all costs if he or she is to remain undetected. A fraudster therefore does whatever is necessary to maintain the required covenants.

- **Are bad situations being swept under the rug?** A fraudster convinces colleagues and managers that "the house is not on fire" when it actually is. A fraudster is sure to have a story that makes the worst situation look positive.

- **Have earnings been on an accelerated decline or at unprecedented levels of growth?** With a horizontal ratio analysis (a side-by-side comparison, year by year), a fraudster has his or her trend analysis homework done. A fraudster has to create events to explain why there is a decline. Trends are a fraudster's friend, since the fraudster needs to create past and forward thinking to avert concerns when earnings decline. Fraudsters create events to explain unprecedented growth.

- **Are inventory levels increasing?** Cost of goods sold divided by average inventory measures the rate inventory being used on an accrual basis. Fraudsters make sure that the numbers meet the targets and stay in line with historical trends.

- **Are profit margins and bottom lines competitive with overall market pressures?** Gross profit divided by sales equals the number of dollars produced by every dollar of sale. An organization has a targeted gross profit margin, and the longer it is in business, the more historical support it has available. The counterpart to net profit is net margin (i.e., net profit before taxes divided by sales), which measures the profit produced by every dollar of sale that the organization has set. The longer an organization has been in business, the more historical support is usually available. These simple checks on profits should be performed, and the results should be monitored. A fraudster does his or her homework to be able to say why other organizations are allegedly undercutting their numbers. Fraudsters always have answers for why the profits are down, or they manipulate the numbers to meet the projected targets.

- **Has the organization had significant investments or losses?** A fraudster blames the economy, the investment adviser, or anyone else related to the numbers.
- **Do Wall Street analysts, investors, and other external interested parties need favorable earnings?** Fraudsters try to satisfy speculative pressures in order to remain undetected. It is often when these pressures can no longer be satisfied that everybody wakes up to find there is a problem.

There are several things that a fraudster must know to avoid getting caught. Conversely, an organization must know that the fraudster knows these things in order to catch him or her. The fraudster knows the following:

- An organization's business model, especially for one or two products.
- An organization's customer base, especially when the firm is dependent on one or two customers.
- Whether the manufacturing, merchandising, or services processes are at full capacity.
- How to make inventory and other assets seem obsolescent. How to keep an organization in a long extended cycle.
- What organizational licenses are revocable or which ones are at risk of nonrenewal.
- Whom to exploit during an organization's rapid growth and expansion.
- How to constantly present overly optimistic earnings forecasts.
- How to manipulate processes based on external economic conditions.
- Whether an organization is having a difficult time collecting receivables (i.e., the fraudster makes sure the numbers meet the targets and stay in line with historical trends).
- Whether an organization is being faced with new or expanding competitors.
- An organization's sales and production backlogs.
- Whether an organization is looking for a strategic partner to merge with.
- Whether there is an inventory increase without a comparable sales increase.
- Whether an organization has been exposed to material tax adjustments.
- Any material litigation between stockholders and management or others.
- Whether publicly traded organizations have been suspended or delisted from a stock exchange.

Fraudsters often look to develop relationships outside the office with related parties who do business with the organization. These outside relationships often present opportunities for the fraudster to gain access to value, which could come back to the fraudster in the form of favors, presents, discounts, and kickbacks. Because these transactions occur away from the organization, they are difficult to uncover because the company's records will not capture the details necessary to prove the fraud. Both the fraudster and the vendor are motivated to keep the secret hidden from the organization.

Fraudsters also tend to know whether an organization uses multiple auditing firms or frequently changes auditors. When possible, a fraudster makes sure the organization is not giving the auditors all the data they need. Similarly, fraudsters know whether their organization uses different legal firms or changes its legal counsel frequently. They attempt to make sure that no litigation involves them or has the potential to expose their fraud. They also tend to know whether the organization does business with a large number of banks or changes banks frequently and whether the organization has problems with regulatory agencies.

The more complex an organization's structure is, the easier it is for a fraudster to camouflage his or her actions and blend in. Fraudsters can steal identities, passwords, and/or building passes to enter fraudulent transactions. They watch the turnover from employee hiring and firing and always know the real gatekeepers of internal controls as well as what level of trust people have.

If you have a good industry because of the economic environment, that will make it easier for the fraudster to commit fraud. However, the fraudster will know how to act in a bad industry as well.

Fraudsters know how to take advantage of an organization's processes in both good times and bad. They tend to know the accounting practices necessary to perform their fraud. They know to avert large year-end or unusual transactions, and they are the first people to recognize that accounting practices are extremely aggressive. They make sure records are poorly kept, and if they are in the right department, they try to make sure that the accounting department is understaffed or staffed with new and untrained employees. They try to create an atmosphere of inadequate disclosure and unusual accounting policies.

Fraudsters need a behavioral environment that creates conflict through contradiction. Their bookshelves may be filled with books indicating strong ethics, but fraudsters are more concerned with making a deal than following the proper rules. Fraudsters find ways to conceal their criminal or questionable backgrounds. They make sure no one knows about their poor credit history or their financial status. They try to hide that they are living beyond their means. And many times in investigations, it becomes apparent that fraudsters have various personal habits that may encourage them to commit fraud, like gambling, sex, alcoholism, or drug addiction, or they may borrow money constantly. Look for these potential signs in your organization's people, especially those in trusted positions.

Fraudsters tend to display their personal feelings. They may be extremely active in their communities and perceived as a positive role model. They may say they are being treated unfairly by the organization or act resentful toward their superiors. They may act frustrated. When fraudsters display these characteristics, traits, and behaviors, the 800-pound friendly gorilla needs to determine whether these behaviors are the beginning of the justification to commit fraud that may lead the fraudsters to get away with accessing and using organizational value for their own self-interest. They take advantage of operations and cover up their actions. They get close to suppliers and other key people in an organization. They fail to inform the other people in a process about the rules that would enable these people to detect, deter, and prevent fraud.

Fraudsters engender a rapid turnover of key people who might catch on to what the fraudsters are doing. Fraudsters typically do not like to be absent from work, and if they are required to take vacations, they will plan around them. In addition, a fraudster knows who is absent and is aware of the periodic rotations or transfers of people into his or her process. All of these details confirm that fraudsters need to know all and see all to manipulate and outdo an organization's system.

Fraudsters usually dominate any process they control and fail to make proper executive-type disclosures. Fraudsters have often been at one job for a long time and feel comfortable. The level of trust they have been assigned has not been adapted or reviewed at regular intervals, and the appropriate checks and balances are not in place or enforced.

The fraudster likes to maintain either clean and detailed but deceptive books, sloppy books, two sets of books, or no books at all in order to frustrate an investigation and remain undetected.

The 800-pound friendly gorilla keeps a watchful eye and ear on the people in the organization. Know your people before one of them becomes the next fraudster.

SUMMARY

The examples in this chapter are not intended to represent all of a fraudster's potential characteristics, traits, and behaviors. There are many types of organizations, opportunities, and people in the world, but the examples offered in this chapter should begin to make you aware of the types of things to look for and assess, whether you are working on a team or are part of an investigation.

An organization has to teach its people what a fraudster's traits and actions may look like. It has to create awareness in as many people as possible, since it is not realistic to expect one person to prevent fraud. The more people in the organization who can raise fraud awareness, the greater the organization's chances of exposing a fraudster.

An organization that develops people who enjoy the success of others more than their own and who put the interests of others above their own will successfully detect, deter, and prevent fraud.

Most fraud perpetrators inside and outside an organization tend to give themselves away through guilt or stupidity, provided someone in the organization is watching.

There are more than 450 species of venomous snakes, and 250 of them are capable of killing a human being. Once snake venom has entered the body, it spreads through the bloodstream. Exhibit 4.4 should give you an idea how one fraudster going undetected in an organization can potentially ruin the whole structure by weakening the ladder and eventually causing it to come tumbling down. To help deter, detect, and prevent fraud, be aware of each employee's traits, actions, and role in the processes of your organization.

Along with creating 800-pound friendly gorillas, the organization needs to create awareness within its people before fraud occurs. The organization needs to create proactive rather than reactive supports. Providing these supports can be accomplished by understanding the needs and skills of your employees as well as the necessary tools they need to perform their duties. Make sure to properly supervise them at all staff levels. Assume that even the most trusted employee can become a potential fraudster, given the right circumstances.

 ## ONE-MINUTE FRAUD MYSTERY ANALYSIS

Have you established where the greed exists in this case? Remember, you are the fact finder and need to think divergently. Here are some of my thoughts on this chapter's mystery based on my experience in the field:

- **Allegation.** The job payments exceed the work completed although billing indicated that the work was completed.
- **Probable cause.** It appears that some type of overbilling has occurred based on the percentage of work completed and change orders. Also, at the

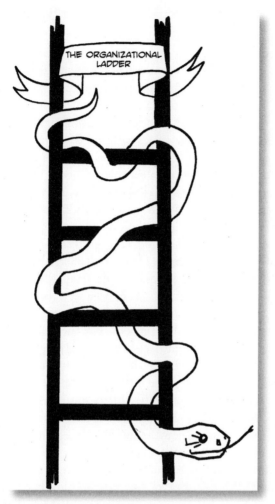

EXHIBIT 4.4 The Organizational Ladder

time of the phone call from State of Bridges, Inc., Dipper and Two-Timer were in the Bahamas.

■ **Action.** Further questioning is necessary. The approach you should take is a cautious one. While you want to treat Jim Dipper, Tim Two-Timer, and John Ripley as people of interest, you need to use the 800-pound friendly gorilla approach when investigating them. Identify the level of socialization and relationships that exist among these parties. Who has a clear understanding of the organizational business process? Who is the potential ring leader? Is he acting alone? Who else may be involved (Chuck Finley)? Is the relationship among them limited to this contract, or is it ongoing? The owner of State of Bridges, Inc., Anthony Oversight, brought the problem to light. Is he credible? Look into his background. Do not rule out victims or parties who bring the problem to light. Rule them out by using proper due diligence. Examine where the greed exists that enables the fraudster to start justifying his rationalization to commit fraud. Are there external influences? Look for lifestyle changes. Look for conflicts of interest. Know your answers before you ask critical questions by having a well-thought-out and planned approach.

- **Preparation.** Make sure you have adequate knowledge of how the construction billing is performed. A thorough understanding of percentage of completion and completed contact accounting knowledge is needed.
- **People of interest.** Jim Dipper, Tim Two-Timer, Anthony Oversight
- **People-with-knowledge interview plan.** Dipper should be interviewed, since we do not know whether he or Two-Timer is the real leader. The likely choice would be Two-Timer before Dipper, since the customer is asking for a status, but interviewing Dipper first would cause less suspicion. To investigate Dipper, speak with Chuck Finley, his prior boss. Then interview John Ripley, the CEO of Catch Me if You Can Inc. Have Ripley identify the accounting people involved and interview them, too, without letting Dipper know. Then go to State of Bridges Inc. to speak with Anthony Oversight, and again ask to speak to the accounting personnel without anyone else knowing. Depending on how the interview goes with Oversight, possibly interview people from Brooklyn Bridge Inc.
- **Documentary evidence.** Review a copy of the contract as well as the invoices and billing. Look at the general ledger and bank statements, canceled checks and deposits, and project completion reports.
- **Formulate opinion.** Potential types of fraud in this case are the following: breach of fiduciary responsibility (having a duty to an organization but doing something that is not in its best financial interest), conspiracy (agreement with another person to cause a crime to be committed), and conflict of interest (acting on behalf of another while having a hidden bias or self-interest adverse to the interests of the other). Excess billings appear to have resulted in modifications in the form of change orders or normal contract billings that were front-loaded and paid before the work was completed. Dipper was engineering the bridge for the client, State of Bridges Inc., specifically with Two-Timer, with whom he appears to have

a comfortable relationship. Ripley bestowed a significant level of trust on Dipper (possibly because they had things in common). The payments in the process could have been intercepted or made outside the organization's books and records. Either Dipper or Two-Timer could have approved suppliers or other contracts in order to take a cut, or perhaps Dipper physically skimmed the checks and destroyed the change orders or manipulated the percentage of completion numbers.

The 800-Pound Friendly Gorilla Suggestions for Catch Me If You Can Inc.

The client, Brooklyn Bridges, Inc., created a fiduciary relationship with the general contractor, State Bridges, Inc., which subcontracted, Catch Me if You Can, Inc., This created the potential for conflicts of interest when State Bridges failed to maintain the proper oversight. The need to examine State Bridges is key since it has a fiduciary responsibility to protect its client's, Brooklyn Bridges, Inc., interest.

The presence of weak controls and a lack of 800-pound friendly gorilla monitoring allowed the fraud to occur. Giving too much authority to the person(s) responsible also creates the opportunity for fraud. Here is what the organization could have implemented to reduce the risk of fraud:

- Having Human Resources check more closely on potential employees' histories through a more detailed background check.
- Looking for potential conflicts of interest.
- Monitoring the responsibilities given to people with access to the value.
- Implementing higher levels of sign-offs with multiple signatures for the approval process of both the percentage completion reports and change order billing.
- Instituting a third-party independent site engineer to perform inspections to determine completion percentages and change order requests.
- Segregating the collection of the billing from the actual billing.
- Calling references from other projects.
- Insuring against risk by instituting that the job is bonded for performance, payment, and material. Maintaining weekly meetings in which accounting takes the cost to complete (which should be signed off on by the supervisors at the project locations) and adds it to actual costs spent to date to test the expected gross profit margins. This ensures that billing is not in excess and identifies change orders.

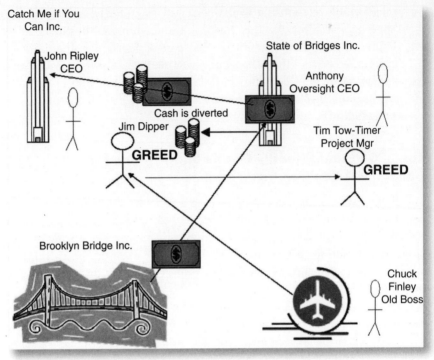

EXHIBIT 4.5 Catch Me If You Can Inc. Drawing

A Simple Picture

Let's take a look at Exhibit 4.5 and identify where the value is exposed. Try to sketch a similar picture of your take on the organizations we have discussed in the fraud mystery in this chapter. How does it compare to Exhibit 4.5?

Where does the greed exist in Exhibit 4.5? This exhibit shows Brooklyn Bridge, Inc. (the customer) giving money to State Bridges, Inc. (the general contractor) and then Catch Me If You Can, Inc. Somehow, Jim Dipper is intercepting the funds before they are received by Catch Me If You Can Inc. (the subcontractor). Two-Timer appears to be approving payments on the over billing and change orders submitted by Dipper. As you can see by the simple drawing, the customer Brooklyn Bridge, Inc. relies on State Bridges, Inc. to oversee the construction project and payment process. The greed exists between Dipper, the project manager of Catch Me If You Can, Inc., and State Bridges, Inc.'s project manager, Two-Timer, since they have the ability to generate additional change orders and determine progress completion for the payments (the value) as well as approve them.

NOTES

1. Alyson Krueger, "12 Statistic-Driven Ways to Make Lasting First Impressions," Gecko Hospitality, December 16, 2012, http://www.geckohospitality.com/geckoblog/job-interview-interviewing-tips.
2. Biannual ACFE studies on fraud and other independent studies consistently point to the existence of a whistleblower or an anonymous reporting program as the strongest prevention or detection tool in an organization's toolbox.
3. Paula Reed Ward, "Plead Guilty or Go to Trial?" Pittsburgh Post-Gazette, March 27, 2006, http://www.post-gazette.com/pg/06086/677199-85.stm#ixzz1loJyux00. Lawyers say the system unfairly rewards one and penalizes the other.
4. Ron Kurtus, "Personal Character Traits Important in Achievement," School for Champions, November 9, 2007, http://www.school-for-champions.com/character/personal_traits.htm.
5. U.S. Department of Labor, "Soft Skills: The Competitive Edge," http://www.dol.gov/odep/pubs/fact/softskills.htm.

CHAPTER FIVE

The Dynamics of Business

Everything Is Related—from People to Processes to Outside Influences

All is connected . . . no one thing can change by itself.

—*Paul Hawkin, environmentalist, entrepreneur, journalist, and author*

People in organizational processes have external standards, or benchmarks, that are established for them by credit rating agencies like Moody's, Standard & Poor's (S&P), Fitch, and Risk Management Association (RMA).[1] This helps potential fraudsters to understand the landscape of numbers the industry expects them to meet, so they can maintain the targeted perceptions, remain undetected, and create the value needed to steal. These credit agencies are worth discussing because they can create a level of comfort by stating that a company is rated AAA and is thus strongly creditworthy. It is often these types of ratings that investors, creditors, the public, and government agencies look to in determining organizational risk. However, these credit agencies do not attempt to detect fraud and simply rely on the numbers presented to them by the same people (management, possibly including potential or actual fraudsters) in the organizations they are rating.

What are the conflicts of interest that exist between credit agencies and the organizations they rate? Neil Weinberg, the chief editor at *Forbes*, revealed that by "providing huge payoffs to their salespeople, banks were aggressively pushing new products to increase volume. Soon, banks were packaging loans and reselling them to Wall Street, who then passed the loans to investors. The ratings agencies were getting huge payoffs to play along and rate the investments as high quality so investors continued to buy blindly."[2] Ironically, financial communications can change drastically if a substantial fraud that management fails to detect or disclose is allowed to occur in an organization's process. Where were the credit risk assessments about the many financial products that contributed to the financial meltdown of 2008? Where were the credit and fraud risk assessments on Enron, WorldCom, and all the others?

Benchmark comparison tools, audited financial reports, or any financial communications serve only as guides. We need to apply imagination to create the necessary forward thinking that can prevent fraud in an organization. Albert Einstein said, "Imagination is more important than knowledge. For knowledge is limited to all we now know and understand, while imagination embraces the entire world, and all there ever will be to know and understand."[3] Organizational management needs to stop thinking in an information silo that is incapable of linking the various people in the organizational processes and instead apply an approach that considers the possibility that people can decide to commit fraud. Create imaginative thinking and ask yourself how fraud can be perpetrated within the process and by whom.

The various control procedures that are in place are often performed by the very same people who develop the financial information and complete the checklists or questionnaires that are submitted to the ratings agencies and become the basis for the assessment of the organization's creditworthiness. The same people also give the information that leads to the preparation of financial statements that are prepared by the auditor or accountant, who states that these have been prepared in accordance with GAAP. It is reasonable to assume that anyone can expose the organization to the risk of fraud, because the same people who create the numbers often oversee the controls.

All financial reporting and disclosure represents a specific period and is static because it addresses past results and is not intended to be forward looking. There is no guarantee that organizations will repeat the results reflected in a financial report and disclosure. One significant transaction can change everything. For example, the death of a significant executive or a Food and Drug Administration (FDA) approval or disapproval of a new drug can affect an organization's value. Therefore, we need to maintain and increase organizational value with forward thinking, imagination, and the application of what-if scenarios to our organizational processes. We have to look at the various benchmarking data methods, such as financial and metric performance indicators, as static representations of data. The ratios and benchmarks generated from an organization's financial communications are often purely historical. Since a single unanticipated event can lead to extreme devastation, or vast profitability, to an organization, so financial communications should include data that are representative of the past, present, and future. Without the trusted people in an organization maintaining the proper ethical tone from top to bottom in regard to these measurements and forecasts, they mean nothing.

Fraudsters can create speculation using static indicators because they know where they have to be in order to remain under the radar, since the industry standards have been established for them to follow. In other words, they have been given a virtual road map. Since financial communications are developed for specific times and transactions that have already taken place, the fraudster can manipulate static measurements to meet whatever return (standard) is to be expected by the user of the financial information. Essentially, the fraudster changes the necessary transactions in order to cover up manipulations.

Established budgeting and ratio analyses in a financial statement communication may or may not expose the potential for fraud to exist, but looking at the people behind the development of the numbers will. Can the employees explain the variations and changes in the proper context by correlating them to the data used to generate the budgets or ratios? Are the budgets realistic, or do they give the fraudster an opportunity to transfer funds or spend more than is available?

Examining management's basis for the underlying assumptions in the development of a budget is critical in deterring fraud. If there is an ongoing run of continued growth or unprecedented returns, what if it stopped? Would the organization remain in existence? Are the growth and unprecedented returns that create investor interest maintainable? These hypothetical questions assess the risk of fraud.

The fraudster loves when there is no transparency or the numbers are difficult to understand. When no one is asking questions, the fraudster can more easily remain undetected. Public outrage often decides when fraud should be brought to light. But it is the organization's responsibility to discover fraud before it is brought to the public's attention. Organizations should not wait until there is public outrage to do something about fraud. A proactive method is always better when detecting, deterring, and preventing fraud.

Let's look at a municipal budget in New Jersey as an example. I am familiar with a town's $160 million budget, and I act as a member of that town's finance committee. We found that most taxpayers did not understand the tax rates or why their real estate taxes increased. Many taxpayers just assumed that when the cost of living goes up, so do their taxes. The committee decided that the taxpayers needed to understand where their tax dollars were being spent, so we explained the complex budget to them. The taxpayers had a better understanding and became more interested in the budget. They also began to ask the right questions to create transparency and hold the elected officials accountable. Once the taxpayers became informed, monitored the budget, and held the elected officials accountable, property tax increases started to become more reasonable. Similarly, people within organizations need to become informed about fraud and have a simple understanding of how, when, and where it can take place in order to deter it.

Without creating an interest and effectively communicating with the average person, fraud will exist. Organizations need to be proactive and work toward preventing fraud rather than hoping it does not occur or dealing with it after the fact.

Look at the expectations of the organization from sources such as the board of directors, shareholders, Wall Street, rating agencies, banking institutions, and regulatory agencies (who are creating the organization's reputation). By understanding these expectations (and, in turn, the value in an organization) and what people may need to do to alter information to meet the expectations, you will often expose potential fraud risk. It may be unprecedented targeted earnings, expectations for Wall Street investors, or lending type covenants (conditions in the loan agreement to which the borrower must adhere or the loan will be considered in default) for creditors that create and maintain organizational value and offer the fraudster opportunity for committing fraud.

Therefore, the people who hold trusted positions are the gatekeepers, maintaining the moral and ethical structures in an organization. These trusted people must maintain the organization's true value. Deciding on the level of trust and creating accountability is critical to detecting, deterring, and preventing fraud.

This chapter features the following:

An overview of the business relationships within the organizational processes and the level of trust that people have been given.

Pointers on understanding the relationship between financial and nonfinancial numbers and on looking at key performance indicators and those who have created them.

An explanation of how budgets are worthless as a fraud prevention or detection tool when fraud is built into the numbers by the people formulating the budgets.

A discussion of how fraudsters keep manipulated numbers under an organization's radar because they understand the needs of the organization, both internally and externally, as well as the people in its process.

A discussion of how fraudsters stay under the radar, avoid revealing red flags, and keep people from asking the right questions.

LOOKING AT BUSINESS RELATIONSHIPS FROM a fraudster's perspective is no different from developing a sound business plan. The steps you use to develop your revenue-generation process are the same ones you need to assess your people's performance. The benchmark to use is the level of trust you have assigned to the people in your organizational process.

Everything in an organization is based on a score or a financial measurement established for employees to meet. Whether it is an incentive bonus based on sales goals or earnings targets to meet Wall Street expectations, conflicts may exist. Organizations need to establish a trusted system. Financial measurement results mean nothing without trust in the people generating the numbers and presenting them. What the measurements mean and how they are conveyed are important. The average person should be able to understand them.

For instance, budgets are organizational estimates based on an assumption that all outcomes can be predicted, which is not necessarily true. In most budget systems, flexibility remains in order to allow for adjustments to the budget processes. The New Jersey municipal budgets, for example, have the flexibility to adjust the budgeted numbers in the first three months of the year. They also have the ability in the last two months of the year to transfer money between various line items that could overinflate or underinflate them. A fraudster can modify the numbers and move them to a different line item to gain an advantage in the future. You need to watch for modifications of budgeted line items and keep an eye on the people with the authority to make them.

Responsibilities assigned to individuals in your organization should not exceed their capabilities; this could lead to unintentional fraud by way of mistakes or could create an opportunity for a fraudster to exploit a weak point in the organization. Even with capable people, the greater the responsibility an individual has, the greater the potential for fraud, and hence the greater the need to put 800-pound friendly gorillas in place (controls, segregation of duties, periodic background checks, etc.). When organizational processes are transparent and you educate people on the process they are involved in, the organization is less likely to be corrupted by the power it assigns. It is always good practice to measure the level of trust (or power) given to your people and make sure it equals their responsibility. Without a balance between trust and responsibility, fraud can exist.

 ## ONE-MINUTE FRAUD MYSTERY: ACCRUAL INC.

It is 2008. Revenue growth has slowed, and Accrual Inc.'s stock price has fallen. The company expenses as a percentage of the total revenue increased because the growth rate of the company's earnings dropped. This means that Accrual Inc.'s earnings might not meet Wall Street analysts' expectations. John Debit, the CFO, was instructed by Theodore Dollar, the CEO, to find a way to meet the profit estimates in order to avoid the stock price from falling further, so Debit has decided to start classifying certain operating expenses as long-term capital investments. Reclassifying $1 million that was paid to lease data network lines to capital assets from operating expenses provided the company another $1 million in additional net revenues to meet Wall Street's earnings estimates. These newly reclassified assets were paid to lease data network lines from other companies. The reclassification thus turned a $500,000 loss into a $500,000 profit.

Debit instructed Jackie Ledger, the controller, to have her staff make the appropriate journal entries to capitalize the data line leases by crediting the expense in the income statement and to reclassify them as investment activity on the balance sheet, labeled "fixed assets data lines." The SEC has received an anonymous tip on its hotline about Accrual Inc.'s inflated earnings and has retained you to determine whether there is any merit to the allegations.

 ## CONTROL-POINT LINKS AND ACCOUNTABILITY

What goes into a process is not always what comes out. Exhibit 5.1 shows the CEO asking the CFO if the transaction was recorded in the system.

What the CEO does not know is how many people actually touched the transaction. By identifying points in the organizational process such as when the salesperson gets the jobs, when the billing department invoices the jobs, and when the accounts receivable department collects the payments, we create the necessary actions to deter fraud. The 800-pound friendly gorilla makes sure the salesperson, billing employees, and accounts receivable department personnel are not circumventing or overriding the proper processes and protects the areas where the organization's value is vulnerable to fraud by making sure there are no breaks in its chain of people. The 800-pound friendly gorilla makes sure that what goes into the process is equivalent to what comes out.

A control plan segregates responsibilities with the belief that it can stop fraud, yet everyone in the process needs to remain linked. For instance, salespeople need billing people to bill, and billing people need receivable people to collect. Even with an 800-pound friendly gorilla at both ends of the process, you cannot detect, deter, and prevent fraud if there is a break or a weak link in the chain of responsibilities.

An organization needs to establish trust throughout the responsibility chain and evaluate the links by designing tests that make sure the process is not altered. The people along the way then know that someone is watching what is

EXHIBIT 5.1 Accounting for a Transaction

put into the process and that someone on the other end knows what should be coming out. As author Steve Covey said, "Begin with the end in mind."[4] If you have trusted people at the end of the process knowing what signs and results to look for, you can detect, deter, and prevent fraud. An organization is only as strong as its weakest link.

 ## THE LAYERS OF TRUST

On March 14, 2001, Moody's Risk Management Services (MRMS) and RMA announced that MRMS had granted a license to enable RMA to analyze its data using Moody's RiskCalc. This default modeling software was designed to determine the probability of default. However, the Enron scandal was revealed in October 2001, and in September 2008, Lehman Brothers—a 185-year-old Wall Street institution—filed for Chapter 11 bankruptcy protection from its creditors. Where were the Moody's, S&P, Fitch, and RMA credit analysis predictions that these failures would occur?

These failures continued to remain undetected for as long as they did because the credit agencies did not factor in the potential conflicts of interest within the securitization groups or the multiple entities created by Enron's management team to keep debt off the balance sheet. The idea that one can measure past performance is a reasonable premise, but it is not an exact science. Analyzing the past may help, but it does not always predict future performance. It is only one measuring stick, and you need to take all factors into account when planning for the future. You can never be 100 percent accurate in your future predictions because of the multiple complexities that exist in the organization's global environment. You can be imaginative in your rationale and apply forward thinking that sees beyond the numbers and people's influence on them but, as Neil Weinberg stated, "Corporate fraud is committed when the tone is set that fraud is acceptable. If a company rewards bad behavior, then employees will behave badly."[5] As noted earlier in this book, numbers don't lie, people do.

You should be aware of the significant frauds that occurred at Enron, WorldCom, Adelphia, Rite Aid, and Tyco, because history has a tendency to repeat itself (e.g., the similarities between Charles Ponzi, whose name has been given to the type of fraudulent scheme he concocted in the 1920s, and Bernie Madoff, who admitted in December 2008 that the wealth management arm of his business was an elaborate Ponzi scheme). These fraud cases represent some of the largest financial scandals in history. They represent great case studies from which you can learn how organizations are exposed to fraud and how to prevent making the same mistakes in your own organization. The aforementioned companies, some of which are considered icons of the modern economy, were decimated primarily because fraud was perpetrated by the highest levels of management. In addition, these meltdowns brought to light the problems within one of the most respected professions in the world: accounting.

The accounting profession has come under considerable scrutiny because of these frauds, yet the principles and rules that were broken in these cases were in place well before any of the fraudulent events occurred. The Enron incident shows how devastating fraud can be, since it essentially resulted in the "big five" accounting firms becoming the "big four."

Because accounting rules do not govern morality and they are no guarantee against fraud, an organization cannot assume that it is protected from fraud simply because it abides by fundamental accounting principles. This is why an organization must take proactive steps to deter, detect, and prevent fraud by developing an 800-pound friendly gorilla presence. So what is wrong with organizations today? What can be done to keep fraud from recurring? These frauds happened in part because a double standard existed within the organizational process (i.e., the rules did not apply to everyone uniformly). Some people were indifferent to the fact that things weren't adding up, as long as they were receiving a paycheck or an investment return. Accountants are the gatekeepers, and if an organization does not have ethical accountants who adhere to the rules, fraud will continue to exist.

When companies pay people well and Wall Street returns are maintained, everything seems fine and no one is interested in the fine print of the processes. Fraud is incredibly dynamic, but one thing is certain: People at any level are always at the root of fraud. Even if one person is the ultimate mastermind, many links in the organizational chain are required for a fraud to be perpetrated and for the mastermind to achieve his or her fraudulent goals.

When things go wrong, the first step is often to look at the process, the system, and then the people. New legislation is often introduced that only addresses the process and ignores the people; when an effective strategy would do the opposite. Unfortunately, the government cannot legislate morality, only good leaders can inspire it within their organization. Paying attention to the people who enact the processes is very important and should be done at regular intervals, whether or not a fraud is committed or suspected. Are you looking at the people and the processes only when something goes wrong? People have personal pressures and needs that often make them complacent in the workplace, but they do not just wake up one day and decide that committing fraud would be a cool thing to do. It is more complex than that. Looking at both the people *and* the processes is essential.

RESPONSIBILITY CHAINS

Successful organizations recognize that all job functions are connected. Let's do a chain analysis that begins with the board of directors and flows all the way down to the mail room employees. What happens if the chairman of the board does not receive an important document from the mail room clerk, such as a litigation document against the organization? If the document is not delivered, a link in the process chain of the organization has been violated. Let's say the mail room clerk takes the legal document and profits from it. This personal profit also negatively affects the organization. It is not always the people at the top who manipulate an organization's process; the people at the bottom can compromise the process just as easily.

Does the mail room clerk deliver all of the bills to the accounts payable department? What about the checks sent to the accounts receivable department? Are the bank statements given to the person who reconciles the accounts? All of the job responsibilities that make up the links in an organizational chain should be examined to find out where the opportunities exist to cause a break in that chain. Organizations often fail to examine why a person behaves a certain way in these job responsibilities. It is essential for an organization to understand the job responsibilities in its structure as well as the forces that influence people's behavior, perceptions, decisions, and interpretations while performing their job functions. For that matter, do executives or other people in the organization have access to the mail room or influence over the mail room clerk that would permit them to intercept mail intended for others? The mail clerk's position can be a great place to position an 800-pound friendly gorilla.

In the book *The Soprano State*, many references are made to the fact that corruption was rampant in the organization (state and local governments in New Jersey) in question.[6] Most interesting is that the people in the organization who were interviewed said that business had always been done that way. They just assumed that fraud was acceptable because it had been going on for so long.

The bottom line is that anyone can be involved in perpetrating fraud, in the smallest business to the largest organization. No matter how small or big an entity may be, it is the people within it who are responsible for creating the breaks in the chain of responsibility. Successful organizations will find remedies to prevent the breaks from happening. Where fraud intrinsically and traditionally exists in an organization is where leadership is needed to effect change and avoid the notoriety associated with organizations such as those featured in *The Soprano State*. Once fraud is allowed to exist, there will be significant barriers and hurdles to overcome that are associated with years of improper practice and tradition.

 ## A FAILURE IN MANAGEMENT

If we examine the recent mortgage scandal, we see the following elements: the government deregulating lending requirements, people (consumers) wanting to own homes with little to no money down, and bankers creating a process that gave mortgages to people with subpar credit for little to no money down. The media also participated, promoting the good life and stating that home ownership was at a record high. Investors were on board, since real estate was skyrocketing and they had heard that mortgage-backed securities were safe and provided the returns they desired. People who were previously not ready for home ownership suddenly found that they could purchase homes that were beyond their means, and the banks and mortgage brokers were able to make lucrative profits. In short, every link in the chain had its needs being met. It is a very complex model, but when it's broken down by identifying the responsibilities of each link in the chain, the points of greed and potential fraud can be determined.

However, regardless of which scandal you analyze, it is management who is failing. Managers have not maintained the proper ethical chains of responsibility. If not directly through their own actions and processes, they have failed through a lack of proactive oversight. Before the more recent mortgage meltdown, there were Bernie Ebbers of WorldCom and Dennis Kozlowski of Tyco (men at the very top of the organizational chain). Under their management, every level of the chain of responsibility was broken. They helped to create the necessary mayhem for fraud to exist within every layer of their organization. And now that the employees at World Com and Tyco have lost their retirements, do you think they would perpetrate the corrupt processes in the same way all over again, or would they expose the company's day-to-day wrongdoings? Hindsight is 20/20, so we can be sure that someone would have spoken up and become a remedy to detecting, deterring, and preventing fraud in these organizations sooner if they had a way to change the course of history. Therefore, one of the most effective fraud-fighting tools is to develop awareness in each organizational process of the ethical expectations of each position and the potential consequences of frauds to instill a dedication to fight fraud. To do this, organizations must maintain a chain of defined responsibilities.

Managers tend to get the biggest share of the corporate earnings pie. Sometimes it is proportionate to their contribution to the organization, but what if it is imbalanced and does not meet public scrutiny? In order to answer that question we need to review some typical management objectives:

- Doing what is best for a company (i.e., fiduciary responsibility).
- Creating and maintaining shareholder value.
- Establishing an ethical tone at the top (i.e., setting a good example for employees).
- Making sure an organization's flow remains connected (i.e., there is one big organizational chain).
- Being a good corporate citizen (i.e., maintaining and showcasing the proper ethics).

These responsibilities are sometimes difficult to maintain because some of them compete with one another. It can be a constant battle to maintain a balance. For instance, it is problematic to establish a strong ethical tone at the top when many businesses focus only on today's results, ignoring the future impact of decisions on tomorrow's profitability. Companies have been known to lay off thousands of employees just to hit the targeted Wall Street numbers, such as in recent cases involving Bank of America, Cisco, and Hewlett-Packard. When these types of layoffs happen, does high-level management take a pay cut? In most cases, the answer is no.

These types of layoffs may make investors happy, but what about the employees who remain at the companies? Usually their morale is greatly deflated, and they question why they should remain loyal to an organization that is focused on external profit pressures and not its employees. These questions create a negative workplace and propagate opportunities for fraud. Employees left behind are asked to pick up the slack for those who were cut, yet are uncertain about their own futures and fear is never a positive motivator. Employees may think, "Well, if they can get rid of Johnny, then it is only a matter of time before I am let go!" This can lead to a rationalization such as, "So why not take what is rightfully mine to protect my family?"

 ## MORE THAN THE BOTTOM LINE

One of the biggest drivers of fraud perpetrated by management is the belief that all that matters is the bottom line results (i.e., the generation of wealth by manipulating the bottom line numbers to create the necessary diversion to preserve their own self-interests). Two strategies for minimizing the opportunity for fraud in management include:

1. Maintain a log that indicates key dates, such as when earnings reports are due, and identify who has the responsibility to report the numbers, as well as who they are reported to.
2. Identify triggers and the people who oversee the processes. Knowing who can override them gives management a road map to review its objectives.

Most management gets paid for performance, and performance has historically been measured on a short-term basis (i.e., what you have done for me lately?). What would happen to a CEO who was willing to forgo short-term (two to five years) profits to build a better business that would potentially catapult future revenue beyond that period? In my opinion, which unfortunately is true of business models lately, that CEO would probably be let go. The pressure to make money now would more than likely be too big to overcome. This pressure is an identifiable trigger.

When times are tough, many companies turn to areas such as research and development (R&D) to cut costs, thus preserving the bottom line. They protect the short-term bottom line by sacrificing future earning potential because essentially the new product pipeline will be empty. Once the short-term hurdle is cleared by cutting R&D, a real problem surfaces: There is nothing new in the pipeline to drive future growth.

However, does senior management really care, since the long-term effect will be on someone else's compensation and not its own? People in current management are usually focused on their own self-interest and have a live-for-today attitude. This trigger is greed. If current management has a short-term perspective when an organization needs to maintain a future perspective, it creates an atmosphere with conflicting goals. Have these conflicts been brainstormed and developed with input from all levels of an organization, or are these goals being instituted by short-term thinkers whose compensation is based on performance in the next few months?

One of the best examples is government, which runs in four-year cycles. The executive and legislative politicians are motivated to portray a positive image to the public about their particular four-year term, even if this may not be the case and their actions may have a negative impact on the future. Fraudster politicians may manipulate budgets, cut manpower, or even transfer funds, which focus on current appearances, not long-term goals. Because voters often have a short-term memory, master manipulators in government will even sacrifice one or two years' ratings just to create one optimal year, which usually occurs just in time for elections. This cycle continues on a four year basis. Here the value is not monetary, but rather, votes. Yet the same fraud motivation exist, the preservation of one's self-interest (greed) over others, in this situation the voters, caused by the absence of 800-pound friendly gorillas to hold people in government accountable.

The short-term focus on organizational financial performance and the solutions to achieve the financial measures provide an excellent environment for the building blocks of fraud to thrive. Recording trigger events in a journal with the people who are linked to them is a useful method of helping to deter and prevent fraud. In the example above, how is revenue generated? Is there a need for R&D to maintain the future revenue stream?

Identifying the greed that leads people to make short-sighted decisions will show you where fraud can exist in your organization. It is not uncommon in today's organizations to have very mobile management. In fact, you seldom find a senior manager who has been with the same organization for a long period of time. With compensation tied to short-term value, the motivation is to do well now and let the next person deal with the long-term consequences. The rationale is that you should get paid today, since nobody knows or cares what will happen tomorrow. Unfortunately, the investing public looks for short-term rewards and instant gratification rather than more long-term goals.

But the value of an organization is the present value of future cash flows and not just the earnings and cash flows from the current year, so ensuring robust future cash flows should certainly be worth a lot. Investors (or the market) drive up stock prices based on the organization's speculated future performance. Investors are, more often than not, looking into the future for expected results, so make sure your organization projects its business into the future with well-documented presumptions that are frequently monitored. The following outline lists additional risk factors that lead to organizational failures:

- **Ineffective board of directors.** Organizations have this problem because of limitations in skills or competence (with the nonexecutive directors, as well as a restricted ability to monitor and control senior executives effectively. If organizations are composed of boards that are blind to risk, the boards cannot be allowed to develop lucrative self-serving incentives without addressing these risks.
- **Poor leadership on ethic and culture.** This results from double standards.
- **Defective communication.** This creates an ineffective organizational environment and removes the transparency that is needed to deter, detect, and prevent fraud.
- **Availability of information.** Excess complexity is caused by the level of design through technology, the procurement processes, and the manufacturing and assembly processes.
- **Political balance.** This must be achieved with upper-level management executives.
- **Inappropriate incentive bonus schemes.** These do not match the intended bonus achievement with an organization's standards.
- **Lack of internal information.** This stems from internal audit or risk management teams that report on risks originating from higher levels in

the organization. It must not be ignored. Where were these internal auditors when Enron and WorldCom failed?

All of these risks tend to be associated with corporate failures but are triggered events that can and should be monitored by the 800-pound friendly gorilla.

OUTSIDE INFLUENCES

Two important influences that organizations need to analyze are investors and society. Organizations are constantly strapped with unrealistic expectations from investors. Investors today have been conditioned to believe that the returns recognized (either real or fabricated) by businesses in the past will continue forever. No one believes anymore that what goes up must come down, and the Wall Street spin doctors have ways of maintaining the speculative bubble.

Fraud is triggered by unsteadiness in the speculative value of an organization, its success, and what is necessary to maintain it. If it seems too good to be true, it usually is. Remember to apply "caveat emptor" (buyer beware). When investors are made aware of a fraud, they can single-handedly devastate your organization in a number of ways, such as by selling stock, instituting litigation, or cutting funding.

Nothing has fundamentally changed in the business environment to sustain higher and higher returns, yet these speculative outlooks still exist. Whether we are speaking of Tulip Mania in 1637 (see Chapter 2) or Bernie Madoff in 2008, it is people who created these frauds, based on formed values caused by speculations. From 1950 to 2009, the market had a real total return of approximately 7 percent.[7] This could continue for 30 more years, so it is important to test the assumptions that analysts are relying on to predict long-term returns in your company and make sure that they are achievable.

The influence of market analyst information on individual and institutional investors has also complicated the problem of preventing fraud. Moody's, S&P, and Fitch influence investors' perceptions. An example of the influence of rating agencies is with Enron. Enron's rating remained at investment grade four days before the company went bankrupt, despite the fact that credit rating agencies had been aware of the company's problems for months.[8]

But RMA's annual statement studies provide comparative data that come directly from the financial statements of small and medium-size businesses that are customers of RMA's member institutions.[9] Therefore, today's organizations should not solely rely on third parties to determine the speculative value surrounding them. With the availability of RMA data and the Internet benchmark, your organization has an easy and reliable way to flag irregularities on a macro level.

The market is fueled by speculative emotion. If a business does not reach its numbers, then its stock price suffers. No one invests in an organization's history of earnings unless that history is going to continue. It really does matter whether the long-term prognosis is good or whether the organization has a strategy to maintain its value that sets it apart from its competition. It all depends on those numbers and meeting the expectations of Wall Street, and most people who fit the executive profile will do what it takes to make these numbers, sometimes costing the company dearly in the long run.

Think about the greed evident in the desire of some executives to preserve their compensation even in the face of catastrophe. A Bloomberg article states, "Lawmakers in both parties have expressed outrage at New York–based AIG's decision to pay $165 million in executive bonuses after taking government money. AIG also budgeted $57 million in 'retention' pay to former employees, according to a March 2 filing with the Securities and Exchange Commission."[10]

These potential conflicts of interest exist in good times and bad. The executives in this instance were always managing expectations rather than the actual organizational process.

In terms of investors, it makes sense that when times are good, people invest, and when times are bad, people leave the market. During the downturn in 2008, investors left the market, creating a significant drop in the Dow Jones Industrial Average: On September 29 of that year, the Dow Jones dropped by 778 points, or 7 percent, which is considered to be the most significant drop in Dow Jones history.[11]

At that time, investors should have been buying low. But it would suffice to reason that there were companies still claiming to be doing higher than the expected returns. It is necessary to investigate returns that are not in alignment with the market; examine them very closely, if returns are too good to be true, they probably are.

You may be wondering what this has to do with fraud, but it is all related. The investor is driven by the analyst, but they both drive the market, which in turn places huge pressure on organizations and their management. Organizations want to please investors and, in return, are rewarded by the market. They must do this consistently, regardless of business cycles, both externally and internally. There are many other variables that can affect things.

Hence, there are consistent pressures to do what it takes to meet expectations, no matter how askew. The most successful organizations will not plan to boost sales just to create an expected bottom line. Successful organizations will execute attainable and sustainable plans so they will not be put in a position of having to make up for everything. Organizations in that position become ripe for fraud, and they cannot make up for lost ground without manipulation of the current results. Management is thus placed in a position where truthful reporting will diminish organizational value as stock prices drop, but organizational value can be sustained or enhanced through the commission of a fraud.

A similar example is that in most parts of the United States, it is commonplace to find people living beyond their means. The national debt in the United States is astronomical.[12] This mind-set perpetuates higher levels of spending than income would dictate. It is not hard to see why annual wages are not covering the extravagant spending of some Americans. This level of spending is exacerbated by constant high-pressure marketing that encourages inflated lifestyles and relies on debt to finance instant-gratification needs.

Organizations have to consider these outside influences when evaluating risk. Would someone in the chain of responsibility easily resort to perpetrating a fraud because of an economic need or desire to live beyond his or her means? "Keeping up with the Joneses" eventually comes back to hurt not only the people playing the game but others, too—perhaps even all of us, as we saw during the recent mortgage meltdown that began in 2007 that required billions of taxpayer dollars to bail out the banks.

In general, the stock market allows for the leveraging of investments through buying stock on margin (or borrowing). This means that if you own 100 shares of a company's stock at $10 per share, you can use those shares as leverage and buy another 100 shares on margin (again, basically borrowed). If the security you bought with borrowed money decreased in value past a certain point, you would be forced either to add more money to your account or to sell off the shares of stock to cover the margin call. In the 1920s, for instance, a buyer had to put down only 10 to 20 percent of his or her own money and thus borrowed 80 to 90 percent of the cost of the stock.[13]

Capitalism facilitates an environment where the ego has the opportunity to flourish and where people constantly one-up one another and reward those who succeed. The pressure people feel in this system can result in their resorting to actions that are sometimes unfair. Besides thinking about the investors hurt by recent organizational frauds that have led to recent organizational failures (bankruptcies), we should think about the employees of those companies.

These employees often hold large sums in company stock acquired through various stock option plans tied to years of service or as part of an incentive-type bonus plan. Incentive plans have the potential to raise conflicts of interest and create an atmosphere ripe for fraud, since the message is, "Produce, and we will give you more stock and ownership."

As the employee gets more of the organization's stock, they also receive a greater incentive to see the stock value increase. A *New York Times* article pointed out the following:

> "Over the past decade an increasing amount of the compensation had been given in stock and stock options," said Robert Willens, a tax expert who worked at Lehman from 1987 to this year. "Employees were paid in restricted stock that took several years to vest. Stock was granted at the current price."[14]

One of the reasons employees end up holding so much of their company's stock is that they hear (around the watercooler) and see (through Wall Street buying) the performance of the stock going through the roof but ignore one of the most vital principles of investing: diversification. Employees at companies bankrupted by recent scandals did not review the proper checks and balances when looking at their own compensation. Greed made them fail to ask what would happen if their organizations' stock prices came down.

Do you think that greed is bad? Not everyone thinks so. For instance, in the 1980s, the Nobel Prize–winning economist Milton Friedman discussed how capitalism actually needs greed to be present to establish free markets because there is a symbiosis between them.[15]

But besides investors (who are often employees with stock option incentive plans), accountants and auditors influence an organization's potential for fraud. The public accounting profession is supposed to be the protector of investors and the integrity of the companies that make up the market. The auditor's job is not to detect frauds but to assist organizations that are developing adequate internal controls to prevent fraud by testing the management implemented controls. At most, auditors evaluate existing controls and report to management and the governance group any significant deficiencies or material weaknesses exposed through the audit. Auditors are not management. If they were, they would not be independent, and that would violate the general accounting standards.

Auditors and accountants are not independent if they do not adhere to the general accounting standards. This can be difficult when the companies they are working for pay for their services, which in turn pays their salaries. Therefore, this relationship to an organization inherently creates the potential for fraud, in my opinion, if there is not a clear adherence to the independence and other applicable professional standards.

Nevertheless, auditors need to be above outside influence. Organizations should not be able to entice an accountant with increased billing to influence the results to satisfy the desired expectations. The auditor or accountant must be willing to lose a client who asks him or her to compromise accounting principles and rules. The mind-set of the auditor or accountant cannot be that of a client advocate. As the writer Upton Sinclair said, "It is difficult to get a man to understand something when his salary depends upon his not understanding it!"[16]

External factors such as Sarbanes-Oxley attempt to improve auditing and accounting independence, but without trusted employees and the right checks and balances of the 800-pound friendly gorilla, organizations will not succeed in improving independence. The internal audit function has to be placed in the organization independently to maintain governance over the various dynamics.

 ## ORGANIZATIONAL FAILURES

Understanding organizational failures stemming from fraud is very important. If opportunity and pressures alone caused the fraudster to act, then everyone in the corporate world would be a fraudster. So what drives people to commit fraud? Exhibit 5.2 illustrates the dynamic.

You can add all the pressure and opportunity rocks to the fraudometer that you want, but until the rationalization rock is added, you will not have a fraud. Organizations need to focus on people's rationalizations to commit fraud in order to figure out how they can detect, deter, and prevent it. Do the people in your organization believe that the rationalization rock is too heavy to add because of the effective communication and ethical tone created by the organizational environment? A fraud that is easy to rationalize is easy to perpetrate. Here is a list of what may be lacking in an organizational process that creates a ripe environment for fraud:

- ▪ **Monitoring of management.** Fraud is easy to perpetrate when a company lacks the necessary skills and competence to effectively monitor and control its senior executives and board members. Who and where were the directors of Enron, Tyco, and WorldCom when those frauds were going on?

- **Understanding of greed.** Fraud is easy to perpetrate when people in an organization, from top to bottom, fail to engage in important risk assessments, such as what are the risks to reputation or the risks in failing to watch the changes in regulations as they are related to reward and opportunity.
- **Leadership in ethics and culture.** An organization cannot have double standards in its various processes and dealings. A top-down code (i.e., what is preached is practiced) is the key. Are leaders and other employees ignoring sound principles and satisfying the wrong self-interest?
- **Communication.** Not maintaining effective communication with vendors. An example would be poor communication about a faulty part that never finds its way to the appropriate level of senior management until it is too late. Always be looking for potential conflicts of interest.
- **Simplicity.** Are your projects immensely complex in terms of information technology, procurement, manufacturing and assembly, or the political balance between executives and team members? Sign-offs should add assurance, not complexity, to an organizational structure.
- **Controls.** Do the bonus schemes disregard the existing controls and focus on achieving results? Are they, in essence, an incentive to commit

EXHIBIT 5.2 Rationalization

fraud? Never allow people to put their self-interest over the interests of the organization.

■ **Internal audits.** Effective risk management and adequate reporting originates at the higher levels of an organization and makes its way to the lower levels of the business through example and controls. Management must also pay attention to any red flags raised by internal and external compliance.

Let's apply these bullet points to the recent example of the insurance giant AIG. In terms of organizational failures, AIG is a pretty spectacular example. In the insurance world, it was one of only two major players in the sector who maintained an AAA rating.

When reviewing how AIG failed, keep the following important facts in mind:

■ AIG grew to become the world's largest insurance group, reaching a peak market capitalization of $213 billion in 2001 at an extremely fast pace. (This is a red flag, by the way, begging the question of whether the growth is sustainable or speculative.)

■ By the end of the third quarter in 2007, AIG had consolidated its assets, which totaled $1.072 trillion, and the shareholders' equity was $104.07 billion.

■ In early 2008, AIG was the eighteenth largest public company in the world.

Business dynamics can change with a simple wrong turn. In the case of AIG, it seems that the lack of the necessary skills at the board of director and senior management levels allowed things to get worse. In 2009, just one year after AIG reported it was the eighteenth largest public company in the world, it was reporting an annual loss of nearly $100 billion, which required the federal government to bail it out with a loan of $182.5 billion.

AIG had chosen not to understand the fraud risks associated with the overriding need to increase its profits by 15 percent per year in an extremely competitive environment. Wall Street expectations were not realistically aligned with the organization's abilities, because of the speculative bubble and the need to develop unsustainable growth.

So when did it begin to go wrong? At the time, New York State attorney general Eliot Spitzer accused the company of bid-rigging with insurance brokers. This added a lack of leadership in ethics and culture to the mix, even though nothing was ever proven. The more serious allegation against AIG was that it had produced misleading accounts and used spurious reinsurance policies to inflate the profits that were substantiated. One executive went to jail, and the company paid $1.6 billion to settle civil charges, while former board chairman Maurice "Hank" Greenberg personally paid $15 million to settle SEC charges that he had altered AIG's records to boost results between 2000 and 2005.

As with any speculative intangible bubble, share prices fell, and the company lost its AAA rating. When the rating of a company is lowered, it is required to post additional cash collateral (reserves), which ultimately reduces liquidity. AIG's problems then became really evident when the subprime lending crisis came to light. AIG had a credit default swaps portfolio that the company had never planned to be exposed to the level of defaults that came to be, which caused a devastating devaluation of the portfolio.

This, then, is where an extreme lack of communication comes into play. The assumed risk-free source of speculated wealth that had been created was, in fact, a liability of epic proportions.

AIG is a perfect example of greed manifested as a desire to pursue profit at almost any cost. Red flags were everywhere in the AIG situation. Not only were the returns too good to be true, the tone at the top was also a bad one. The nonexecutive directors were often friends or colleagues of senior managers. The processes they were participating in were intricate instead of simple. All of these red flags in an organization can be utilized when assessing fraud risk. Enforcing these systems and deterring the various rationalizations that are found when analyzing the red flags will help to detect, deter, and prevent fraud.

UNDERSTANDING CASH FLOWS

The dynamics of business are complex. With an emphasis on the bottom line, earnings numbers, and an understanding of how these numbers can be manipulated, detecting, deterring, and preventing fraud is really just a matter of understanding cash flows. Regardless of the existing level of control or the amount of profit, a solid control of the cash must be created.

Using the **direct cash flows method**, we can understand a business's cash flows relatively quickly by simply reviewing the financial statements showing cash received and cash paid out without accruals. Whatever the revenue stream of an organization, the revenues must eventually be received, and there are related expenses that generate that revenue.

Simply following the direct flow of cash received and spent is often where the risk of fraud exists. Using the direct cash flows method for searching for unreported income, you can compare all identifiable cash sources that are termed cash inflow (or cash received), with all identifiable cash uses that are termed cash outflow (or cash payments and disbursements). If an outflow is greater than an inflow, it is—at a minimum—an indicator that income may have gone unreported. This could also mean that the company is hemorrhaging cash, building inventories, or having trouble collecting accounts receivable. Further fact finding by the 800-pound friendly gorilla is necessary.

You can also use an **indirect cash flows method** to detect fraud. This takes into account the accruals and eventually works back to cash. One indirect cash flows method for determining unreported income is the **net worth method**. Net worth is determined by deducting total liabilities from the total value of assets. This method compares the change in net worth during a certain period with the reported income during the same period. The statement looks at the changes in current assets and current liabilities that reflect the accrual-based adjustments. Current assets minus current liabilities equals working capital. If you made money from operations, your cash should increase. However, if you lost money from operations, the 800-pound friendly gorilla should recognize it immediately.

In several situations it is necessary to look for hidden income by determining whether the income reported by the organization is reflective of the actual cash received. In a fraud-minded organization, the 800-pound friendly gorilla searches for instances of unreported income *before* a fraud occurs. The types of analyses indicated above follow the sources of cash and are used in divorce, bankruptcy, contract disputes, and fraud investigations. Unreported income searches should not be a reactive response to a creditor withholding credit. Waiting for red flags to be raised before initiating searches is not going to help you catch fraud before it occurs. Remember to perform these searches *before* they are necessary, to create a proactive approach to reducing the risk of fraud.

A traditional method of identifying unreported income is to review tax returns, financial statements, bank statements, or other reports purported to represent income. However, these documents mean nothing if the 800-pound friendly gorilla is not in place to check the level of trust bestowed on the people all along the way in the process and ensure that adequate controls exist to provide assurance that no manipulation has been allowed to occur among the steps.

Exhibit 5.3 shows my take on an organization's cash flows. The model in Exhibit 5.3 is oversimplified, because ultimately, without cash flows, the fraudster cannot exist, regardless of the dynamics of the business.

Exhibit 5.3 shows a side-by-side cash-flow model. Owners' lifestyles are a direct result of the organizations they work for or created, unless they have other means of generating income besides the income received from that organization (e.g., inheritance or other income, legal or illegal). When reviewing an organization's cash flows, the 800-pound friendly gorilla is looking not only at the dynamics of the organization but also at the dynamics it creates for the key people involved in it.

Both models start with beginning cash at the start of the fiscal year being analyzed. Although the accounts that we examine here may be different for the organization than for the key person, the effects on cash are the same. The first effect on the organization is the cash related to the operations (i.e., the organizational processes that generate the revenue) versus the main income that a key person derives from an organization. The latter includes both salary and bonuses); we want to separate the base salary, associated with the job responsibility, from the incentive-driven bonuses. Thus, we are able to compare the organization's profits to the key person's salary and bonuses.

The organization has a few steps to take in arriving at the true cash flows generated by the operations—for example, adding back items that are not cash, such as depreciation and other nonoperating transactions, as well as adjusting it back to the cash basis by examining the changes in working capital and either adding back or subtracting (depending on the effect in cash).

Both the organization's key executives and trusted people in the process will make the financing decisions. The 800-pound friendly gorilla should be looking at these financing decisions to make sure they are justified, fit the overall direction of the organization, and contain no existing conflicts of interest. The 800-pound friendly gorilla asks the following:

- Are the financing purposes being matched?
- Is the long-term financing occurring for long-term thinking and not just to improve cash flows by removing short-term borrowing or payables?
- Does the key person have the income to support the financing being provided (and is it easily verified by a tax return)?
- Is the organization in financial trouble? Does it need to infuse capital? Remember that key-person borrowing should raise a red flag when infused into an organization, because the investment in the organization would increase working capital. Make sure infusions are for positive reasons and not to keep a sinking organization afloat.

The organization should also look at normalizing expenses to the necessary levels to get a true read of the cash flows being generated by the operations

EXHIBIT 5.3 Organizational Cash flows Model

Organizational Cash Flow	Key Personnel Cash Flow
Cash Balance Beginning	**Cash Balance Beginning**
<u>Net Income</u>	<u>Salary</u>
Noncash Adjustments	**Distributions**
Depreciation/Amortization	Business Distributions
Total Noncash Adjustments	**Total Distributions Received**
<u>Working Capital Changes</u>	
Accounts Receivable Increase (Decrease)	<u>**Investing Inflow (Outflow)**</u>
Accounts Payable Increase (Decrease)	Interest Income
	Dividend
Total Changes in Working Capital	Capital Gains
Operating Activity Cash Inflow (Outflow)	Investment Purchases
	Investment Sales
<u>**Investing Inflow (Outflow)**</u>	**Total Investment Inflow (Outflow)**
Purchase Equipment	<u>**Financing Inflow (Outflow)**</u>
Total Investing Activities	Borrowing
	Repayments
<u>**Financing Inflow (Outflow)**</u>	**Financing Investment Inflow Outflows**
Borrowing	
Repayments	

(Continued)

EXHIBIT 5.3 (Continued)

Organizational Cash Flow

Issue Stock

Dividends Payable

Total Financing Activities

Total Change in Cash

Ending Cash Balance Before Adjustments

Personal Expenses (Not Allowed)

Discretionary Spending

Normalizations

Officer's Salary

Benefits

Bonuses

Travel and Entertainment

Total Normalizations

Ending Cash Balance Adjusted

Key Personnel Cash Flow

Other Income

Total Other Income

Personal Expenses

Normal Reoccurring (Rent, Mortgage, Utilities)

Total Personal Expenses

Discretionary Spending

(Yacht, Car, Fur Coat, etc.)

Total Discretionary Spending

Ending Cash Balance Before Adjustments

of the organization. An organization should submit itself to an annual valuation review, which makes all the necessary adjustments to determine if it is more valuable or less valuable than the previous year.

Like monitoring an organization's equity changes (growth), a key person's net worth and value analyses should be prepared to determine how they increased from the previous year. The 800-pound friendly gorilla asks whether the key person's income from the organizational process makes sense, or is it excessive. The U.S. Department of Housing and Urban Development requires a lender to maintain a certain net worth to remain a lender. The key people should be required to maintain a level of net-worth documentation that will enable them to remain transparent to the average person, and in a way the average person can understand. Politicians have to file a financial disclosure, and so should the key personnel who have access to an organization's value. In fact, all people in an organizational process who have access to value should be given an annual review beyond the one they received when they were hired. Every January 15, all personnel should have to file financial disclosures.

The remaining analyses that the 800-pound friendly gorilla should perform involve expenses that are not required to operate the organizational process. Some examples are travel and entertainment and other discretionary spending. When examining it from the key person's side, the 800-pound friendly gorilla looks for purchases, such as luxury items, and flags any unsupportable lifestyle changes.

Keeping a close watch on the cash flows in an organization on all levels, including how cash flows between it and its key personnel in terms of lifestyle and net worth changes, creates just the right 800-pound friendly gorilla effect to detect, deter, and prevent fraud.

 SUMMARY

The 800-pound friendly gorilla does not like to overcompensate executives, but that does not stop boards that are not up to the task of governance to virtually give away the organization's value. The compensation of executives is disclosed but is usually buried in annual reports, so the interest and outrage needed to deter what some might call a legal fraud (a fleecing of the shareholders) does not happen.

In my opinion, most accounting professionals are trained to look for inside frauds rather than macro-frauds, such as stock manipulations, or outside frauds that never make it into the financial reports or disclosures. When you talk about manipulating ratios, margins, and earnings, you are talking about inflating results that are often intangible. Most accounting professionals are trained to look for things like straw (fictitious) vendors, and they set up controls to prevent stealing tangible items in order to determine whether these frauds affect the organization's value. The organization and its professionals need to create a different level of thinking and develop a global approach rather than continue the same old thinking that the fraudster already knows how to manipulate.

This chapter has presented a lot of information that can seem a bit daunting. But the simple fact is that you need to work on your organization and how you oversee its processes. This can make you feel like the weight of the world is on your shoulders (see Exhibit 5.4).

We mentioned greed as a motivating factor for committing fraud. Greed exists because of the hunger that is created by the dynamics of people, institutions, and foundations in businesses, with unrealistic short-term goals replacing much needed long-term planning and processes and chains of responsibilities that have gone askew. Unfortunately, the speculations that are created come down like a sledgehammer and at the expense of the shareholders or external parties.

Organizations need people to manage their processes. Think of this expression from the English poet John Donne in 1624: "No man is an island, entire of itself; every man is a piece of the continent, a part of the main."[17] To be successful in detecting, deterring, and preventing fraud, an organization needs to keep its people from thinking that they are their own islands, without any oversight. The transparency and checks and balances described in this chapter will help every individual to maintain the integrity of his or her part in the chain of responsibility before fraud occurs.

 ## ONE-MINUTE FRAUD MYSTERY ANALYSIS

Have you established where the greed exists in this case? Remember, you are the fact finder and need to think divergently. Here are some my thoughts on this chapter's mystery, based on my experience in the field:

- **Allegation.** There is an inflated net income, possibly created in order to meet Wall Street earning expectations.
- **Probable cause.** The cause is not entirely clear, but a tip about the discrepancies came in from an anonymous source.

**Most people feel like they are carrying
a lot of weight on their backs.**

EXHIBIT 5.4   Weight of the World

- **Action.** Further questioning is necessary. The approach you should take is a cautious one. While you want to treat John Debit (CFO), Theodore Dollar (CEO), and Jackie Ledger as people of interest, you need to use the 800-pound friendly gorilla approach when investigating them. You need to understand the level of socialization and relationships that exist among these parties. Who has a clear understanding of the organizational business process? Who is the potential ring leader? Who else may be involved (staff accountants)? Is the relationship among the parties limited to this transaction, or is it ongoing? The SEC brought the problem to light based on a tip. Is the tip credible?

Look into it. Do not assume that the victims are not involved. Rule them out by doing proper due diligence. A tipster may be trying to get revenge. Examine where the greed exists that enables a fraudster to start justify the rationalization to commit fraud. Are there external influences? Look for lifestyle changes. Look for conflicts of interest. Know your answers before you ask critical questions by having a well-thought-out and planned approach.

- **Preparation.** Talk with the auditor (interview external sources first). If there is an internal audit team, make sure you talk to its members, with the board of directors' knowledge and input.
- **People of interest.** Board of directors (i.e., policy makers), CEO, CFO, controller, accounting staff, internal auditor, audit committee.
- **People-with-knowledge interview plan.** The interviews should be done in the following order: external auditor, board of directors, internal auditor, audit committee, accounting staff, controller, CEO, and CFO.
- **Documentary evidence.** Review the invoices and contracts for data lines as well as the corporate, board meeting, and audit committee minutes. Research the company's stock price history (e.g., through Yahoo! or Google Finance). Research the company's audited financial statements and review the information for other companies in the industry to establish industry standards. Check credit rating data (Moody's, S&P, Fitch, and RMA) and other economic data.
- **Formulate opinion.** Accrual Inc.'s stock prices are falling, and its credit agency rating is being jeopardized, which means higher interest rates and cash flows pressures. The CFO and CEO appear not to have maintained the proper ethical tone at the top. The CFO appears to have manipulated the income statement and the balance sheet by electing to capitalize expenses so that they appear to be an asset instead of treating the cost as a current period expense. This inflated the company's earnings and increased the fixed assets to maintain the earnings expectation of Wall Street, and it appears that the earnings have been manipulated within a reasonable degree of accounting certainty.

The 800-Pound Friendly Gorilla Suggestions for Accrual Inc.

Create divergent thinking by asking yourself who was the tipster? Was it a former employee whose stock options were expiring? Was it a current employee who did not get his or her bonus or granting of stock or options? Or was it someone in the organization who is uncomfortable with the way financial reporting and disclosures are being prepared? What was the motivation behind the fraud? Was a gun being held to someone's head, or was someone's job threatened? Was it simply to gain a higher result for the organization's stock price for someone's personal interest?

Knowing the people of interest and the facts and circumstances behind the fraud is extremely difficult when the tip is anonymous. You will now need to develop strong documentary proofs because there is no physical witness. The 800-pound friendly gorilla has his work cut out for him and needs to go undercover. The following are suggested actions to reduce the risk of fraud:

- Establish a fraud hotline, or make sure people have someone to go to report fraud if a hotline does not exist.
- Create an unexpected fraud monitor in a space, such as a janitor or a repairman, who has an understanding of what to look for.
- Monitor the responsibilities given to people with access to the value.
- Make sure that all capitalization of expenses meets the applicable standard requirements of GAAP or IFRS. Compare them to tax depreciation regulations and to any timing differences the methods utilized, so they are reconciled. If the assets cannot clearly be considered capitalized, the determination of what should be capitalized should be done independently by the external auditors, the board of directors, and the established organizational internal auditors.
- Make sure that the chart of accounts that is established clearly identifies the proper expense accounts and capital accounts. A proper chart of account is a must and should be reviewed as frequently as necessary to maintain its accuracy. Also make sure that the account describes the transaction accurately.
- Check the list of the organization's established ethics from top to bottom.
- Determine whether the assets have tangible (physical or touchable) value verse intangible (intrinsic or untouchable) value and obtain proper fair market valuations.
- Ask applicable what-if imaginative questions (e.g., Are the organization's earnings sustainable?).

A Simple Picture

Where does the greed exist in Exhibit 5.5?

The expectation of Wall Street to meet earnings is imposed on the CEO (Theodore Dollar), and creates the need to manipulate earnings to satisfy those expectations, in turn fostering greed. The CEO is enabled to perform the manipulation with the help of a qualified CFO (John Debit) and his staff to develop the adequate numbers to meet Wall Street's expectations. Therefore, by a simple examination of the picture, we can see that greed exists not only within the organization but also within the external body, Wall Street. The question is who is greedier: the Wall Street analysts who expect a certain level of returns or the CEO who wants to meet those expectations?

Expectations and enablers are important to consider when analyzing your organization and its potential for fraud. The expectations of an organization often exert pressures that can lead to greed and other rationales for fraud. Enablers are those who allow fraud to exist in your organization. An enabler can be a person on your accounting staff who allows access to secret numbers or a custodian who allows people illegal entry to your building. Only by understanding where the potential for fraud lies can you successfully detect, deter, and prevent it.

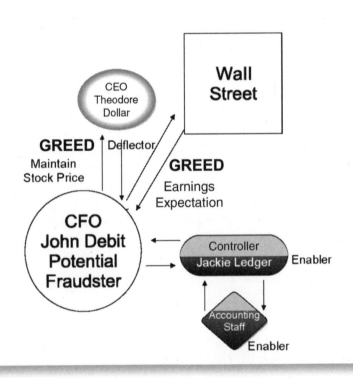

EXHIBIT 5.5 Accrual Inc. Drawing

NOTES

1. Credit rating agencies assess risk. They analyze creditworthiness on a wide range of investments and debts and determine the associated risk. Moody's, S&P, and Fitch control the credit rating market: Moody's and S&P each control 40 percent, and Fitch the remaining 20 percent.
2. Neil Weinberg, text of speech at Bell Memorial Union, Chico, California, http://www.csuchico.edu/cob/_documents/LinkSpring2008.pdf, p. 9.
3. Albert Einstein and Sonja Bargmann, *Ideas and Opinions* (New York: Crown Publishers, 1982).
4. Stephen R. Covey, *7 Habits of Highly Effective People* (New York: Simon and Schuster, 1989), p. 95.
5. Weinberg, text of speech.
6. Bob Ingle and Sandy McClure, *The Soprano State: New Jersey Culture of Corruption* (New York: St. Martin's Press, 2008).
7. "S&P 500: Total and Inflation-Adjusted-Historical Returns," Simple Stock Investing, http://www.simplestockinvesting.com/SP500-historical-real-total-returns.htm.
8. Amy Borrus, "The Credit-Raters: How They Work and How They Might Work Better," *BusinessWeek*, April 8, 2002.
9. "Annual Statement Studies," Risk Management Association, www.rmahq.org/tools-publications/publications/annual-statement-studies.
10. Jonathan D. Salant, "AIG Bonuses Contemplated in '08, TARP Inspector Says," Bloomberg, March 19, 2009, http://www.bloomberg.com/apps/news?pid=newsarchive&sid=aBwUb_K6GQ7s.
11. Harry Bradford, "10 Worst Single-Day Drops in Dow Jones History," *Huffington Post*, August 5, 2011, http://www.huffingtonpost.com/2011/08/05/dow-jones-biggest-drops- falls_n_919216.html#s323006&title=10_August_4th.
12. To calculate the U.S. national debt in real time, go to http://www.usdebtclock.org.
13. Jennifer Rosenberg, "The Stock Market Crash of 1929, About.com, http://history1900s.about.com/od/1920s/a/stockcrash1929.htm.
14. Geraldine Fabrikant and Eric Dash, "For Lehman Employees, the Collapse Is Personal," *New York Times*, September 11, 2008.
15. *The Phil Donahue Show*, 1979, http://www.youtube.com/watch?v=RWsx1×8PV_A.
16. Upton Sinclair, *I, Candidate for Governor: And How I Got Licked* (Berkeley, CA: University of California Press, 1994).
17. Wikiquote, *John Donne*, http://en.wikiquote.org/wiki/John_Donne.

CHAPTER SIX

Understanding the Accounting Process

Accuracy is the twin brother of honesty; inaccuracy, of dishonesty.

—*Nathaniel Hawthorne, writer*

Property may be destroyed and money may lose its purchasing power; but character, health, knowledge and good judgment will always be in demand under all conditions.

—*Roger Babson, business theorist and founder of Babson College*

People present the greatest fraud risk within an organization. People are also often the most critical resources for maintaining a successful organization. Consider the forensic accounting equation called APE (assets minus people equals equity), which we introduced in an earlier chapter. It is important to recognize that people in the organization represent the greatest liability. You can use APE instead of the traditional accounting equation of assets minus liabilities equals equity. Think of where APE can be substituted in your normal accounting for debits and credits. Again, we have entered the world of the 800-pound friendly gorilla, as people create obligations within organizations. If these people are not monitored properly, it can severely impact the assets. Therefore, we need to examine the people who have the ability to incur these liabilities if we are to detect, deter, and prevent fraud while still maintaining the organization's value. Find the right nonaccountant gatekeepers to place in the process in order to make sure the real number stories are being told. The ultimate goal is to create effective accounting communications that an average person can comprehend. Understanding the people behind the original accounting equation of assets minus liabilities equals equity is the proactive thinking of the 800-pound friendly gorilla.

An example of the 800-pound friendly gorilla is found in the movie *The Breakfast Club*. The character named Bender asks the school's custodian, Carl, "How does one become a janitor?" Carl appears to have a firm but friendly relationship with the kids, talking to them without being condescending yet maintaining his professionalism and authority. He lets them know that he is aware of more than they think he is, remarking, "I look through your letters, I look through your lockers. . . . I listen to your conversations; you don't know that, but I do. . . . I am the eyes and ears of this institution, my friends." In this case, Carl is acting like an 800-pound friendly gorilla. He is effective because the students don't suspect that he is monitoring them. Create 800-pound friendly gorillas that are not visible to the fraudsters, in addition to the visible ones (this keeps the fraudsters off balance). You can apply this to your organization. Make the people who are least likely to be thought of as your eyes and ears the monitors in your organization so that the fraudster cannot manipulate them.

When was the last time you ran an algorithm to understand how the people in your organization communicate? See Exhibit 6.1 for an example of how to determine the internal and external communication processes happening in your organization. Next, see the documentation flow analysis in Exhibit 6.2.

It is imperative for an organization to have established and disseminated specific documentation policy controls in its practices. These documents are critical for detecting and proving fraud. The person responsible for receiving the documents needs to date stamped and paginate them if there are multiple pages. The person receiving the documents should not be in a position to alter the documents but should merely forward them to the person responsible for addressing the documentation received. After the document is properly recorded and the necessary action taken by the responsible party, the document should be placed in a secure area with the proper controls in place. Keep in mind that a document can be in paper form or electronic. An organization must have established retention and destruction policies in place that comply with the applicable laws.

Organizations should schedule daily morning meetings with the people in the organizational process to establish the daily responsibilities to be performed. These meetings should recap the previous day's results and set forth the goals for the next day. Having 10- to 20-minute brainstorming sessions on how to improve the results from the previous day and ensuring that there are no weak links in the organizational chain improves communication.

A big part of detecting fraud is employing people who understand accounting language so they can interpret whether the numbers story being told by a

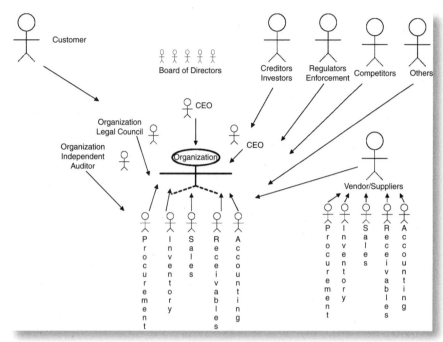

EXHIBIT 6.1 Communication Processes

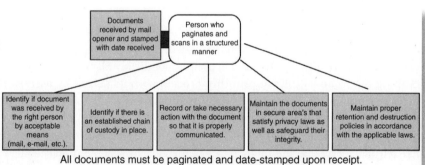

All documents must be paginated and date-stamped upon receipt.

Receptionist or mail opener must maintain date received of each and every item that is received.

EXHIBIT 6.2 Documentation Flow Analysis

potential fraudster is fact or fiction. This chapter helps you to understand accounting processes that are important when detecting, deterring, and preventing fraud.

This chapter features the following lessons:

How knowing the people within your organization's accounting process cycle is imperative to being able to detect fraud. .

Examining how people in your organizational process act at different times.

How different accounting demands can affect a fraudster in the organizational process.

Understanding the fraudster's position within the accounting process to expose potential schemes and scenarios.

How to focus on your trusted people by examining who has access to exposed value.

T HIS CHAPTER HELPS YOU TO understand the people who make the debits and credits in your organization's accounting process. Make a list of all of the people who are involved in the organization's accounting cycle and recording process so you know who has the opportunity to perpetrate fraud by manipulating the accounting and communication process. An example would be a foreman who has his workers paint his house, and he approves overtime on the company payroll to pay for it.

The organization's 800-pound friendly gorillas need to examine people in defined durations of time to generate recordable and accountable results. Defining specific durations of time helps an organization to link its business processes with the people who have the greatest access to the value, because everything then becomes clearly measurable. Expose the accountability by creating limited windows of controlled activities that do not allow a fraudster to blend into the organizational process.

Fraudsters know what accounting information is needed to avoid detection and to access an organization's value. An organization needs to recognize how people act when faced by different demands, conflicts, and time constraints. Linking an organization's accounting process with its people by assessing their performance in controlled activities with unsuspecting observers helps to ensure that they maintain the proper ethics.

Train the people in the process and throughout the organization to think like a fraudster by making them aware of the various schemes and scenarios in which the opportunity for fraud exists. It is important to learn from the past. There are a slew of frauds that have occurred and serve as great learning tools. Where did past organizations fail to maintain a proactive approach to fraud? We need to make sure that the people in our organizations know what fraud looks like so they can understand how it can exist. It is equally important for employees to have an understanding that the 800-pound friendly gorilla is knowledgeable of fraud opportunities and schemes; this will lead to an increased likelihood of detection. Training and testing the people in your organization is a key part of fraud prevention. A suggested action would be to put in your employee handbook that random tests may be performed to ensure that the company's controls are not being circumvented.

Think like a fraudster by identifying areas in the accounting process that have to be manipulated for a potential fraud to remain undetected. We typically label and identify the things that fraudsters should be cautious of and ultimately provide them with a road map for remaining undetected in the organization. Always keep fraudsters guessing. Make sure the people monitoring the accounting functions understand the red flags that may signal fraud.

Furthermore, the monitors of your organization should not be obvious. A good monitor is one whom a fraudster would not suspect. Give the monitors easy ways to communicate so they are comfortable reporting violations. Remember that tips are the number one way fraud is caught. People may be the cause of fraud, but they can also be your biggest fraud deterrent. Detected frauds become deterrents for future frauds.

 ## ONE-MINUTE FRAUD MYSTERY: SNEAKERS ARE US INC.

A purchase order for 10 pairs of sneakers, costing about $570 with shipping, is received by Patty Precision, the sales manager of Sneakers Are Us Inc. The order is from Overseas Inc., a company it has not previously done business with. Precision informed the client salesman, Charlie Cash, that certified payments must be received by Western Union before shipping. Cash said Steve Doubledip, the salesman from Sneakers Are Us Inc., had explained the company's policy for establishing new accounts, specifically with international entities like Overseas Inc., that orders are to be in cash until a credit approval has been processed by the Sneakers Are Us Inc. credit department.

When the money order arrived, it was accompanied by three counterfeit watches that were amazing brand-name replicas. Attached was a note that read, "We can increase your profitability by selling our watches." The money order was received by Tommy Trustworthy in accounting but had been addressed to Doubledip, who apparently already opened the incoming mail and forwarded the money order internally. Trustworthy posted the money order, deposited the funds in the company cash account, and informed Precision that the money order funds had been received. Dennis Delivery, in the warehouse, was notified by Precision to ship the goods. No mention of the three counterfeit watches was made.

Precision received a phone call from Sam Slinky, the sales manager from Overseas Inc., asking if she liked the watches, thanking her for fulfilling the sneaker order, and saying that he looked forward to doing a larger volume of business with her and her company. Precision calls you, a forensic accountant, and asks you to investigate the call and the watches.

 ## UNDERSTANDING THE SALE OF GOODS

The future of detecting, deterring, and preventing fraud revolves around "negotiated truths" and the understanding that anyone and everyone are capable of committing fraud. "Negotiated truths" are essentially rationalized mistruths. This includes both lies (intentional falsehoods) and inadvertent mistakes made by misestimating and the like. Let's say that you tell your boss that he or she will have a report by 3 p.m. but you do not deliver it until 3:15 p.m. Technically, you created a mistruth (see Exhibit 6.3). A University of Massachusetts researcher found that 60 percent of people lied at least once during a 10-minute conversation and told an average of two or three lies.[1] Organizations cannot allow "negotiated truths" that can develop into the wrong ethical tone. Organizations should hold friendly and open meetings to maintain a more cooperative tone.

The accounting process is literally the organization's highway. With a good road map of the process, the fraudster can easily manipulate and access the organizational value. This is where opportunities for fraud can exist, and it is where the correct tools will allow the organization to deter, detect, and prevent fraud. Therefore, an important step in dealing with fraud is to ensure that the accounting process is being analyzed by all levels of people in an organization. Accounting has to go beyond the process of recording the numbers. The people in the process have to maintain the proper controls, or the accounting records will not be accurate and therefore not worth the paper they are printed on. One way to determine that controls are operating as designed is to have people in your organization who are the least likely to be 800-pound friendly gorillas (remember *The Breakfast Club* example) monitoring the process and keep the accounting reports credible.

For example, having a company maintenance man in the accounts receivable department with his eyes and ears observing the process and reporting it to

EXHIBIT 6.3   Mistruths

Copyright © 2012 James Lee

you will give you a more accurate description of what goes on day-to-day than sending in an internal or external auditor will. You may be wondering how a janitor would know what to look for. You would provide the janitor with a list of what to look for. When an auditor is present, potential fraudsters go into defensive mode. To keep your financial reporting credible, put potential undercover gatekeepers in place to observe the people in accounting to identify any behaviors associated with potential fraudsters so that management can adjust the level of trust (and authority) bestowed upon them and mitigate a perceived fraud risk.

The organization should closely monitor accounting because it is involved in the reporting of all of an organization's transactions; as a result, the people in accounting have access to a lot of organizational value. See Exhibit 6.4.

People in the accounting process are clerks, managers, bookkeepers, data entry employees, credit managers, staff accountants, and they also include the CEO, CFO, controller, treasurer, and anyone with the right level of access (e.g., managers and executives at remote locations) to make entries to an accounting recording system. These are the people who will likely interact with fraudsters in an organization, if they are not accomplices or the actual fraudsters themselves. Internal auditor are *not* part of the accounting process; they are a control element that reports directly to the board. They should be *prohibited* from making entries into any accounting records.

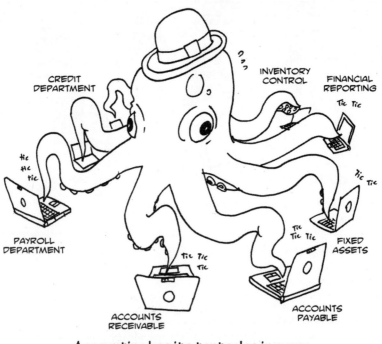

Accounting has its tentacles in every
organizational transaction.

EXHIBIT 6.4 Accounting

The accounting cycle includes identifying, recording, and communicating the organization's business transactions. Keep in mind that business transactions are the result of organizational processes that create organizational value. A typical accounting cycle scenario is this: After the transactions created by the processes of your organization are analyzed, they are posted to various journals, then posted to a general ledger account that accumulates the totals for a specific period being analyzed. The general ledger balances are put into a trial balance to make sure that debits and credits equal; this becomes the unadjusted trial balance. The unadjusted trial balance is part of what is often called a *worksheet*. The unadjusted trial balance is further journalized and posted for adjusting entries like prepayments and accruals to create an adjusted trial balance.

The next step in the financial communication process involves the preparation of financial statements from an adjusted trial balance. The financial statements consist of the income statement, which reflects an organization's operational and net income for a specified period; a statement of retained earnings (the owner's equity statement or partner's capital), which is the scorecard and represents the remaining share available for the equity owners; and the balance sheet, which is a snapshot of the financial condition of the organization for a specific date.

The cash flow statement is the final financial communication, generated by comparing the current year's balance sheet and the previous year's balance sheet; it is not developed from the accounting worksheet that leads to the adjusted trial balance. I have distinguished this financial communication because it is often the least understood, yet it provides the most beneficial information from a forensic perspective because it shows the net changes in cash.

The organization finalizes the process by journalizing and posting closing entries to create a postclosing trial balance so the process can be reset and the cycle can begin all over again. Keep in mind that the accounting process does not consider the level of trust that people have been given, nor is it designed to find fraud without specifically implementing appropriate levels of control and proper oversight.

Therefore, the focus should be on discovering accounting fraud before the damage is created by the fraud. This requires real-time bookkeeping controls. For instance, the most basic bookkeeping controls would have flagged the WorldCom scam by simply requiring a mandatory review of any revisions to the entries before they were actually made. That's right: the most *basic* bookkeeping controls. At the very least, when an organization's transaction changes exceed cumulative thresholds, they should be approved by the 800-pound friendly senior level managers. Furthermore, journal entries proposed by senior level managers should be approved by the comptroller, CFO, or other executive-level officer. Organizations should be required to visibly display detailed bookkeeping controls and have them independently evaluated by accounting firms other than those who audit their financial statements.

Helping your people to gain an understanding of the debits and credits required to properly reflect the transactions of the organization will deter fraud. If the fraud is on the books, it is because there has been a manipulation. But if the fraud is off the books, no accounting record is even made. Understanding what should be debited and credited exposes these unreported transactions as well. Using an acronym to remember the accounting language of debits and credits is extremely helpful. The one I use with my accounting students is EARLS: expenses, assets, revenues, liabilities, and stockholder equity.

Exhibit 6.5 shows how EARLS is useful for understanding debits and credits using a T account in which the normal balance (increase) side of the account places the E and A on the left side of the account and the R, L, and S on the right side. To increase the E and A accounts you need to *debit* them. To increase the R, L, and S accounts you need to *credit* them. You should make note that when dealing with accounting, the debits are totaled on the left side of the T account, and the credits are totaled on the right side, regardless of which account you are analyzing.

The debits and credits in the accounts indicate the normal balance for those accounts. It does not mean that a debit balance account cannot be credited, or vice versa for a credit balance account. For example, a liability account normally has a credit balance. When the liability is paid, you would debit the liability account and credit cash. The cash account normally maintains a debit balance.

Accounting is a double-entry system, which means that the debits and credits made in the accounts for each transaction must balance. Thus, the total debits will always equal the total credits, which is the fraudster's biggest hurdle when perpetrating a fraud. Fraudsters have to make sure that all of the accounts involved in a potential fraud are balanced. Do the accounts in your organization balance?

In addition to understanding the debit and credit aspect of the T account, we need to train people on which accounts get debited and credited with each transaction in an organization's processes. It is important that people understand what these postings mean to the organization's value. Training your people to understand the process they are involved in will give them the ability to communicate potential improper postings.

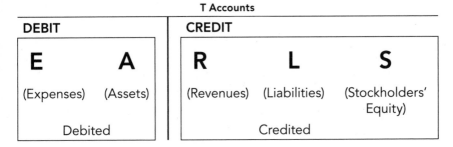

EXHIBIT 6.5 EARLS

Source: Pedagogy in Action, http://serc.carleton.edu/sp/library/visualizations/
examples/48567.html

Exhibit 6.6 shows another acronym to help you understand the accounting cycle and remember the classifications of accounts: LASER (liabilities, assets, stockholders' equity, expenses, and revenues). Fraudsters know the proper classifications of the various accounts and the transactions of an organization's processes. They know how to manipulate accounting to cover their tracks so that the fraud remains undetected, but tracing the transactions by using T accounts can lead to a detection of fraud.

The world operates in cycles (or capsules of time), and accounting is no different. The accounting cycle is the way an organization generates a reporting period to properly reflect the necessary transactions to determine the value created by the process. A baseball game generally has nine innings, so there is an end point that enables a result to be recorded. Similarly, organizations have daily, monthly, quarterly, semiannual, and annual reporting cycles as end points that designate when the results to be recorded.

Merchandising and manufacturing organizations generally have the same types of adjusting entries that a service organization does, and they reflect them within specified periods to create measurable results. The way to tell merchandising and manufacturing apart is by understanding the inventory being maintained. A merchandiser is a reseller of goods, also known as a retailer or wholesaler, whereas a manufacturer makes the goods.

In both cases, the inventory needs to be further reviewed to determine whether an organization is using a either a perpetual inventory system (as the sale occurs) or a periodic inventory system after a physical count. Perpetual inventory systems record the cost of goods sold as the sales take place, and the only sure way to verify their accuracy is to perform a periodic physical count, which is typically done at the end of the year. In either inventory system, the employees will be required to make an additional adjustment to reflect any difference discovered after the physical count is compared to the general ledger. This is where a fraudster is likely to be exposed, since in a misappropriation fraud there is often inventory missing. In a stock manipulation fraud, overstated inventory is one way to improve periodic operating results to meet or beat investor expectations.

I once was taking an inventory count for a gas station that included cases of oil stored in boxes. The boxes were lined up evenly in rows, and I just happened to lean against a box at the end—and fell through. The fraudster at the company never figured I would lean against a box in the farthest corner. It turned out that the party was selling the oil and pocketing the cash. This appeared to have been going on for years, but without a physical count, the fraud would never have been detected. Since the oil was secondary to the sale of gas, it was viewed as immaterial, and therefore no one was paying attention. This illustrates how important it is to monitor your inventory as well as your people.

Inventory is a critical component in a manufacturing or merchandising organization's ability to generate operational cash flows. Typically, inventory

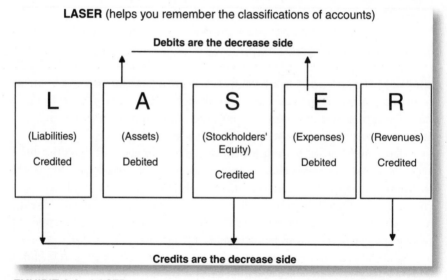

LASER (helps you remember the classifications of accounts)

Debits are the decrease side

L	A	S	E	R
(Liabilities)	(Assets)	(Stockholders' Equity)	(Expenses)	(Revenues)
Credited	Debited	Credited	Debited	Credited

Credits are the decrease side

EXHIBIT 6.6 LASER

Source: Pedagogy in Action, http://serc.carleton.edu/sp/library/visualizations/examples/48567.html

represents items that are going to be sold to generate revenues. But what about the supplies you use in your organization, like copy paper and ink cartridges? These may be called *prepaid supplies* rather than *inventory* and stay on the balance sheet, which means they do not reduce the value of the organization until it is added to the expenses on the income statement. On the balance sheet, a debit is an asset and increases organizational value, whereas on the income statement (i.e., the statement of operations), a debit is an expense that reduces an organization's value. Proper accounting treats supplies as expenses based on when they are used.

A fraudster will find ways to manipulate the use of inventory for his or her own personal use or to sell it off to generate cash. If the copier cartridge is used, it is treated as a legitimate operating expense. If the inventory goods are used to make a sale, the cost is treated as a legitimate cost of sale. The accounting record is the same in the sense that both remain on a balance sheet as an asset until they are used, at which time they are treated as expenses in an income statement.

A fraudster could manipulate these accounting entries to keep the items on the balance sheet, which would create incorrect financial reporting, since the profit would appear higher. By applying honest debit and credit language to this scenario, you see you have an asset that is debited, which means you need an offsetting credit to balance the entry, which in this case is a credit to income. Fraudsters increase an organization's assets and make the profit appear higher than it should be.

Crazy Eddie Inc. (see Chapter 1) had established a strong relationship with the vendor Wren Distributors.[2] Crazy Eddie was Wren's largest customer, purchasing more than 10 percent of its merchandise from Wren and accounting for 35 percent of Wren's revenues. To successfully inflate the inventory, Crazy Eddie would ask Wren to ship $3 million to $4 million in merchandise before the end of the year but not to bill for it until after the auditors completed the year-end audit. The merchandise was included in the year-end inventory count but was not posted to accounts payable, since it was not billed. This meant that on the year-end date there would be no money owed to Wren. The company had a $3 million to $4 million increased inventory asset account on the balance sheet, with no corresponding liability because a corresponding accounts payable entry was not recorded.

Remember the basic accounting equation (assets minus liabilities equals equity)? Basic accounting dictates that the correct entry would be to debit inventory and credit accounts payable. If Crazy Eddie did not credit a liability account, then what account did it credit? It credited sales, so not only did the company increase its assets, it also increased its earnings by $3 million to $4 million.

When inventory is sold, it is credited to a revenue account on the income statement; this revenue account is ultimately closed at the end of the period and goes to the entity's retained earnings. The accounting equation says that assets minus liabilities equals equity, which includes a retained earnings increase. In this case, equity increased a liability account (which also has a credit balance). Assets, a debit balance account, increased, and the equity, a credit balance account, increased, which enables the accounting equation to balance. The mere shifting of a liability from the balance sheet to the income statement or the nonreporting of a liability can mislead the reader of the financial communications. We often do not pay attention to these incidental revenue generators because they are perceived as immaterial compared to more significant revenue generators. Supplies are often viewed in a similar manner. The problem is that if you do not address these situations, you are allowing an inappropriate organizational tone to potentially develop. All it takes to commit these types of frauds is a simple misclassification of accounts. All organizations, whether merchandisers, manufacturers, or service organizations, are required to make accounting entries that ultimately affect their financial statements. This is why it is important to know the people in your organization.

The next area to review in an organization is what formal income statement is being used. An income statement (also called a *profit and loss statement*) shows your business's performance over a defined period (usually monthly, quarterly, semi-annually, and annually). The income statement reports sales revenues minus costs of goods sold minus all other expenses, which then equals profit or loss. A balance sheet shows your financial position at a specific moment in time (usually at the end of the month or the end of the year). The balance sheet reports assets, liabilities, and capital. Assets must always be equal to liabilities and capital (which is also called *equity*). The cash-flow statement reconciles the income statement and balance sheet by reconciling the change in cash. Not all organizational money received or spent shows up on the income statement or the balance sheet. The cash flow statement links the two. More important, it shows where the money came from and where it went.

It is also important to review whether an organization is using the multiple-step or single-step income statement. The multiple-step income statement shows several categories in determining net income, which includes the cost of goods sold, net sales, and gross profit. The manufacturer adds another step in the cost-of-goods-sold section called the *cost of goods manufactured*. The operating expenses are deducted from the gross profit to determine the net income.

In addition, there may be nonoperational sections for revenues and expenses that result from secondary or auxiliary operations, as well as gains and losses that are unrelated to the operations. As you can see, there are multiple areas in which people have access to an organization's value. These various accounting categories identify transactions for recording and ultimately communicate to the intended users both internally and externally.

Gross profit margin is a percentage calculated by subtracting the cost of goods from the net sales and then dividing that number by the net sales. Desired gross margins are determined by an organization. You should ask yourself how often and by whom are these margins checked. The answer is a critical red flag, if not aligned with an organization's desired results. Not only is it a tool for detecting and preventing fraud, it is the critical measurement used to ensure that the organization is meeting its targeted goals. If a company or one of its competitors has a 25 percent average margin established by an industry, and your calculation leads to a different finding, it should make you wonder why. Whenever you can establish an independent comparison, like established industry percentages, you have a quick way of exposing potential frauds. Can organizations manipulate gross profit? Exhibit 6.7 shows that there are multiple ways a fraud can take place.

When auditors find misstatements while performing an audit, they are responsible for making an assessment. They alone must determine whether the misstatement represents an error or a fraud. Errors are not deliberate. Fraud contains evidence of intent to mislead. For the record, generally accepted auditing standards (GAAS) direct the reporting to at least one level of management above the highest ranking person who could be involved in the potential fraud. The irony is that an auditor who finds fraud reports it to the appropriate person in the organization, but what if that person is involved in the fraud?

Keep in mind that the dollar amount of the misstatement does not make a difference when assigning a badge of fraud. It does not make any difference if the intentional misstatement is material or immaterial; fraud is fraud. If fraud is left unaddressed, this sends an improper message and negatively affects the ethical tone of an organization.

Here are some common errors you will typically come across:

- **Inadvertently taking an expense and charging the wrong account**. For example, an advertising expense shows up as an amortization expense. The two accounts are next to each other on the chart of accounts, and the

234 ■ Understanding the Accounting Process

EXHIBIT 6.7 Where Is the Fine Line?

Accounting Errors	Accounting Irregularities		Areas of Thinking	
Unintentional mistakes	Intentional mistakes	Inventory cost determination		
Followed GAAP	Aggressively followed GAAP			
Capitalized (mathematical, calculation, or misinterpreted)	Aggressive capitalization	Amortization vs. expense	Period to write-off	Defer vs. expense
Write-downs (change in estimate)	Write down so that in future there's less impact on balance sheet and earnings	Collections	Acquisition	Discontinued operation
Earnings (mistake)	Earnings manipulated			
Revenue (mistake)	Revenue fictitious	Revenue recognition timing		
	Income smoothing			
Financial statement mistake	Financial statement fraudulent			

data entry clerk could have made a simple keystroke error. A fraudster's best defense is being able to say that any error was a mistake. Fraudsters know exactly how to position accounts so that if they are caught, they can just say, "I hit the wrong key."

Another example, common to the side-by-side account, is to make the accounts transposable (i.e., two digits are reversed). If any two adjacent numbers are transposed, the result of subtracting one from the other can be evenly divided by nine. For example, if a fraudster knows account 250 (the prepaid contract account) is on the balance sheet and account 520 (the service expense) is on the income statement, posting expenses to the 250 account instead of the 520 will lead to the overstating of income. But 520 minus 250 divided by 9 equals 30; this rule is used to quickly find errors by accountants and others trying to reconcile balances. If caught, a fraudster will simply claim that someone transposed a number.

■ **Using an unreasonable accounting estimate for allowance for bad debt expense.** The person who makes this mistake may have simply misinterpreted the facts by making a bad or incorrect conclusion or prediction. The allowance for bad debt arises because GAAP calls for the matching of revenue and expenses in the same financial reporting period. In this case, each period would have a certain amount of credit sales recorded as bad debt. That way, revenue is not overstated in the current period.

Businesses use many different methods to estimate bad debt. A common method is to allocate a percentage of gross sales to bad debt. The percentage can be an industry average or the actual percentage of bad debt to gross sales experienced by the company in the past. Some companies allocate all invoices that are past due more than 120 days to bad debt. The manipulation of accounting estimates is one way that the organization can manage reported earnings and the fraudster knows it.

■ **Incorrectly applying accounting principles in accounting records so they are flawed.** Recording an asset at its cost rather than its market value is an example of an accounting principle (in this case, the historical cost principle). Make sure the company hasn't inadvertently made an adjustment to increase the value of an asset (such as land or a building) to its appraised value rather than its cost. It is never appropriate to change the value of a fixed asset on the balance sheet from its original cost.

 ## DECEPTIVE DATA

We need to understand that the term *assets* also includes intangibles, like patents depletable. In recent years there has been fair value accounting through FASB rule 157, "Fair Value Measurement," and more scrutiny with rules 141, "Revised 2007 Business Combinations," and 142, "Goodwill and Other Intangible Assets." However, this area is often neglected by fraud detectors when determining fraud in an organizational process.

Keep in mind that here you are looking at two cash-flow areas that are not part of operational cash inflow and outflow; you are looking at cash flow from investing activities and financing activities, which is often not understood by most people who rely on financial communications, because the interested parties are usually concerned only with the bottom-line earning results.

WorldCom was able to manipulate its earnings by changing the cash-flow category from an operating to an investing cash-flow activity. In July 2002, WorldCom provided the SEC with a detailed statement that the company knew about its accounting problems. In that statement, WorldCom explained that in 2001 and the first quarter of 2002 it had taken line costs, which were mostly fees associated with its use of third-party network services and facilities, and wrongly classified them as capital expenditures. By transferring these obvious expenses into capital expenditures, WorldCom clearly violated basic accounting principles and perpetrated a fraud.

What people ensure that assets are tangible and are maintained and used solely for business purposes? Who is responsible for the classifying of assets? Are these assets business assets or personal assets? Do the assets exist? When was the last time the assets were physically inspected? Are the assets causing health and safety issues? Are the assets inefficient because of old technology? Does the organization invest in infrastructure, and is it well maintained? You can clearly see that a fraudster can thrive in the assets category and remain undetected for years. Fraud occurs when someone purposefully produces deceptive data. You need to be on the lookout for two types of fraud:

1. **Misstatements because of fraudulent financial reporting.** In this type of fraud, the management or the owners are usually involved, and the fraud is facilitated by overriding the internal controls. The fraudster knows where the weak links in the process are and overrides them.
2. **Misstatements because of the misappropriation of assets.** This type of fraud is usually perpetrated by nonmanagement employees. The fraudster outright steals organizational value and makes sure the effect of his or her actions is not on the books or else doctors the books to cover the trail.

Fraud can take the form of the falsification or alteration of accounting records or financial statements. The deliberate making of a mistake when coding expense checks is fraud. So is intentionally booking a lower allowance for bad debt than is deemed unreasonable by normal estimation methods. The fraudster knows what documents will help cover the trail, like a bogus invoice or a created collection correspondence showing an allowance decreased or increased, depending on how the letter was written.

Fraud also includes intentional omissions of significant information. For example, if a company knows that its largest customer is getting ready to close its doors and doesn't disclose this fact, it is fraud. Not properly disclosing loss contingencies is another example such as when a company doesn't disclose that it is likely to lose a lawsuit brought against it, and the damages can be reasonably estimated.

Of course, the theft of assets such as cash, inventory, or equipment is also fraud. Paying personal expenses out of the company checking account is fraud. Another example is taking company computers home for personal use.

COMPUTERIZED FRAUD TECHNIQUES

If you depend only on data mining or techniques on how to find fraud with your computer, you are not going to successfully detect, deter, and prevent fraud. Data mining and other computerized tools can search for attributes of a fraud faster than humans can, but it takes humans who are knowledgeable of both the transactional data being searched and the types of attributes that could indicate red flags for fraud to make the software work for you. Complex transactions require accounting records to capture the attributes necessary to detect fraud. The computer-generated results still need to be manually analyzed by people. Each organization's accounting varies, depending on the types of transactions in which it is engaged. There is no standardized system that meets every requirement; therefore, the trusted user should select the one that is most appropriate. The more sophisticated your documenting needs are in determining a fraud, the stronger your accounting structure should be. Unfortunately, most frauds are usually outside the computerized world, or the perpetrators have covered their tracks using technological methods and are long gone.

To make a computer do anything, someone has to write a computer program. To write the computer program, the person has to tell the computer, step by step, exactly what to do. The computer then executes the program, following each step methodically, to accomplish the goal. Whoever is telling the computer what to do also gets to choose how the computer is going to do it. This is where computer algorithms come in. An algorithm is the basic technique used to get a job done.

For example, let's say that you have a client coming to your office, and he or she needs directions. Here are two algorithms that you might give the client for getting to your office.

The Car-Service Algorithm

1. Go to the car service at Third Street.
2. Get in the car.
3. Give the driver the office address.

The I-Pick-You-Up Algorithm

1. Be outside your office in 15 minutes.
2. Get in my car.
3. Arrive at the office.

Each of these algorithms accomplishes the same goal, but each does it in a completely different way. Each algorithm also has a different cost and a different travel time associated with it. Taking a car service, for example, is probably the fastest way, but it's also more expensive. The pickup option is definitely less expensive, but it certainly is much slower. Your choice of algorithm is based on the facts and circumstances. Every algorithm has advantages and disadvantages in different situations.

Sorting is one area where a lot of research has been done, because computers are tasked with a good number of work sorting lists. For example, here are five different algorithms that are used in sorting:

1. Bin sort
2. Merge sort
3. Bubble sort
4. Shell sort
5. Quick sort

If you have a million integer values between 1 and 10 and you need to sort them, the bin sort is the right algorithm to use. If you have a million book titles, the quick sort might be the best algorithm. Knowing the strengths and weaknesses of the different algorithms helps you in picking the best one for the task at hand.

Organizations are faced with the need to keep accurate track of debits and credits on a daily basis. The actual design and process is the key, and the ability to alter the design and process can only be done by trusted people in order to maintain integrity.

These days, access to accounting is easier because of the increase in the development of information technologies and software to aid businesses. However, many times these developments are upgraded, and this can create a diversionary opportunity for any fraudster. When a computer is upgraded, for instance, it could easily be stated that falsified numbers were changed by the computer or that the numbers were lost.

Computers appear to make financial record keeping so simple that even nonaccountants can utilize them to report a transaction rather than having to rely on people who truly understand the effect of the transaction. It is often said that computers do not make mistakes, only people do. But nothing could be further from the truth. Although there can be human error in the input, what about the assumption often made that the software will safeguard the organization against fraud? If that were the case, why do organizations need antivirus software, fire walls, and information technology personnel to protect the data's integrity? What about the possibility of a back door that the fraudster discovers? The correct algorithm must be written with a beginning and an end that does not allow a back door or a design change without authorization, or it will be impossible to remove the potential for fraud from a recording function. We need people with 800-pound gorilla oversight to ensure the data's integrity.

We appear to have replaced human oversight with reliance on technology, which is clearly evident when one looks at the growth of identity theft today. From the need to have virus protection on your computer at work and at home to the speed at which millions of dollars can be manipulated with a single keystroke, it is all too clear that fraudsters can benefit from technology.

An accounting information system (AIS) collects, stores, and processes financial and accounting data used by a company's decision makers. An AIS is generally a computer-based method for tracking accounting activity and is often used in conjunction with information technology resources. The resulting statistical reports can then be used internally by management or externally by other interested parties, including investors, creditors, and tax authorities.

AISs are composed of multiple components. Questions to consider when looking at AIS operations include the following:

- What users will operate them?
- Who designs the procedures and instructions involved in collecting, managing, and storing the data?
- How are the data related to the organizational processes handled?
- What software applications process the data?
- What information technology infrastructure, beyond the actual physical devices and systems, allows the AIS to operate and perform its functions?
- What internal controls and security measures have been implemented to safeguard the data?

A typical accounting cycle consists of the following steps:

- Analyzing the transactions
- Journalizing the transactions
- Posting transactions to ledger accounts
- Preparing trial balances
- Making adjustment entries
- Preparing an adjusted trial balance
- Preparing financial statements and appropriate disclosures

Furthermore, there is journalizing and posting the closing entries and preparing the after-closing trial balances. These are performed once the financial communications for the previous steps have been completed.

At first glance, accounting does not appear to be difficult, but when you look at it closely, there can be thousands or millions of transactions, depending on the situation. A high volume of repetitive transactions may appear to be simple. This can often result in an organization's people becoming complacent. Even one little mistake or inaccuracy can corrupt an entire accounting cycle, requiring tedious analysis from the very beginning of a process to the end to find and correct a mistake. Every successful fraudster is counting on this.

There are many people inside and outside an organization who can manipulate the value of an organization. By following the arrows in Exhibit 6.8, you can see where the people in a process meet.

Preserving the integrity of automated accounting software and documenting the authority levels of its users to read or make entries into the system are key controls necessary to the prevention, deterrence, and detection of fraud.

 ## OPERATING EXPENSES

After you understand the accounting related to the sale of goods, you can review the operating expenses. Operating expenses affect the measuring of net income for an organization. After you consider the operating expenses, you have to consider the activities that generate these expenses and ask whether they are necessary to create a revenue stream. You need to identify the nonoperational items that do not directly relate to your organization's main revenue streams. An example of nonoperating income or expenses would be a gain or loss on a sale of investments (assuming the organization is not in the business of investing).

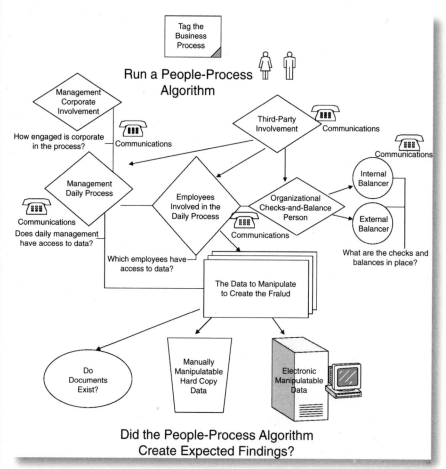

EXHIBIT 6.8 The People in the Process

If the income statement is a single-step income statement, the transactions are classified into two categories: revenues and expenses. In this scenario, there is one step required to determine net income or net loss.

The next area is the balance sheet as it applies to the merchandiser, manufacturer, and service organization. The main difference among these is the way the inventory is reflected in the current-asset section of the balance sheet. On a manufacturer's balance sheet, the inventory is disclosed in greater detail than on one for a merchandiser or a service organization. The manufacturer will break down the inventory into three categories, in order of liquidity: finished goods, work in process, and raw materials. All items on a balance sheet should be listed in order of liquidity, with cash always first, since it is obviously the most liquid (if no restrictions are in place).

Inventory Systems

Determining the cost of goods sold under a periodic inventory system involves using separate accounts to record freight costs, returns, and discounts. In addition, a running account of changes in inventory is not maintained the way it is in a perpetual inventory system. The balance in ending inventory, like determining the cost of goods sold for the reporting period, is calculated at the end of the period. The format for using a periodic inventory system is as follows.

Let's look at a cost-of-goods-sold section for the year ended December 31, 2012. The section would be labeled "cost of goods sold." The first category listed here would be the beginning inventory, which is really the previous reporting period's ending inventory. If the inventory in the beginning is not accurate, then the numbers that are subsequently reported will also be incorrect. What safeguards are in place?

After listing the beginning inventory in a merchandising company, you would add the purchases made within the period and reduce them for returns, allowances, and discounts (which should be maintained in separate accounts). Who oversees the returns and discounts in your organization? It is important to look at the returns, allowances, and discounts to determine if the percentages are in line with the management estimates. This would be much more difficult to analyze if the accounts were combined. Does your organization combine or reduce the purchase account? These numbers are added and subtracted, resulting in net purchases. We then add freight-in costs and get the cost of goods available for sale. Is the available inventory meeting the customer demand?

After the beginning inventory, net purchases and freight-in are added to get the cost of goods available. You then subtract the ending inventory from the cost of goods available to determine the cost of goods sold.

Cost of goods sold is subtracted from the net sales to arrive at the gross profit (margin). The steps to examine in a periodic inventory system are purchases of merchandise, what returns and allowances occurred, what discounting was given, and verification of the inventory accounts of goods on hand at the beginning and end of an accounting period. Watch the contrapurchase accounts, which are subtracted from purchases to produce net purchases, and the freight-in is then added to the net purchases. The cost of inventory on hand under the periodic inventory method is determined by a physical count.

A problem with periodic inventory systems is the cost of goods sold from the sale of merchandise are not recorded when the sales are made, the way they are in a perpetual inventory system. There is no attempt on the date of sale to record the cost of the merchandise sold until the end of the period after a physical count. As a sale is recorded, no adjustment would be recorded for the cost of goods sold. For a cash purchase, cash is credited. For a credit purchase, accounts payable is credited.

The perpetual inventory system posts to the cost of goods sold as each sale occurs. The reason for a physical count in a perpetual inventory system is to verify the accounts records with the physical existing inventory. If the two do not agree, there may be a fraud.

One of the most difficult accounting tasks for an organization is determining in what period particular revenues and expenses should be reported. This is an area often utilized by a fraudster to create a fraud. The International Accounting Standards Board (IASB) and the FASB recognize this problem and are currently working together to develop a common procedure to develop a revenue recognition project in which the intent is to provide organizations with guidance in recording these transactions more consistently and credibly over a proper period.

Accrual-Basis Accounting

Accrual-basis accounting is applied under GAAP and IFRS to record the transactions that change a company's financial statements in the period in which the transactions occur. Both sets of principles agree that cash-basis accounting is not in accordance with their standards, and both divide the economic life of an organization into artificial periods. This is referred to as the *time period assumption*.

IFRS requires a company to present a complete set of financial statements, including comparative information, annually. Any time you give comparative information, you are communicating to the readers of the statement in a better context, since they can see the change from one period to another. Does your organization present its financial statements properly?

There are more than 100 GAAP rules dealing with revenue recognition that are industry-specific. IFRS primarily uses a single standard. GAAP's revenue recognition principle requires that companies recognize revenue in the accounting period in which it is earned. GAAP's expense recognition principle requires that efforts (expenses) be matched with results (revenues).

There is a large disparity in the amount of detailed guidance for revenue recognition. The revenue recognition principle required by GAAP is similar to that of

IFRS. The problem is that the interpretations of the rules are made by people, and as this book has stated repeatedly, people are going to do what is best for themselves. Revenue recognition fraud is a major issue in the U.S. financial reporting system. The same situation occurs in other countries, as evidenced by the revenue recognition breakdowns in cases such as the Dutch software company Bann NV, the Japanese electronics giant NEC, and the Dutch grocer Ahold NV.

The specific standard for revenue recognition under IFRS is International Financial Reporting Standards (IAS 18). This standard uses the probability that the economic benefits associated with the transaction will flow to the organization selling the goods, providing the service, or receiving the investment income. The revenues and costs must be capable of being measured reliably. GAAP requires the person making a report of the revenue to determine what revenue is *realized* or *realizable*. This means determining what revenue was received and what revenue is expected to be received. The other determination that needs to be made is whether the revenue used as the basis for revenue recognition was *earned* or *unearned*.

A basic step in the revenue recording process is to closely analyze each transaction for its effect on the accounts involved. This involves making sure that transactional information has been recorded in the appropriate journal. Then the transaction should be transferred from the journal to the appropriate accounts in the ledger. I stated this earlier when explaining EARLS. The act of entering an amount on the left side of an account is called *debiting* the account, and making an entry on the right side is *crediting* the account. If the debit amounts posted to any ledger account exceed the credit amounts, an account has a debit balance. When the reverse is true, the account has a credit balance.

The effect of debits on an asset is an increase, and the normal expected balance in that account is a debit. Therefore, a credit will reduce the asset. What are the accounts involved in your organization's investigation? If you have liability accounts, a credit increases the balance and is the normal balance. Therefore, a debit will reduce a liability. Assets and liabilities are balance sheet accounts.

Retained Earnings

Examples of equity are retained earnings and the owners' or partners' capital accounts in partnerships. Retained earnings are increased by a credit, and the normal balance is a credit. Debits to retained earnings decrease their balances (dividends for organizations and for proprietorships and partnerships are the owners' or partners' draws). Equity accounts are increased by net income and capital contributions. If expenses exceed revenues, you have a net loss, which will reduce these accounts with a debit. Which accounts in your organization are you investigating? Do the balances of these accounts make sense, and who are the people making these entries?

Journals and Ledgers

A journal, or book of original entry, is where accounting transactions are initially recorded. There can be multiple journals, but the most common journal is the general journal. The journal makes several significant contributions to the recording process and is the one place that shows the complete effect of a transaction. The accounting requirement is that the journal maintain a chronological record of the transactions. This is where we can detect, deter, and prevent fraud, because the debit and credit amounts for each entry can be easily compared. The process of entering transaction data in the journal is known as *journalizing*. Having more than three accounts in one journal entry is referred to as a *compound entry*.

This is where the organizational process begins, and if an organization is to deter, detect, and prevent fraud, it needs to make sure there are people who are outside the journal maintenance function who check these journal entries, like an 800-pound friendly gorilla. A ledger is where all accounts are maintained by an organization. By keeping all of the data about changes in account balances in one place, you gain a useful source of data for management interpretation. Typically there are three columns: a debit column, a credit column, and the running balance (determined after each transaction).

The procedure of transferring journal entries to the ledger accounts is referred to as *posting*. A well-maintained general ledger will reflect the entered amounts in the appropriate columns of the account (debit or credit), the date, the journal page, and a description in the reference column of the journal. Is your journal posting up-to-date and reconciled? An unreconciled, unposted, and out-of-date general ledger is a flag for fraud and should be investigated.

A basic technique of fraud investigation is to retrace the steps involved in an organization's recording process. When you are investigating a process, the first step is to understand the organization's transactions and how they are reflected in the books and records. Start by knowing the accounts that are affected by the transaction. Once you have a basic understanding of the accounts, ask the following: Have the transactions been recorded? Then do a debit and credit analysis to see if the transactions are balanced, as required by the double-entry accounting rules. Determine if the amounts, dates, descriptions, and data are correct.

As we discussed a bit earlier, the use of a T account is very helpful in following the flow of transactions (see Exhibit 6.9).

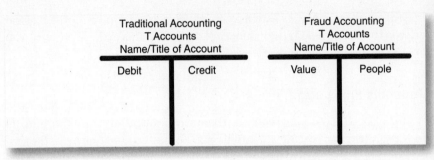

EXHIBIT 6.9　T Account 1

The comparison between a traditional T account and the one we have just discussed can be best demonstrated using accounts receivables (see Exhibit 6.10).

Accounts receivable frauds can involve inventory, bad debt reserves, sales returns, sales discounts, and other accounts, but by using the T account analysis, we can connect the dots. The fraud T account is a fraud detector's best friend, because it charges us with following the money trail. A simple T account analysis, coupled with an understanding of an organization's value and the people with access to it, is the best fraud detector when dealing with accounts receivable value manipulations (see Exhibit 6.11).

 ## BALANCED PRINCIPLES

Make sure your people's principles are in balance. The forensic T account for accounts receivable shown in Exhibit 6.12 illustrates that we do not solely rely

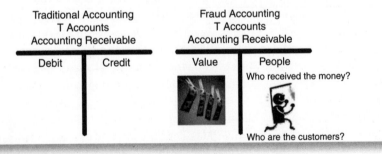

EXHIBIT 6.10　Accounts Receivable Comparison

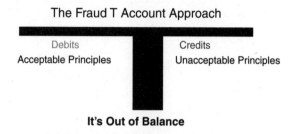

EXHIBIT 6.11 The Best Fraud Detector

on the numerical aspects but rather focus on the inferences that make the transaction a candidate for a fraud examination.

In addition to using T accounts, using a flowchart like the one in Exhibit 6.13 for accounts receivable creates a visual aid of the flow of the transactions. It will help you to find any links in the process chain that are broken and analyze the people in the trusted positions. Make sure you consider how the transaction originates from the process and whether the results are accurate or have been altered.

Add people's names to the flowchart by indicating who received the invoice and in what form it was received. Create an 800-pound friendly gorilla dynamic by showing all of the people in the organization the flowchart of the transactions and who has been entrusted with the responsibility. This is to safeguard the organizational value, since the trusted people have been made visibly responsible.

A trial balance lists the accounts and their balances and is used to prove the mathematical equality of the debits and credits after posting. A trial balance does not prove that the organization has recorded all transactions or that the ledger is correct. Errors that can occur include the following: Transactions are not journalized, a correct journal entry is not posted, a journal entry is posted twice, incorrect accounts are used in journalizing or posting, and offsetting errors are made in recording the amount of a transaction.

Adjusting entries are made in order for revenues to be recorded in the period in which they are earned and for expenses to be recognized in the period in which they are incurred. Adjusting entries are required every time financial statements are prepared or errors are made. Adjusting entries that can be used

EXHIBIT 6.12 Accounts Receivable Fraud—T Account

Debit the T Account for a Sale	Credit the T Account for Funds Received
Is the sale valid?	**Is collection valid?**
(a) Not sold to related party	(a) Was full amount received?
(b) Customer pays within terms	(b) Was payment received on time?
(c) Any unusual discounts or returns	(c) Is customer within terms?
(d) Terms of sale are not usual	(d) Were there any discounts or returns?
Who are the people involved?	**Who are the people involved?**
(a) Salesperson, sales manager	(a) Salesperson, sales manager. Flag if either is involved, because neither should be.
(b) Collection manager	(b) Collection manager. Is he or she involved in a write-off decision or recording function?
(c) Accounts receivable manager and staff	(c) Accounts receivable manager and staff
(d) Accounting department staff, controller, and CFO	(d) Accounting department staff, controller, and CFO
Are there frequent journal entries or adjustments?	**Are there frequent journal entries or adjustments?**

by a fraudster include deferrals (prepaid expenses or unearned revenues) and accruals (of revenues or expenses).

Deferrals that are prepaid expenses are recorded as assets until they are used or consumed. The passage of time or through use and consumption leads to them being recorded as expenses. An asset-expense account relationship exists with prepaid expenses. Keeping an expense on the balance sheet as an asset will reflect higher net income and working capital. Without proper adjustment, the assets will be overstated and the expenses understated. The adjusting entry results in a debit to an expense account and a credit to an asset account. Typical prepaid expenses include supplies, insurance, rent, and interest.

A fraudster will use various deflection techniques to hide and disguise a fraud. Let's take a look at the following six deflections.

The first fraud deflection utilizes timing issues. This is based on the assumption that the economic life of an organization can be divided into periods, whether interim (monthly, quarterly or semiannually) or annual. By shifting the assets, liabilities, revenues, and expenses to different periods, the fraudster can manipulate the financial results as well as hide the misappropriation of the organizational value. Make sure you examine in multiple periods and establish

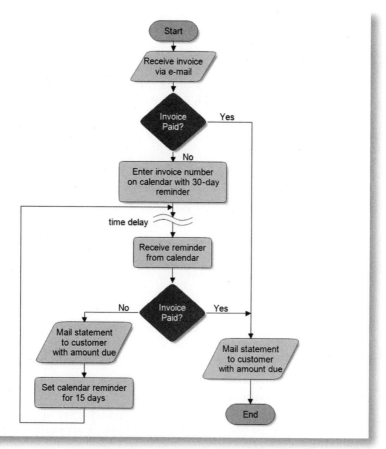

EXHIBIT 6.13 Accounts Receivable Flowchart

Source: RF Flow 5, http://www.rff.com/process_mapping.htm

trend analyses of five years or more. This will help to expose unusual or deceptive transactions such as abnormally high rent expense in one accounting period and no rent expense in the next accounting period.

The second fraud deflection utilizes accrual-basis versus cash-basis accounting. Using the accrual basis to determine net income means recognizing revenues when they are earned (rather than when the cash is actually received) and recognizing expenses when they are incurred (rather than when they are paid). Under cash-basis accounting, companies record revenue when they receive the cash and record an expense when they pay out the cash. Look at the real cash in the organization. Simple examples are where a fraudster makes up fictitious accounts receivable or does not accrue accounts payables.

The third fraud deflection is recognizing revenues and expenses. The revenue recognition principle requires that companies recognize revenue in the accounting period in which it is earned. The expense recognition principle requires that efforts (expenses) be matched with accomplishments (revenues). Expenses are matched with revenues in the period when the efforts are expended to generate the revenues. Fraudsters love to misapply this principle by recognizing revenue when they should not or deferring expenses that should be listed as expenses. Simple examples are when a fraudster creates a sale that never actually occurred or does not expense an incurred cost on the income statement but instead capitalizes it on the balance sheet.

Where is the organization's ethics oversight? Abuse of the revenue recognition principle has become an all too common occurrence in recent years. Organizations are being accused of saying that a sale that occurred at the beginning of one quarter really occurred at the end of the previous quarter in order to achieve the previous quarter's sales targets. What is motivating sales executives and finance and accounting executives to participate in activities that result in an inaccurate reporting of revenues?

The same reward bonus systems based on the ability to target sales goals cause these rationalizations. Wall Street makes its targeted earnings expectations well-known to the accounting and financing people in an organization. Wall Street also makes it clear that failing to meet these targets will lead to the organization's stock price falling. As a result of these pressures, executives sometimes knowingly engage in unethical efforts to misstate revenues. Because of the increase in financial statement fraud, the Sarbanes-Oxley Act of 2002 made the penalties for such behavior much more severe. But penalties alone will not stop fraud; you need ethical people.

The fourth deflection the fraudster uses is depreciation, which is the process of expensing the cost of an asset over its useful life in a rational and systematic manner. It can be the purchase of equipment or a building. This involves any asset having a life greater than one year (long-term). Depreciation is an estimate rather than a factual measurement of the cost that has expired. On the balance sheet, accumulated depreciation is offset against the asset account. Depreciation expense is debited and a contra-asset account, accumulated depreciation equipment, is credited. The difference between the cost of the asset and its related accumulated depreciation is referred to as the *book value* of the asset. The fraudster can manipulate the useful life or the true cost or can shorten or lengthen the asset life to whatever scheme he or she has planned.

The fifth deflection involves unearned revenues. Unearned revenues are the result of receiving payment for a service before the service has been performed. The fraudster could hide earned revenues by posting them as a liability to unearned revenue on the balance sheet; a liability-revenue account relationship exists with unearned revenues. In this situation, liabilities are overstated and revenues are understated. The fraudster delays revenue so he or she can maintain the appearance that the revenue will continue over several periods, while deferring tax liabilities. The correct adjusting entry results in a debit to a liability account and a credit to a revenue account, which would increase net income.

The sixth deflection, and the fraudster's favorite, is to use basic adjusting journal entries. Are the adjusting entries ensuring that revenues are recognized in the period in which they are earned and that expenses are recognized in the period in which they are incurred? Is that what the fraudster wants you to perceive? We know that an organization needs to make adjusting entries every time it prepares financial statements, but so does the fraudster. The same goes for deferrals (prepaid expenses and unearned revenues). These expenses, paid in cash, are recorded as assets before they are used, consumed, or expired, either with the passage of time or through use (supplies, insurance, rent, interest). Maybe expenses have been used and not recorded, or maybe they have been deferred by capitalizing. This is where we need to review who in the organization has access to create these deflections.

Gift cards are popular with marketing executives, but they create accounting questions. Should revenue be recorded at the time the gift card is sold or when the card is used by the customer? Suppose a customer purchases a $500 gift card from Clothing Inc. on December 21, 2011, and gives it to his wife on December 25, 2011. On January 3, 2012, the customer's wife uses the card to purchase clothes. When do you think Clothing Inc. should recognize the revenue, and why?

According to the revenue recognition principle, companies should recognize revenue when it's earned. In this case, the revenue is not earned until Clothing Inc. provides the clothes. Thus, when Clothing Inc. receives cash in exchange for the gift card on December 21, 2011, it should recognize a liability, unearned revenue, for $500. On January 3, 2012, when the customer's wife exchanges the card for merchandise, Clothing Inc. should recognize the revenue and eliminate $500 from the balance in the unearned revenue account. If we had a fraud situation, the revenue would be recognized when sold. As long as the gift cards continue to sell, the fraud would perpetuate until no more gift cards were available to be issued.

BALANCE SHEET COMPONENTS

A classified balance sheet becomes more useful when we understand its sub-classifications. Assets are broken down into current, long-term, property, plant and equipment, intangibles, and other subclassifications. Liabilities are broken down into current and long-term. Equity consists of capital stock and retained earnings (which includes owners' equity and partners' capital).

Current assets are assets that a company expects to convert to cash or use up within one year. Current assets are listed in the order of their liquidity. The operating cycle (usually one year) of a company is the average time that it takes to purchase inventory, sell it on account, and collect cash from the customers. Long-term investments are generally investments in stocks and bonds of other companies that are held for many years. Property, plant, and equipment are assets with relatively long useful lives (more than one year) that an organization is currently using in order to operate. Intangible assets do not have physical substance yet are often very valuable.

Current liabilities are obligations that an organization has to pay within the coming year. Long-term liabilities are obligations that an organization expects to pay after one year. An equity section varies with the form of business organization. In a sole proprietorship, there is one capital account. In a partnership, there are separate capital accounts for each partner. In a corporation, the owner's equity is called *stockholders' equity* and consists of two accounts: capital stock and retained earnings.

The balance sheet is presented in report form with the assets shown above the liabilities, and then equity. It may also be presented in account form, with the assets section placed on the left and the liabilities and owner's equity section on the right.

A fraudster can create a deflection with a balance sheet reversing entry. This is an entry made at the beginning of the next accounting period. The purpose of reversing entries is to simplify the recording of a subsequent transaction related to an adjusting entry by reversing entries for accrued revenues and accrued expenses.

 ## STATEMENT OF CASH FLOWS

We talked a good deal about cash flow in Chapter 5, and probably the most important fraud prevention financial statement is the statement of cash flows. The primary purpose of this statement is to provide information about an entity's cash receipts and cash payments during a given period. In essence, it shows the inflow and outflow resulting in the net change in cash. By showing the flow of cash, this statement takes the legs out from under a fraudster when it is properly prepared and maintained.

The information in the statement of cash flows helps investors to assess an organization's ability to generate future cash flow, pay dividends, and meet obligations as well as reconcile the difference between net income and net cash provided (or used) by operating activities, cash investing, and financing transactions during a given period. The successful organization properly classifies its cash flow.

The statement of cash flows classifies cash receipts and cash payments into the following three classes:

1. **Operating activities.** These include cash effects of transactions that create revenues and expenses and thus enter an organization's determination of net income.
2. **Investing activities.** These include the acquiring and disposing of investments, lending money, and collecting loans.
3. **Financing activities.** These involve liability and stockholders' equity items; they include obtaining cash from issuing debt and repaying the amounts borrowed as well as obtaining cash from stockholders and providing them with a return on their investment.

A successful fraudster will misclassify cash-flow items into the wrong categories.

The statement of cash flows also contains significant noncash transactions, including the conversion of bonds into common stock and the acquisition of assets through the issuance of bonds or capital stock. These transactions are individually reported at the bottom of the statement of cash flow, or they may appear in a separate note or supplementary schedule to the financial statements. This gives fraudsters the necessary cover to remain undetected by converting debt into equity after the organization's stock has been manipulated.

The general format of reviewing the three classes in the statement of cash flows is to go from operating activities to investing activities and then to financing activities. A thorough review generally should follow the format of the financial statement by examining each class of cash transactions. The net cash provided or used by each activity is totaled to show the net increase or decrease in cash for the period. The net change in cash for the period is then added to or subtracted from the beginning-of-the-period cash balance, and any significant noncash investing and financing activities are reported in a separate schedule at the bottom of the statement.

The statement of cash flows is prepared from three sources:

1. A comparative balance sheet
2. The current income statement
3. Additional information

The first step in preparing the statement of cash flows is to determine net cash provided or used by operating activities. This step involves analyzing not only the current year's income statement but also comparative balance sheets and selected additional data.

The second step is to determine the net cash provided or used by investing and financing activities. All other changes in the balance sheet accounts must be analyzed to determine their effect on cash.

The third step is to compare the net change in cash on the statement of cash flow with the change in the cash account reported on the balance sheet to make sure that the amounts agree.

In the first step, the operating activities section must be converted from an accrual basis to a cash basis. This may be done by either the indirect method or the direct method. Both methods arrive at the same total amount for net cash provided by operations, but they differ in disclosing the items that make up the total amount. The indirect method is used extensively in practice even though the Statement of Financial Accounting Standards No. 95 has expressed a preference for the direct method to be used.

Indirect Method

The first step in the indirect method is to determine the net cash provided or used by the operating activities. Under GAAP, the accrual basis of accounting is used, which allows for the recognition of revenues when earned and expenses when incurred.

In order to determine the cash provided from operations, it is necessary to report revenues and expenses on a cash basis. This is determined by adjusting net income for items that did not affect cash. The operating section of the statement of cash flow should begin with net income or loss; add or deduct items not affecting cash (like expenses for depreciation, amortization, depletion, losses on a sale of equipment that are added to net income, and gains on a sale of equipment that are deducted from net income); and show the net cash provided by the operating activities. Continuing to determine the net cash provided by the operating activities, deduct increases in specific current assets other than cash from net income, and add decreases to net income. Similar increases in specific current liabilities are added to net income, and decreases are deducted from net income.

The second step in the indirect method involves determining the net cash provided or used by investing and financing activities from changes in non-current accounts reported on the comparative balance sheet and in selected additional data. For example, if the account—in this case, land—increases by $100,000, and the transaction data indicate that land was purchased for cash, then a cash outflow from an investment activity has occurred. If a different account, common stock, increases by $500,000, and the transaction data indicate that additional capital stock was issued for cash, then a cash inflow from a financing activity has resulted. The redemption of debt and the retirement or reacquisitions of capital stock are cash outflow from financing activities.

The third step in the indirect method is to determine the net change in cash on the statement of cash flows, using the change in the cash account reported on the balance sheet to make sure that the amounts agree.

Free cash flow describes the cash remaining from operations after adjustment for capital expenditures and dividends. The formula for free cash flow is as follows:

$$\text{Free cash flow} = \text{Cash provided by operations} - \text{Capital expenditures} - \text{Cash dividends}$$

If you want to stop fraud, you need to figure out what an organization's free cash flow is.

Direct Method

When preparing a statement of cash flows using the direct method in the operating activities section, include only the following:

- Major classes of cash receipts from sales of goods and services to customers.
- Interest and dividends on loans and investments and cash payments, including those to suppliers, to employees, for operating expenses, for interest, and for taxes.

Exhibit 6.14 shows the formula for computing cash receipts from customers.

EXHIBIT 6.14   Sales Revenue

Increases	Decreases
Increase in accounts receivable	Decrease in accounts receivable
	Normal account balance is a credit

EXHIBIT 6.15   Cost of Goods Sold

Increases	Decreases
Increase in inventory	Decrease in inventory
Decrease in accounts payable	Increase in accounts payable
Normal account balance is a debit	

This reflects the actual cash received by an organization and has removed the accrual deflection available to the fraudster. Short of stealing and not putting the funds in the company, the fraudster cannot manipulate the organizational value here without being exposed.

Exhibit 6.15 shows the formula for computing cash payments to suppliers. Exhibit 6.16 shows the formula for computing cash payments for operating expenses.

Exhibit 6.17 shows the formula for computing cash payments for income taxes.

Whether the cash payments are to suppliers, for operating expenses, or for income taxes, the actual cash paid by an organization is accounted and has removed the accrual deflection available to the fraudster. Short of stealing and not recording the expense properly in an organization's books, a fraudster cannot manipulate the organizational values here without being exposed.

After completing a cash-flow analysis from operating activities, the net cash provided or used by investing and financing activities is generally determined from changes in noncurrent accounts reported on the comparative balance sheet and selected additional data, just as in the indirect method.

The final step is to determine the net increase or decrease in cash by determining the difference between cash at the beginning of the year and cash at the end of the year.

Utilizing a cash-flow approach removes the main accounting deflections perpetrated by some of the biggest fraud cases in recent history, including WorldCom, Tyco, and Sunbeam (small home appliances). With the proper accounting in place, it would have been evident that the cash flow of these

EXHIBIT 6.16 Operating Expenses

Increases	Decreases
Decrease in prepaid expenses	Increase in prepaid expenses
Increase in accrued expenses payable	Decrease in accrued expenses payable
Normal account balance is a debit	

EXHIBIT 6.17 Income Tax Expense

Increases	Decreases
Decrease in income taxes payable	Increase in income taxes payable
Normal account balance is a debit	

organizations was not being generated by operations. This kind of situation is one that no organization can survive for extended periods.

RATIO ANALYSIS

The use of ratio analysis can assist you in uncovering fraud by bringing to light unusual trends and percentages or findings outside an organization's or an industry's established metrics, thereby alerting you to potential areas to investigate.

Liquidity ratios facilitate the identification of whether the company has enough capability to meet short-term obligations and requirements. Current and quick ratios compare current assets and current liabilities and are necessary for making informed decisions. These ratios measure the short-term ability of a company to pay its maturing obligations and to meet unexpected needs for cash.

Profitability ratios—like gross profit ratio, net profit ratio, and operating ratio—give a picture of the profitability position of an organization. These ratios measure the income or operating success of a company for a given period.

Long-term solvency and leverage ratios, such as debt-equity ratio and interest coverage ratio, convey a firm's ability to meet the interest cost repayment schedules of its long-term obligations and show the proportions of debt and equity in an organization's financing. These ratios measure the ability of a company to survive over a long period.

Finally, activity ratios—such as inventory turnover ratios, debtor turnover ratios, and working capital turnover ratios—measure the efficiency with which the resources of a firm have been employed.

Profitability ratios help the users of an entity's financial statements determine the overall effectiveness of management regarding returns generated on sales and investments. As mentioned, commonly used profitability ratios are gross profit margin, operating profit margin, and net profit margin. Gross profit margin measures profitability after considering cost of goods sold, whereas operating profit margin measures profitability based on earnings before interest and income tax expense. Net profit margin is often referred to as the bottom line and takes all expenses into account.

Efficiency ratios measure the effectiveness of management's decision making. They evaluate turnover and the return on investments. Examples of efficiency ratios are inventory turnovers, sales to receivables, and return on assets. Inventory turnover measures the number of times an entire stock of inventory is repurchased, whereas sales to receivables compares trade receivables to revenues. In both types, a higher number indicates a higher level of efficiency when selling inventory and collecting receivables. Return on assets compares net income before taxes to total assets and shows the efficiency of management when using assets to generate profits.

Liquidity ratios help financial statement users evaluate the ability of a company to convert its current assets into cash to meet its current obligations. Common liquidity ratios are the current ratio and the quick ratio. The current ratio is calculated by dividing current assets by current liabilities. According to industry standards, a general rule is to have a current ratio of two, which is two to one or twice as many assets as liabilities. The quick ratio, or acid test, determines a company's ability to pay obligations that are due immediately.

Solvency and leverage ratios judge the ability of a company to raise capital to pay its obligations. Solvency ratios, which include debt to worth and working capital, determine whether an entity is able to pay all of its debts. In practice, bankers often include leverage ratios as debt covenants in contract agreements. Bankers want to ensure that an entity can maintain operations during difficult financial periods. The debt-to-worth ratio calculation is total liabilities divided by net worth. Working capital is calculated by subtracting current liabilities from current assets.

See Exhibits 6.18 through 6.21 for more information on the various types of ratios.

EXHIBIT 6.18 Balance Sheet Ratios

Ratio	How to Calculate	What It Means in Dollars and Cents
Current	$\dfrac{\text{Current Assets}}{\text{Current Liabilities}}$	Measures solvency: the number of dollars in current assets for every $1 in current liabilities. For example: A current ratio of 1.76 means that for every $1 of current liabilities, the company has $1.76 in current assets with which to pay them.
Quick	$\dfrac{\text{Cash + Accounts Receivable}}{\text{Current Liabilities}}$	Measures liquidity: the number of dollars in cash and accounts receivable for each $1 in current liabilities. For example: A quick ratio of 1.14 means that for every $1 of current liabilities, the company has $1.14 in cash and accounts receivable with which to pay them.
Debt-to-Worth	$\dfrac{\text{Total Liabilities}}{\text{Net Worth}}$	Measures financial risk: the number of dollars of debt owed for every $1 in net worth. For example: A debt-to-worth ratio of 1.05 means that for every $1 of net worth that the owners have invested, the company owes $1.05 of debt to its creditors.

EXHIBIT 6.19 Income Statement Ratios

Gross Margin	$\dfrac{\text{Gross Profit}}{\text{Sales}}$	Measures profitability at the gross profit level: the number of dollars of gross margin produced for every $1 of sales. For example: A gross margin ratio of 34.4% means that for every $1 of sales, the company produces 34.4 cents of gross profit.
Net Margin	$\dfrac{\text{Net Profit before Tax}}{\text{Sales}}$	Measures profitability at the net profit level: the number of dollars of net profit produced for every $1 of sales. For example: A net margin ratio of 2.9% means that for every $1 of sales, the company produces 2.9 cents of net profit.

EXHIBIT 6.20   Overall Efficiency Ratios

Sales-to-Assets	$$\frac{\text{Sales}}{\text{Total Assets}}$$	Measures the efficiency of total assets in generating sales: the number of dollars in sales produced for every $1 invested in total assets.
		For example: A sales-to-asset ratio of 2.35 means that for every $1 invested in total assets, the company generates $2.35 in sales.
Return on Assets	$$\frac{\text{Net Profit before Tax}}{\text{Total Assets}}$$	Measures the efficiency of total assets in generating net profit: the number of dollars in net profit produced for every $1 invested in total assets.
		For example: A return on assets ratio of 7.1% means that for every $1 invested in assets, the company is generating 7.1 cents in net profit before tax.
Return on Investment	$$\frac{\text{Net Profit before Tax}}{\text{Net Worth}}$$	Measures the efficiency of net worth in generating net profit: the number of dollars in net profit produced for every $1 invested in net worth.
		For example: A return on investment ratio of 16.1% means that for every $1 invested in net worth, the company is generating 16.1 cents in net profit before tax.

EXHIBIT 6.21   Specific Efficiency Ratios

Inventory Turnover	$$\frac{\text{Cost of Goods Sold}}{\text{Inventory}}$$	Measures the rate at which inventory is being used on an annual basis.
		For example: An inventory turnover ratio of 9.81 means that the average dollar volume of Inventory is used up almost 10 times during the fiscal year.
Inventory Turn-Days	$$\frac{360}{\text{Inventory Turnover}}$$	Converts the inventory turnover ratio into an average "days inventory on hand" figure.
		For example: A inventory turn-days ratio of 37 means that the company keeps an average of 37 days of Inventory on hand throughout the year.

EXHIBIT 6.21 (*Continued*)

Accounts Receivable Turnover	$\dfrac{\text{Sales}}{\text{Accounts Receivable}}$	Measures the rate at which accounts receivable are being collected on an annual basis. For example: An accounts receivable turnover ratio of 8 means that the average dollar volume of accounts receivable are collected eight times during the year.
Average Collection Period	$\dfrac{360}{\text{Account Receivable Turnover}}$	Converts the accounts receivable turnover ratio into the average number of days the company must wait for its accounts receivable to be paid. For example: An accounts receivable turnover ratio of 45 means that it takes the company 45 days on average to collect its receivables.
Accounts Payable Turnover	$\dfrac{\text{Cost of Goods Sold}}{\text{Accounts Payble}}$	Measures the rate at which accounts payable are being paid on an annual basis. For example: An accounts payable turnover ratio of 12.04 means that the average dollar volume of accounts payable are paid about 12 times during the year.
Average Payment Period	$\dfrac{360}{\text{Accounts Payble Turnover}}$	Converts the accounts payable turnover ratio into the average number of days that a company takes to pay its accounts payable. For example: An accounts payable turnover ratio of 30 means that it takes the company 30 days on average to pay its bills.

One potential problem with ratio analysis is that a smart fraudster is also aware of this tool and may be falsifying financial data as part of his or her fraud to keep the ratios in line with benchmarks to avoid detection.

BUILDING A CASE: DOCUMENT ORGANIZATION, DATA ANALYSIS, AND LIFESTYLE ANALYSIS

In the investigation of potential frauds, one of the biggest problems is keeping track of the amount of paper generated from a business's transactions. Good organization in complex cases is essential and includes the following:

- Segregating documents by either witness or transaction.

- Making a "key document" file for easy access to the most relevant documents.
- Establishing a database early in cases involving a large amount of information.

Data analysis is also important in building a case of fraud. The following items are typical examples of data analysis queries that can be performed by data analysis software on accounts payables:

- Comparing the disbursement made with the paid invoice that should have been previously matched to the purchase order. Only use original documentation, third-party-obtained copies, or certified true copies when comparing source documents.
- Summarizing large invoices by amount, vendor, and so on.
- Identifying debits to expense accounts outside set default accounts.
- Reconciling check registers to disbursements by vendor invoice.
- Verifying vendor 1099 requirements.
- Creating vendor detail and summary analysis reports.
- Reviewing recurring monthly expenses and comparing them to posted or paid invoices.
- Generating a report on specified vouchers for a manual audit or investigation.

Also, when involved in a fraud investigation case, you need to make sure your people can adequately answer the classic questions of who, what, where, when, why, and how. They should know the answers to the following:

- Can you please tell me about your job?
- Can you please tell me about the operation of your department?
- What do you think about this problem (i.e., whatever the specific situation is)?
- Can you describe the procedures to me?

In addition, the following searches listed are useful in developing background information to build or investigate cases (where permitted by law):

- Performing credit header searches to confirm address and Social Security number information.

- Reviewing state and federal criminal court records and statewide criminal convictions to uncover past criminal problems presaging similar difficulties.
- Reviewing licenses for aircraft mechanics, pilots, physicians, CPAs, lawyers, and other license-oriented positions to ensure that basic job requirements are met in the appropriate circumstances.
- Obtaining consumer credit reports for the purposes of employee selection, retention, and promotion.
- Obtaining public filings such as bankruptcy filings, tax liens, and judgments to identify adverse financial matters that can serve as potential motivators for fraud, defamation, and embezzlement.
- Reviewing the visible activities of employees, such as when a prospective or current employee drives a personally owned vehicle or an employer-owned vehicle in furthering the interests of the employer. Such activity may expose an employer to liability for damages. In this example, driving records could be checked.
- Verifying basic information on job qualifications through educational and employment-history records.
- Using software such as CaseMap, Xanalys Suite, and i2 Analyst's when appropriate.
- Reviewing computers, both personal and work. Crimes committed with and against computers include computer and computer component theft, system intrusions, software piracy, and software theft. Computers can also be used to facilitate a crime. When this occurs, the computer is known as the tool or instrument of the crime. In such cases, examiners commonly encounter computers that have been used in offenses such as the solicitation of minors in chat rooms, check fraud, and counterfeiting.

Finally, income and expense analysis can uncover unsupported lifestyles or significant lifestyle changes in members of an organization. When computing the comparative net worth of members of an organization, use the expenditures method, including these steps:

1. Establish the subject's known expenditures for the relevant year. Expenditures include the use or application of funds for any purpose, including deposits to bank accounts, purchases of major assets, travel and entertainment expenses, and payments of loans and credit card debts.
2. Identify all sources of funds available to the subject, including loans and gifts, as well as cash on hand from previous years.

3. Compute the difference between the amount of the suspect's expenditures and his or her known income to determine the amount attributed to unknown sources.

SUMMARY

In general, successful fraud theory consists of the following steps:

1. Analyzing the available data
2. Creating a hypothesis
3. Testing the hypothesis
4. Refining and amending the hypothesis

To do this, one needs to understand accounting methods and people's roles and responsibilities within the process and cycle of accounting.

This chapter has included a lot of information. Sometimes keeping track of all this information can seem intimidating, especially when you are genuinely concerned about stopping fraud. Trying to keep track of everything the fraudster does can seem like trying to ride a whale in the ocean (see Exhibit 6.22); it's a daunting and dangerous task. But by keeping in mind the basic concepts of this book (such as the idea that you should focus on people), you will be better equipped to detect, deter, and prevent fraud.

AICPA defines accountancy as "the art of recording, classifying, and summarizing in a significant manner and in terms of money, transactions and events which are, in part at least, of financial character, and interpreting the results thereof."[3] Accounting has been around for thousands of years, with the earliest accounting records dating back more than 7,000 years to the Assyrians in Mesopotamia.[4]

Fraud exists because the "art of recording" is in the hands of people in your organization. Accounting can be a problem because transactions are always evolving and are both controllable and uncontrollable. A successful organization makes sure the accounting cycle and the people in it clearly know that the 800-pound friendly gorilla accepts no mistruths and is watching to ensure that the art of recording is proper.

Remember to place unexpected people within the processes at points where the organizational value is exposed. Put a maintenance person in accounts receivable, a computer programmer in the warehouse, or managers at the water coolers so they can monitor situations for fraud. Having people who

**Trying to account for things the fraudster
does is like trying to ride a whale in the ocean.**

EXHIBIT 6.22   A Whale of Information

keep their eyes and ears open while transactions are being developed is critical. Accounting can no longer simply be the act of recording transactions that
have taken place. Accounting needs to ensure that the most trusted people in
its process are maintaining proper ethics and providing all relevant data in
order to reflect the numbers' real story.

 ## ONE-MINUTE FRAUD MYSTERY ANALYSIS

Can you establish where the greed exists in this chapter's fraud mystery?
Remember, you are the fact finder and need to think divergently. Here are some
of my thoughts on this chapter's mystery, based on my experience in the field:

- **Allegation.** Sneakers Are Us Inc. salesman Steve Doubledip is selling outside the organizational process and went into business himself.
- **Probable Cause.** There was a strange phone call asking about watches and a money order addressed to Doubledip. Precision's immediate call for a forensic accountant raises other concerns.
- **Action.** Further questioning is necessary. The approach you should take is a cautious one. While you want to treat Tommy Trustworthy, Daniel Delivery, Sam Slinky, Steve Doubledip, and Charles Cash as people of interest, you need to use the 800-pound friendly gorilla approach when investigating them. You need to understand the level of socialization and relationships that exist between these parties. Who has a clear understanding of the organizational business process? Who is the potential ring leader? Who else may be involved (identified party at this point of the investigation)? Is the relationship between them limited to this transaction or is it ongoing? Patty Precision brought the problem to light; is she credible? Look into her background. Do not assume that the victims are not involved. Rule them out by using proper due diligence. Examine where the greed exists that enables the fraudster to start the justification for the rationalization to commit fraud. Are there external influences? Look for lifestyle changes. Look for conflicts of interest. Know your answers before you ask critical questions by having a well-thought-out and planned approach.
- **Preparation.** Doubledip needs to be caught in the act—with a camera in a sting operation, possibly—because transactions outside the system are the most difficult to prove. Ensure that the watches exist and prove that he is selling them to your existing customer base.
- **People of interest.** Doubledip, Charlie Cash (Overseas Inc. salesman), Sam Slinky (Overseas Inc. sales manager), Tommy Trustworthy (Sneakers Are Us accountant), Daniel Delivery (Sneakers Are Us warehouse manager), and Patty Precision (Sneakers Are Us sales manager).
- **People-with-knowledge interview plan.** Precision, Trustworthy, Delivery, Slinky (with caution, since he may be involved with Doubledip), Cash (with caution, since he may also be involved with Doubledip), and Doubledip.
- **Documentary evidence.** Review the invoice issued to Overseas Inc. and look at the general ledgers and bank records. Review the note about the watches and the money order addressed to Doubledip. Look at the watches included with the note and all of Doubledip's sale records as well as all inventory sent out by Doubledip's sales delivery staff. Do a review of any

accounts receivables related to Doubledip, customers and examine Double-dip's credit record, and perform a background check and analysis.

▪ **Formulate opinion.** After you examine all of the facts, you will probably determine that Doubledip was running other sales outside the system using the company's organizational processes and contacts to establish credibility, allowing him to have an existing customer base established while employed at Sneakers Are Us, Inc. You may also find that Trustworthy received the watches as a coconspirator.

800-Pound Friendly Gorilla Suggestions for Sneakers Are Us Inc.

At Sneakers Are Us, Inc. salespeople are close to the company's value because they are fulfilling small orders for sneakers and facilitating the sales process. Direct access to merchandise, external merchandisers, and payments (cash, checks, credit cards, wired money, etc.) open up the possibility for fraudulent activities to take place. Without the presence of the 800-pound friendly gorilla at all levels in this company, potential profits are vulnerable to fraud. Even the front line salespeople need to understand the zero tolerance company culture backed up by an 800-pound friendly gorilla presence in the organization. Here is what Sneakers Are Us, Inc. should implement to reduce the risk of fraud:

- ▪ Maintain a whistleblower hotline.
- ▪ Look for potential conflicts of interests
- ▪ Monitor the responsibilities given to people with access to the value.
- ▪ Update background and credit checks for the salespeople as well as others in the process.
- ▪ Maintain a higher level of sign-off in the sales approval process (multiple signatures) that checks the margins to make sure they are maintained. Check the sale price minus cost of goods shipped to determine contribution margin.
- ▪ Require the salespeople to maintain time logs or journals in order to create accountability.
- ▪ Monitor phone numbers to see if numbers being called are generating sales.
- ▪ Require accounting to monitor the sales reports and match them to sales.
- ▪ Make sure the salespeople do not have access to customer payments.
- ▪ Make sure the people with access to organizational value are bonded (to insure against risk).

■ Maintain weekly sales meetings at which sales activity reports are monitored by managers at appropriate levels.

A Simple Picture

Where does the greed exist in Exhibit 6.23? The normal sneakers sale in the mystery creates a diversion for the salesmen and accountants at both companies to deal in watches, which create totally unrelated sales revenue. Both salesmen are using their organizations' phones and other infrastructure for their personal benefit. Using this case as an example, can you tell if your

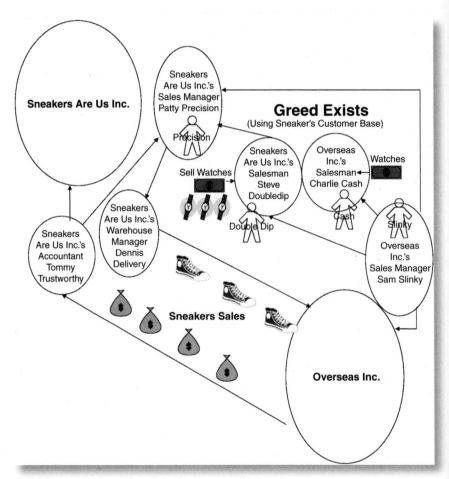

EXHIBIT 6.23 Sneakers Are Us Inc. Drawing

organization's trusted people are conducting certain business actions without your knowledge? The greed exists in the use of the organization's customer base and infrastructure that holds the value. The value can be intangible, which, unlike a tangible physical asset, can be difficult for the 800-pound friendly gorilla to monitor.

See Exhibit 6.23 for a visual offering of some ideas you might find useful in assessing your organization's situation.

 NOTES

1. Robert Feldman, "Study Shows Differences in Types of Lies Told by Men and Women," EurekAlert, June 10, 2002, http://www.eurekalert.org/pub_releases/2002-06/uoma-urf061002.php.
2. San Antar, "Crazy Eddie: The Many Faces of Fraud," White Collar Fraud, http://www.whitecollarfraud.com/947660.html.
3. Ramnik Singh Wahla, *Accounting Terminology Bulletin*, http://www.accountingcourseguide.com/accounting-principles.html
4. G. Thomas Friedlob and Franklin James Plewa, *Understanding Balance Sheets* (New York: John Wiley & Sons, 1996), 1.

7

It All Comes Down to Cash

> Yesterday is a canceled check; tomorrow is a
> promissory note; today is the only cash you
> have—so spend it wisely.
>
> —*Kay Lyons, author*

In all instances of fraud, whatever the scheme or scenario, the result must translate into some monetary value to create the fraud's rationale. Who are the people in the organization? What access do they have to cash (value)? What level of trust has the organization bestowed on them? The organization must put in place the right tools to prevent fraud when dealing with cash—not only in the form of currency, coin, and money orders (which are often the most difficult forms of cash to recover or use to prove intent) but also items and transactions that are convertible into cash. A simple "Oh yeah, I forgot to put the cash in the drawer or prove that I received it" can make intent difficult to prove. You'd better have a camera and/ or an eyewitness for the documentation of cash, since it will most likely not be evident once it has been removed. Add to the complexity the necessary proofs associated with cash, paper checks, electronic checks, automated clearinghouses, electronic fund transfers, lockbox deposits, the factoring of collections through third parties, sweep accounts, debit memos, credit memos, debit cards, credit cards, gift certificates, gift cards, and loan payments—and all often coming out of the organization's one main account—and you have created a multitude of opportunities for the potential fraudster.

Employing the three Ds—diversion, distraction, and deception—and determining where they exist in an organization in respect to cash is essential. Identify the people in your organization who have access to cash and cash equivalents and know where they are in the process so you can enable the appropriate safeguards. Know who receives and makes the payments involving cash in order to detect, deter, and prevent fraud. Who can collect and disburse the funds in your organization? Find out where these people are and whether they have the necessary skills, the proper ethics, or the potential to commit fraud.

This chapter features discussions on the following:

Reviewing your organization to find the people involved in the business processes that create monetary value.

Monitoring the external (outside the organization) contacts of the internal people who have access to monetary value.

Clearly labeling and identifying the procedures and items that a fraudster could use to perpetrate fraud.

Training your people to think like a fraudster in the context of various schemes and scenarios involving cash.

Gaining an understanding of where people can create fraud in a process so you and your teams can catch them.

ALL OF THE PEOPLE in an organization are involved in the business processes that create monetary value (cash). Therefore, understanding the people who have direct access to the value of an organization (cash and cash equivalents) is the best fraud detection, deterrence, and prevention tool. There are management, sales, operating, and support processes (each run by people) to consider. Fraudsters need to understand all of the processes so they are able to get their hands on the cash and/or cash equivalents, and the organization has to be one step ahead of them. Which people are internally involved in the organization's processes and have access to monetary value?

Understand that procurement processes, bill payment, inventory (which can be sold and converted to cash), and payroll (payments to employees) can all be used as diversions and manipulations by fraudsters to create the cash to satisfy their needs. For example, during the process of bill payments for inventory not yet warehoused, the related inventory can be sold for cash. A fraudster will potentially pocket that cash if an organization does not put the proper safeguards in place. One such safeguard could be storing the inventory in a locked environment until it can be warehoused properly. But keep in mind that a fraudster needs to create only slight manipulations or distractions from the everyday business processes to commit fraud.

An organization needs to monitor the external contacts of the internal people in the cash and cash equivalent tree; this includes not only people outside the organization but also others in the organization in different departments. The list is large (Exhibit 7.1 shows a few), because cash is involved in all organizational processes:

- **Management personnel.** Board of directors, owners, CEOs, CFOs, and managers (all levels).
- **Sales personnel.** Sales managers, sales support personnel, cashiers, billing and accounts receivable clerks, collection managers and staff, credit approvers, customer service, controllers, marketing and advertising personnel, external customers, consultants, and professionals.
- **Operations personnel.** Operating managers, operating support personnel, accounts payable clerks, controllers, credit staff, purchasers, requisitioners, treasurers, warehouse workers, inventory personnel, engineers, research and development staff, computer personnel, external vendors, suppliers, service providers, consultants, and professionals.
- **Support personnel.** Administrators, accounting personnel, and maintenance people.

Train the people in your organization to think like a fraudster in the context of various schemes and scenarios by positioning them in the business processes that create cash. This is one way to begin developing a proactive approach to detecting, deterring, and preventing fraud. Make sure the people in your organization know what fraud looks like, since it may be right under their noses. It is important to have trust in an organization, and to do so, you need to have tests that ensure that you have the right people in place. Show people that you know how to catch fraud, reward ethical behavior, and punish unethical conduct.

Clearly label and identify the items and procedures that potential fraudsters can use in perpetrating a fraud (e.g., the controls). Make sure that people understand what the red flags and signs of fraud look like and that they are aware of the consequences of committing fraud. An organization must maintain open communication channels that enable people to feel comfortable reporting the red flags and signs (remember that tips are the number one way fraud is caught).

After you have clearly labeled and identified the red flag items, gain an understanding of where and how people can commit fraud in an organizational process. Develop the necessary proactive thinking to detect, deter, and prevent fraud. An organization must ensure that its personnel understand the consequences of their actions.

EXHIBIT 7.1   Personnel

ONE-MINUTE FRAUD MYSTERY: YANKEE PROPERTY MANAGEMENT

The Yankee Property Management Company receives monthly rents. Its collection policy states that rent is due on the 10th day of each month. On Monday, May 16, 2011, Deb Joint came in with a letter she had been sent stating that she has not paid May's rent. On the same date, Joint's neighbor, Charlie Good, came in with a similar letter. Yankee generates the letter on the eleventh day of the month if the rent has not been received and is distributed by the complex superintendents. The complex consists of eight separate buildings, totaling 320 units of one-, two-, and three-bedroom apartments.

The two tenants had handwritten receipts for paid rent, yet the automated system did not show their payments. They both indicated that they had paid the rent in cash. Joint lives in a one-bedroom apartment and pays $650 per month, and Good lives in a two-bedroom apartment and pays $750 per month. The receipts contained what appeared to be the signature of the receptionist, Jane Currency. Helen Sprint, the bookkeeper, quickly pulled up the ledger accounts in the collection department and found no cash deposits for rent in the specified period for Joint or Good.

Both tenants indicated that they had paid on the morning of Friday, May 6, and that they had given the cash to Darin Golf, the property's operations manager. Golf had told them to see Currency for a receipt. Sprint typically made up the deposits and gave them to Currency to deposit. The deposits were more frequent in the first few days of the month, which would not be unusual since most tenants paid early in order to avoid late charges and collection proceedings.

Golf was responsible for determining the appropriate collection procedures, which included litigation, if necessary, instituted by Johnny Civil, Yankee's general legal counsel (hired by Peter College, the property's owner). Initially, Golf had established a collection letter that Currency, the receptionist, would send if a tenant failed to pay the rent on time. At that time there were five pending collection matters, but Joint and Good were not included in the five.

Whenever late payments had occurred in the past, Golf had spoken to the tenants, and the matter had been resolved relatively quickly. You have been hired by College, the property owner, to investigate the rents. He believes there may have been higher than normal write-offs of rents. Furthermore, the rental income levels have declined by 10 percent, yet the property is fully occupied and has a waiting list of prospective tenants.

HANDLING CASH

No one pays attention to little frauds. The problem with this is that when little frauds are left to accumulate, they can cause even more damage than big frauds. Small frauds are easy to overlook, but if enough build up, they can destroy even the most sound organization. Remember what we said in Chapter 1 about mosquito bites versus shark attacks (see Exhibit 7.2).

Cash frauds are the hardest frauds to detect and can be the most difficult to prove. Do not let cash frauds, no matter how small, go unattended. Cash should be focused on, since all other areas in an organization's processes have to transact through cash or cash equivalents. If you follow the cash, your organization will be on its way to significantly reducing the potential for fraud. Cash frauds are seldom prosecuted and invite arbitrary and discriminatory enforcement.

EXHIBIT 7.2   Pay Attention to Even the Smallest Frauds

In order to really understand the cash process in an organization, we need to review some basic concepts, such as cash flow, or working capital (current assets minus current liabilities). By being aware of the working capital in the organization, we maintain control. Without working capital, an organization cannot continue to operate. Just look at any of the major frauds (such as Madoff or WorldCom) that were exposed when the cash dried up.

Organizations that fail to identify the people responsible for maintaining cash flows are exposed to fraud, which can ultimately lead to the organizations' extinction. The key component of working capital is the actual cash the organization has to demonstrate as sufficient capital with which to operate. Other items can be manipulated, but with cash, you either have it in your possession or you do not.

There are several manipulations a fraudster can make with cash in order to remain undetected. A fraudster will have to manipulate the organization's bank reconciliations and create bogus organizational cash balances. He or she will fail to disclose to the intended users of the information that the cash balances are controlled by others and were previously pledged as collateral for other loans.

The traditional thinking is that we can segregate responsibilities and use prenumbered receipts, checks, deposits, and other controls to prevent fraud in an organization. Such controls often fail not because of their design, but because people do not implement and oversee them properly. Define the key activities involving cash, such as how the organization generates it. Accounting ranks the balance sheet accounts in order of their ability to be liquidated into cash. An organization's cash is the common denominator of all of the processes within it, in some form, whether or not they are readily available.

Organizations need to maintain their daily cash and cash equivalents in order to maintain available short-term funding for their operations. In order for an organization to understand the people who have access to its value, it is important to discuss the sources and uses of cash: where it comes from and the timing of the receipt and payment of funds. Notice that we stay away from common terms like "paying bills" and "selling goods." These types of generic terms are for traditional recorders of transactions and follow GAAP. GAAP does not catch fraud, however; people who know what to look for do.

Changing our examination of sales from income to the source of the funds creates the necessary thinking to understand where fraud can exist. Income has been recorded for the purpose of forming the income statement or the statement of operations. All of these financial communications are for a specific period of time and are used primarily by those who have a financial interest in an organization. A statement of operations means nothing without confirming the sources and the uses of funds.

Cash comprises cash on hand or in an organization's bank accounts, demand deposits, and possibly a petty cash fund. Organizations also have cash equivalents that are short-term, highly liquid investments that are readily convertible to known amounts of cash and subject to another type of risk: changes in value. These types of short-term equivalents are typically certificates of deposits, money market accounts, and treasury bills that can be converted in 90 days or less.

It is essential to understand where and how to safeguard cash and ensure that the accounting records for cash do not allow anyone to override the internal controls over it. Review the people who control the cash receipts or inflow. Your organization cannot disburse money unless you receive money. For organizations to understand receipts, they need to classify them into activities. The first activity is cash receipts from operating activities (derived from the revenue stream sources of the organization). The information needed to determine these inflows is contained in the statement of earnings (or income statement).

The second activity that generates receipts is an investing activity, such as gains (or losses) from investments in the financial markets and operating subsidiaries. Similarly, changes result from investments in capital assets such as plant and equipment. The third activity is cash receipts from issuing stock or debt (loans). These categories will be utilized in cash disbursements (cash outflow).

The most important thing to consider when dealing with cash receipts is that the designated personnel are bonded (or insurable), so if a fraud was to occur, an organization would be covered by a dishonesty insurance policy. It is important to ask the following:

- When was the last time the control people had background checks performed?
- How often are these people trained?
- Are there senior executives who oversee the organizational process independently (e.g., auditors or internal auditors)?
- How often are the people in the cash receipts process tested? Are tests announced, or are they done on a surprise basis?

The typical internal control used for cash receipts transactions often includes designating specific personnel to handle and have access to the cash receipts. Organizations need to ensure that different individuals are assigned to various duties performed in the process of receiving cash, recording cash receipt transactions, and having custody over cash. The documents in the cash receipt process are sales invoices, remittance advices, cash register tapes, and deposit slips.

The cash should be secured in company safes and bank vaults with limited access to these areas. With the affordable cost of video cameras and the ability to monitor through the Internet from remote locations, organizations can now provide a strong deterrent. A recent newspaper article described how a workers' compensation fraud committed by a couple was exposed:

> Acting on an anonymous tip, agents with the U.S. Postal Service's Office of Inspector General went undercover for two months. They used video cameras to document the activities of the couple, who had claimed they could not work because sitting more than 15 minutes caused pain and swelling, records show. The agents followed the husband and wife either alone or together driving, gambling and mowing the lawn, among other activities.[1]

Frauds caught on camera offer strong evidence of intent, which is very difficult to prove when cash is involved.

Personnel who handle cash registers should provide customers with an over-the-counter receipt. Control of over-the-counter receipts is based on the fact that the cash registers are visible to the customers. A daily cash count and daily comparison of total receipts should be performed and signed by at least two parties (three parties, if there is a significant amount of cash). Do not allow multiple people to handle cash from the same point. Cash drawers need to be assigned on an individual basis. It is important to require all personnel who handle cash receipts to take vacations. Another important control is to institute job rotations within the process.

CASH DISBURSEMENT CONTROLS

The principal controls in dealing with cash disbursements are no different from the cash receipt controls previously discussed. Ensuring that the designated personnel are bonded is a necessary control. Another control is to perform background checks annually (not just when the employees are hired). You must train your employees on an ongoing basis. Have senior executives, auditors, internal auditors, and others test the process unannounced. Cash disbursements are an area of high concern for organizations, since there is direct access to value.

In most organizations, cash disbursements are created with a payment by check, rather than cash, except for incidental amounts that can be paid out of petty cash (for small and immaterial items that may arise when maintaining the flow of operations). Control features include assigning specific individuals to sign checks, with at least two signatures required. An organization will have different departments or individuals perform the duties of approving an item for payment and then actually processing the payment.

An organization's documents should maintain a prenumbering system (checks, invoices, deposit tickets, receiving tickets, petty cash vouchers, expense vouchers, and so on) and require detailed support, such as approved invoices or other documents signed by parties other than the party preparing the payment. The more significant the payment, the more signatures the organization should require.

All blank checks should be stored in a safe, and access should be restricted to authorized personnel. The organization should use a machine to imprint the amount on the check in indelible ink, with some unique marking that is not easily replicated. There should be a final cross-check that compares the check amount with the approved invoice before it is issued by the treasurer, who should be the final person to approve the check.

Personnel who have access to cash should be required to take vacations. During a person's vacation, it is a good idea to have an independent person performing the duties to see if there has been any manipulation. I have personally uncovered fraud when asked to monitor clients' cash receipt and disbursement processes.

Background checks should also be conducted with people who have access to cash (value). These background checks should be performed when the employees are hired and annually thereafter.

Organizations can implement a voucher system to further implement control over cash disbursements. A voucher system typically has multiple approvals by authorized individuals acting independently of the accounting process to ensure that all disbursements by check are proper. A voucher system includes the use of authorization forms that are often signed by managers in addition to the personnel who handle the daily processes and that are recorded by the accounting department in a voucher register.

Organizations typically establish a petty cash fund to pay relatively small amounts. The operation of this type of cash fund is referred to as an *impress system*, which involves establishing the cash fund in a separate account (petty cash), making payments from the separate cash fund, and then replenishing the fund. There are accounting entries to establish the cash fund, replenish the cash fund, and post amounts to the proper expense. The reimbursement is made only after the appropriate receipts and supports are provided. This is often an area of abuse since it is used for small amounts. Small amounts that are not monitored can lead to large amounts of fraud. Bonding (insuring) the personnel in charge of these cash funds, requiring vacations, rotating personnel, requiring at least two signatures, and conducting independent reviews that are unannounced are important fraud deterrents.

The bank still remains one of the best controls of cash because it is outside the organization. No matter what happens to the original documents, the bank will be able to re-create the original deposit tickets, checks, and any other transactions it processed, if necessary. The bank also minimizes the amount of currency that must be kept on hand and therefore contributes significantly to good internal control over cash. A check is a written order signed by the depositor directing the bank to pay a specified sum of money to a designated recipient and, once processed, is a permanent record. There are three parties associated with a check: the organization that issues the check, the bank from which the funds are drawn, and the person to whom the check is written.

The bank provides a statement that shows the checks paid, other debits charged against the account, deposits and additional credits made to the account, and the account balance after each day's transactions. These reflect all of the transactions that have been processed through the bank. This is where fraud can be visible, since the bank statement may be different from the organization's books and records. These differences may have legitimate reasons; they may be caused by timing errors or irregularities, but they may also be caused by fraud.

The bank debit memorandum that is included with the bank statement indicates charges to the organization's account, such as a bank service charge, the cost of printing checks, the cost of issuing travelers' checks, and charges for no sufficient funds (NSF check). The NSF check should send up a red flag and be investigated. With each statement, the bank will include a credit memorandum showing items like the collection of a note receivable for an organization by the bank.

The reconciling of the bank account is probably the most important process in the organization, and the third-party bank offers the best independent verification available (assuming that bank personnel are not involved in the fraud). The reconciliation of a bank account is necessary because the balance on the bank statement and balance on the organization's books are rarely in agreement. There may be timing differences, such as items on the bank statement that are not on the books (or vice versa), checks that were written on the books and have not yet cleared (outstanding checks), or deposits that were posted on the books but have not yet cleared (deposits in transit).

The bank reconciliation should be prepared by an employee who has no other responsibilities pertaining to cash. It should be someone who understands all of the transactions, applies professional skepticism, and is not there to simply balance the books. The reconciler is there to ensure that there is no fraud.

Since the bank is an independent third party, reconciling an organization's book balance to the bank's balance will ensure the accuracy of an organization's recorded amounts. The reconciliation will comprise two sections: the cash balance per the bank statement and the cash balance on the organization's books. The steps involved in the preparation of a bank reconciliation include determining what deposits were posted to the books and whether they were deposited in the bank (determine deposits in transit). After the deposits are reviewed, it must be determined what checks were written and posted to an organization's books that did not clear or get charged to the account at the bank.

The reconciler will have to see if the bank statement and the organization's books balance. If they do not reconcile, the bank may have other transactions that an organization's accounting records have not reflected, such as bank service charges or debit card transactions. Any amount the reconciler used in adjusting the cash balance in an organization's books to the bank should be recorded by the organization with the proper supports.

See Exhibit 7.3 on reconciling cash. How is the cash report communicated? Cash on hand, cash in banks, and petty cash are often combined and reported on the balance sheet as cash. Remember that cash is the most liquid asset, and the order of reporting is by liquidity; listed first in the current assets section under the title is cash and cash equivalents on the balance sheet.

 ## CASH AND FRAUD

Now that we know how cash works, where can fraud exist? Look at the funds arising from sales or services to customers. Where did you get the customers from? What percentage of your organization's total sales is derived from those customers? Are they related-party sales? GAAP-based thinking creates a different perspective because it focuses on debiting accounts receivables or cash (depending on whether a sale is in cash or on account) and creating sales when a sale or service takes place. People are often so busy counting the dollars and hitting their goals that they have no idea whom they do business with and who in the organization is responsible for safeguarding the recording process.

EXHIBIT 7.3 Reconciling Cash

Reconcile Cash	
Cash Balance per Bank Statement	**Cash Balance on the Organization's Books**
Correct Bank-Balance Adjustments	**Correct Adjustments to Organizational Records**
	Add: Notes and Receivables
Add: Deposits in Transit	Collected by the Bank
	Subtract: NSF (Bounced Checks)
Subtract: Outstanding Checks	**Subtract:** Service Charges
	Subtract: Debit Memos or Charges (Debit Card)
Add or Subtract: Bank Errors	**Add or Subtract:** Other Bank Items
Correct Balance	Correct Balance

Should Be Equal

The IRS requires the notification of cash deposits through the use of Form 8300. The IRS requires anyone who receives more than $10,000 while conducting his or her trade or business to file Form 8300. The receipt of $10,000 may occur in a single transaction or as a series of related transactions. The same form must also be filed if the cash payments received in a 12-month period total more than $10,000. What people in your organization maintain these filing requirements and ensure that the organization is in compliance?

The IRS defines these transactions as transfers of cash. Included under this requirement are sales of goods, services, real or intangible property, rentals of goods or real or personal property, cash exchanges for other cash, establishments, maintenance or contributions to a trust or an escrow account, loan repayments, and conversions of cash to a negotiable instrument such as a check or a bond. Does your organization receive cash, and where? Does it accumulate more than $10,000 from a client in a related transaction within a 12-month period?

We may be so busy applying GAAP that other regulations slip under the radar. The Form 8300 regulation is very interesting for wholesalers, who may require cash as part of discounts and other special arrangements. Based on my experience, I am sure that many organizations are not even aware of the Form

8300 rule and are most likely not adhering to it, because until there is an audit or a fraud is exposed, no interest has been created. The other reason that the Form 8300 rule may not be followed is that with the advance of technology, cash transactions are becoming rarer and rarer in the business world.

Cash from sales or a provided service must come into a company in some manner. If you follow the cash, then you can detect, deter, and prevent fraud. Keep in mind that accounting is a double entry system—that is, for every debit you make, a corresponding credit of equal value must follow.

The fraud triangle discussed in Chapter 1 is applicable to all international companies. Fraud is international; it occurs everywhere. Some recent major international frauds occurred at Parmalat (Italy), Royal Ahold (the Netherlands), and Satyam Computer Services (India). Any organization, whether public, private, domestic, or international, needs 800-pound friendly gorillas to deter, detect, and prevent fraud.

The following information was determined by the PricewaterhouseCoopers' Global Economic Crime Survey of 2005:

■ Rising economic crime poses a growing threat to companies, with nearly half of all organizations worldwide being victims of fraud in a recent two-year period. Specifically, 44 percent of the remaining companies surveyed experienced fraud in the past two years.

■ Globally, the number of companies reporting fraud increased from 37 percent in 2003 to 45 percent in 2005. The loss to companies was, on average, $1.7 million from "tangible frauds"—that is, those resulting in an immediate and direct financial loss. These included asset misappropriations, false pretenses, and counterfeiting.

Accounting scandals, both in the United States and internationally, have reignited the debate over the relative merits of GAAP (rules-based approach) versus IFRS (principles-based approach). The FASB announced that it intends to introduce more principles-based standards.

In the next section on fraud schemes and scams, think about the FAGAAPA (see Chapter 2) with each example and evaluate each fraud by determining the level of risk in the organizational process featured.

It is recommended to use the contingent liability accounting standards of *probable* (a 50 percent or more chance that fraud exists), *reasonably possible* (a 1 to 49 percent chance that fraud exists), and *remote* (a 0 percent chance that fraud exists). The next step is to identify who the people in the processes are. After that, a close examination of the organization's existing controls must be made.

When the examination of the controls is complete, a determination has to be made about the effectiveness of the controls. The final assessment involves determining the materiality of the fraud. The standard (probable, reasonably possible, or remote) determines the appropriate level of investigation. Every organization needs to develop a zero-tolerance policy toward fraud to be effective in detecting, deterring, and preventing it.

 ## CLASSIFICATIONS OF CASH AND CASH-EQUIVALENT FRAUD SCHEMES AND SCENARIOS

There are a number of classifications of fraud schemes and scenarios, each of which is detailed in this section:

- Accounts receivable valuation (bad debt valuation and write-off) scam
- Lapping of receivables
- Register schemes
- Recording less than received
- Fraudulent or unauthorized discounts
- Kiting (float) scam
- Fictitious sales
- Sales return scam
- Outright theft
- Stealing deposits
- Stealing cash on hand
- Forging checks
- Outstanding check scam
- Voided check scam
- Theft through sales promotions
- Vendor or creditor's "finance your purchase" scam

The Accounts Receivable Valuation (Bad Debt Valuation and Write-Off) Scam

An article in the October 4, 2004, issue of *CPA Journal* about the HealthSouth (a rehabilitation provider) fraud stated that the PricewaterhouseCoopers forensic audit indicated that the company's cumulative earnings were overstated by anywhere from $3.8 billion to $4.6 billion.[2] The forensic audit discovered at least another $1.3 billion in suspect financial reporting in addition to the previously estimated $2.5 billion that HealthSouth acknowledged. The after-the-fact report found an additional fraud of $500 million and identified at least $800 million of improper accounting for reserves, executive bonuses, and related-party transactions.

The receivable-related activities that were reflected in the financial statements contained a relatively large percentage of receivables estimated as uncollectible. This is not surprising, given an industry that is dependent on reimbursements by third parties, such as Medicare and insurance companies (which are always changing). The annual write-offs for uncollectible receivables that were maintained showed no consistency whatsoever. The accounts written off did not match the allowance that was established:

> A memo, dated November 1998, was apparently written by an anonymous HealthSouth shareholder and sent to auditor Ernst & Young. In it, the shareholder alerts the audit firm to alleged bookkeeping violations at the rehabilitation-services company. Reportedly HealthSouth's top lawyer assured its independent auditor that it would conduct an internal investigation of the allegations.[3]

This situation involves the tone at the top. Most receivables transactions result in an exchange in which a seller provides goods and services to a buyer on credit. The sale price is the amount due from the customer. Typically, there is an invoice. Receivables represent claims on customers for some monetary consideration.

Since the organization has not received the cash, it is exposed to a potential write-off if the funds are not collected. Any uncollectible accounts receivable will result in a loss of revenue that requires an adjusting journal entry to the asset's account receivables, which will need to be credited since reductions to asset accounts require a credit to be reduced. This concept refers back to the basic accounting formula, assets minus liabilities equals equity; a decrease in income because of the reduction of revenue ultimately reduces the stockholders' equity. Accounts receivable is decreased by the recording of a bad debt expense or the established accounts receivable becoming uncollectible.

There are two methods of accounting for and recording uncollectible receivables: the direct write-off method and the allowance method.

The Direct Write-Off Method

The direct write-off method does not apply the matching principle, in which expenses are matched to revenues in the same period. This situation creates the fraudster's opportunity to commit fraud. The fraudster merely has to create the perception that the account is uncollectible. The organization writes it off, and no one deems it to be material, so the company takes the reduction to net income. The fraudster is then able to collect the debit directly from the customer (if he or she has not done so already) and walk away with the organizational value.

GAAP states that this method should be used only if the amount recorded as bad debt expense is immaterial. The determination of immateriality is based on peoples' judgment, so make sure the 800-pound friendly gorilla is watching. The defined value for immateriality varies from organization to organization, depending on its net worth or value of receivables. The rationalization may be that if an organization's accounts receivables are in the hundreds of millions, then what is a couple of hundred thousand? Organizations cannot allow this type of thinking to exist.

The Allowance Method

The allowance method is more in line with GAAP, and companies that have material amounts in accounts receivables should use this method. The organization determines the percentage of receivables that will be uncollectible, usually by analyzing historical trends, industry statistics, and market conditions, which are based on judgment. The fraudster loves estimates and hypotheticals. In order to prevent a fraudster from reducing the profits when accounts are written off that should not be, organizations must be aware of those who are monitoring the creditworthiness of their customers.

The allowance method follows two approaches: the balance sheet approach and the income statement approach. The goal is to value an organization's receivables at their future collectible values:

- The balance sheet approach's objective is to reflect an accurate estimate of the net realizable value (NRV). Usually this method is applied based on an aging schedule, using different percentages for the various age categories.
- The income statement approach is also called the percentage-of-sales approach and is considered a more accurate approach in applying the matching principle. When this method is used, the balance in the allowance account is not taken into consideration with respect to the calculation of the current year's allowance, since it is a year-in, year-out computation that creates an opportunity for the fraudster.
- We must understand the NRV of accounts receivables, which is the amount that an organization expects to convert into cash through collections. If a company has $10,000 gross accounts receivables and one customer owes $2,000, which is deemed uncollectible, then the NRV would equal (or "net out" to) $8,000 ($10,000 gross minus the $2,000 uncollectible receivable).

Bad debts are accounts receivables that are likely to remain uncollectible and will be written off and appear on the income statement as bad debt expenses, reducing the organization's net income. A fraudster knows that as part of the process of estimating earnings, an organization needs to make an estimate (based on past records) of bad debt expenses that might be incurred in the current period. Most organizations establish a contra-asset account called a *bad debt allowance*, since it is not likely that all of their customers will pay their debts in full.

To create the necessary deflection, the fraudster will need to increase the percentage of sales to be written off or accounts deemed to be uncollectible. This can be done with or without the client knowing what the fraudster is doing. The most likely scenario of fraud in regard to cash is that a customer will be involved, such as by paying a discounted amount to the fraudster. A customer who is receiving a benefit from a fraud is not going to call attention to a fraud. The taking of payment from a legitimate client would be flagged when the receivables are checked at year's end by an auditor's confirmation process or when a client receives a request for a balance owed that was paid already.

An organization knows it has large uncollectible accounts, but it does not want to reduce its revenues and ultimately its net income. This is most likely to occur when the expected results from the external parties are not being met. If an amount has been written off and then is partly recovered, this is another way a fraudster can conceal a fraud, since this requires another journal entry to be accounted for. A fraudster can collect the recovered portion of the bad debt directly from a customer and never make the adjusting entry in the organization's books to show the payment was received, instead just keeping the money (value) for himself or herself.

Walter Pavlo Jr. and Neil Weinberg's book about the MCI WorldCom fraud, *Stolen without a Gun*, presents an example of using an outside customer.[4] In this case, external telecom wholesalers were used to embezzle funds from MCI WorldCom through a web of false accounting entries, bogus companies, and offshore accounts for collections. Pavlo, a senior manager at MCI WorldCom, took full responsibility for his actions and spent two years in prison for the embezzlement of $6 million from MCI.

The way in which Pavlo and his partners perpetrated the crime was by manipulating the collections on the books. MCI WorldCom would keep a receivable on its books long after the account was deemed uncollectible. MCI World-Com had the help of banks, which were eager for high interest and fees, to finance it all.[5] Organizational neglect enabled Pavlo to take high-flying trips to the Cayman Islands, experience high gala organizational entertainment, go to golf events, get luxury hotel accommodations, and live a fast-lane lifestyle— that is, until the whole organization came crumbling down.

Frauds involving the use of allowance accounts can occur in any organization, including municipal government. Following is an additional example to show how a simple manipulation of an estimated uncollectible receivable can artificially create a surplus or excess cash. As a local budget is developed by a township, the need to estimate the amount of taxes it will collect is necessary, and a resulting contra-asset account is set up for uncollectible property taxes. The estimated uncollectible rate can be highly subjective, and local officials are able to manipulate the collection amount in order to achieve highly variable results in the budget. If an estimate is slightly manipulated lower, it may result in an increase in the tax collection and artificially create a surplus or excess cash. The higher reserves create a potentially higher tax rate that is ultimately passed on to the taxpayer. Positioning the 800-pound friendly gorillas at the point where the contra-asset account will be set up will help to deter, detect, and prevent fraud at the point where the opportunity for fraud exists.

Organizations must follow all of GAAP, especially the principles that involve judgment. Knowing what the industry trends are may not always tell the real numbers story. Be sure you apply the proper principles when bad debt expenses are being applied in an organization, and have an independent check system in place. A debt becomes worthless when the surrounding facts and circumstances indicate that there is no reasonable expectation of payment. The IRS says the following:

> To show that a debt is worthless, you must establish that you have taken reasonable steps to collect the debt. It is not necessary to go to court if you can show that a judgment from the court would be uncollectible. You may take the deduction only in the year the debt becomes worthless. You do not have to wait until a debt is due to determine whether it is worthless.[6]

Organizations should not convert current receivables into long-term debt. They should do the following:

- Examine the receivables and maintain well-documented files.
- Know their customers before they do business with them so that the organizations do not end up with uncollectible receivables.
- Know the people in the process who approve credit and deem an account uncollectible.
- Make sure that the reporting function of bad debt is separate from the personnel who deem the accounts uncollectible and that the personnel recording the transactions maintain detailed documents.

- Ensure that the personnel who deem accounts receivable as uncollectible have high moral character and that the appropriate level of management is involved.
- Be sure the auditor and external parties perform an independent review (send third-party verifications and communications).
- Watch the internal and external individual relationships.
- Look for any unexplained lifestyle changes.
- Examine trends and changes in the accounts receivables on a daily basis.

Organizations must maintain these proactive approaches to detect, deter, and prevent fraud.

The Lapping of Receivables

The lapping of receivables involves the siphoning off of the accounts receivables in the current assets section of a balance sheet (financial communication). The way to prevent it involves identifying, recording, and communicating. Examine the people who might be involved in the scheme by analyzing the following necessary steps:

1. Examine the people who receive the value (payments). Specifically, look at the employees who open the mail and those who receive checks by other means.
2. Look at the people who make the deposits. When was the last time you did an updated background or credit check on them?
3. Examine the employees who are recording the transactions. Is this done independently of the actual receipt of the value?
4. Examine the people who reconcile the accounts and verify that the third-party bank received the funds. Are these people experienced and independent of the value?
5. Examine your external relations, such as those with the customers (send random confirmation test samples) and the banks (what safeguards do they offer?).

This scheme involves cash that is intended as payment for a receivable but which is stolen and replaced by the next payment received. The first receivable collected is used to cover the fraudster's acts, whereas the second receivable collected is recorded to satisfy the original receivable so the fraudster can remain undetected. This pattern repeats for the third receivable in relation to the second, and so on.

This scheme may be compared to a Ponzi scheme, which pays returns to its investors from their own money or from the money paid by subsequent investors, rather than from profit earned by an individual or organization running an operation. Robbing Peter to pay Paul works only until the cash dries up and there are no more Peters to rob.

Monitoring cash flows is essential. Also make sure that the people with access to the cash are subject to independent checks. Segregation of duties without independent checks in itself will not detect, deter, or prevent fraud. Watch the cash and do not be fooled by the accruals. Follow the value throughout the entire process. For each engagement you undertake, draw a mental picture of the process. Look at all of the potential fraudsters in Exhibit 7.4 and draw the connections between the people and the value.

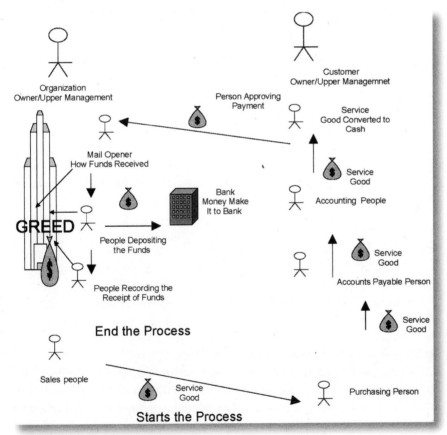

EXHIBIT 7.4 People and Value

As you can see, the value exchange occurs when an organization sells goods or performs services for a customer. The value is not exchanged back to the organization until the customer converts the organization's goods or services into cash by making a payment. Once the goods or services are converted to cash and given back to the organization, the organization needs to focus on protecting the value from a lapping of receivables. The word *greed* in the diagram exposes the organization's process, where the people and the value meet, and where the exposure for fraud exists.

Register Schemes

Register schemes (or skimming, the removal or concealing of cash before the receipt is recorded) are created by the fraudster's thinking of "a dollar for me and a dollar for the organization." When cash is involved, it is very difficult to catch the fraudster and prove intent. Two principle schemes in this category are false refunds and false voids.

1. **False refunds** are fictitious refunds; no merchandise is actually being returned, which results in the overstatement of inventory.
2. **False voids** are overstated refunds; a legitimate refund is overstated, and the excess voided amount is skimmed.

The false-refund fraudster typically performs one of these actions: diverting the credit refunds to a third-party account, which receives a kickback for a portion of the refund, or diverting the refund directly to the fraudster's own account.

A fraudster using false voids makes the sale and keeps the customer's receipt. Later, after the customer is gone, the fraudster uses the receipt to process a false void. The fraudster may need a manager to sign off but can take care of that by forging the manager's signature. The fraudster can use a rubber stamp for voids or can con the manager into believing that it is a legitimate void. The fraudster then takes the money. The opportunity to remain undetected is present, along with a low level of review for multiple transactions. The fraudster has the ability to destroy the transaction, and this works because the typical rationalization of the organization is to not look for fraud.

Organizations must know how a fraudster thinks and must examine any trends in which employees are processing too many reversals. The organization must continually examine refunds and voids in recurring amounts, especially ones that are in round numbers. Are the excessive refunds or voids just below the required levels of review and the person who addresses them? There are many algorithms that can be used to detect patterns in returns and voids, and they should be utilized. These are examples of steps in an algorithm:

- Maintaining a red flag system for multiple refunds for the same merchandise and for refunds or voids with no corresponding sale.
- Requiring management approval for all refunds or voids.
- Having cameras and a visual management presence at the cash registers.
- Restricting access to the control key that authorizes reversing entries.
- Not allowing cashiers to reverse their own sales.
- Keeping journals of all voids and refunds.
- Having a different log-in code for each cashier.
- Requiring a copy of the customer's receipt for any reversal.
- Having someone independent of the cashiers prepare the register count sheets, observe the inventory, and use the perpetual inventory system.

These rules should be followed if an organization wants to detect, deter, and prevent fraud. An organization should also clearly communicate to its customers that they should closely examine their receipts. This could be encouraged by establishing a rule that if the customer does not get a receipt, the purchase is free. Refunds should not be granted without receipts. The organization should make random calls to its customers, inquiring if they are satisfied, why they returned merchandise, and what could have been done better.

Recording Less Than Received

Recording less than received means reducing revenues, which results in less net income. The scam is to alter the sales invoice by recording a lower figure so the amount skimmed remains undetected. This takes place at the point of receiving the cash. The first step in solving it is to identify the transaction and the parties responsible for recording the transaction. Include an analysis of all of the people in the process.

Identify the person who originated the transaction. Since it is a sale, start with the salesperson who made the sale, then follow the process to the creation of the sales invoice and find out who was responsible for creating it. The sales invoice has to be given to the customer, who takes it and ultimately remits the payment to the organization.

Once the payment has been received by the organization, identify the person who received it. Determine if the deposit is made by the same person or a different one. Once the deposit has been made, is it reported by the person

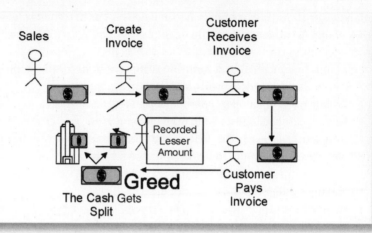

EXHIBIT 7.5   Cash Process

who received the money, the person who deposited the money, or someone different?

Let's look at a simple diagram and identify the people in a process. Exhibit 7.5 shows the personnel in an organizational process. The same person receives the cash and records the cash. Where does the value not make it onto the organization's books? This particular scenario is off the books, making the fraud difficult to catch.

The appropriate actions are to separate the various responsibilities relating to cash, make third-party verification requests to see how much money the customer has sent, observe any changes in the lifestyle of the person of interest, and look for unusual and unexplainable fluctuations in the recorded numbers. It is important to update background changes and monitor any relationships in the process. Organizations should also institute job rotations, mandatory vacations, bondings (dishonesty insurance policies), exit interviews, and unannounced process reviews.

Fraudulent or Unauthorized Discounts

In this scheme, the fraudster makes discount entries on the books and skims the proceeds. An example of this scam would be a fraudster selling goods at full price to a customer, recording the sale at the discounted price on the organization's books, and the skimming the discount. In one scenario, a fraudster discounts an invoice and claims that he or she did it to match a competitor's price. But instead the customer paid the full price, and the fraudster kept the amount discounted.

Another example is a retailer that allows its cashiers to apply discounts to sales without a manager's approval. A fraudster can make a large purchase, receive an improper discount at the register, return a portion of the discount to the employee in cash, and keep the rest. This is why most retailers have 800-pound friendly gorilla protocols in place where managers are frequently called to the register for approval on discounts. Do not forget that 800-pound friendly gorillas need to watch the managers as well.

In both examples, we should look for odd entries and unusual fluctuations posted in the sales discount account in the general ledger.

The Kiting (Float) Scam

Kiting is the process in which separate but related items are grouped together. Check kiting, the most common type, uses float-time to make use of nonexistent funds in a checking (or other bank) account and is considered a form of check fraud. *Float-time* is the amount of time it takes for a check to clear; today most checks are cleared in one day. In check kiting, a check is written from one account for an amount higher than the account balance; then a second check is written from a different account and deposited in the first account to cover the insufficient funds. The purpose of check kiting is to increase the balance of a checking account in order to allow checks that would otherwise bounce to be cleared by the bank. A fraudster would need multiple accounts and a good relationship with a bank to perpetrate this scam.

Another kind of kiting is the process in which separate but related items are grouped, packaged, and supplied as a unit. Think of how fraudsters could manipulate this with computers or goods. The average person would not be aware of the component parts that went into the goods.

For example, does a person buying a computer really know whether the represented components are inside the computer? Are they counterfeit parts? A fraudster would have to be involved in the assembly of the machine and could sell the high-end components and substitute the counterfeit parts. This could be done without upper management's knowledge of the fraud or without anyone normally involved in the assembly process.

It could be done in the manufacturing, purchasing, shipping, or receiving department of a retailer. A scam in the purchasing or receiving department would most likely require the involvement of the vendor or supplier.

Fictitious Sales

In fictitious sales, a fraudster creates counterfeit sales that are recorded as fake accounts receivables, which are eventually written off. The fraudster recognizes revenue in the current period to inflate the sales, and then later he or she writes the sales off in another recording period. This is as simple as crediting sales and debiting accounts receivable in the general ledger. The fraudster's intent is that the sale will never be collected. The fraudster simply debits the bad debt expense and credits the allowance for uncollectible accounts to cover his tracks. Eventually, the account is deemed fully uncollectible, and the allowance for the doubtful account is debited and the accounts receivable is credited. Remember that most accounting frauds are very simple, yet you still need to think outside the box in order to be an effective fraud detector.

The fraudster can send a customer more goods than ordered in a recording period to inflate revenue. When the customer realizes that he or she has received more goods than was ordered and returns the unwanted merchandise, revenue is reduced in a later accounting period, thus allowing the fraudster to continue to remain undetected.

The fraud examiner should determine whether returned goods are present when doing inventory. The examiner should compare sales returns to total sales and look for unusual fluctuations and variances. He or she should visit the organization's customers and obtain their purchase orders and compare them to the organization's related shipping and sales documents.

You should begin your investigation in the sales department where employees create sales orders and determine shipping quantities. When the fraudster inflates sales, he or she uses the sales revenue account in the income statement and the allowance for sales returns account on the balance sheet. The fraudster is using long-term future profitability to generate short-term profits. The increased allowance for sales returns will remain on the balance sheet and reduce income in later periods.

Putting an unsuspecting 800-pound friendly gorilla, such as the computer maintenance person, in the department, who is responsible for collecting the uncollectible debt accounts, and having that person keep his or her eyes and ears open is a simple way to deter, detect, and prevent fraud. Remember, TIPS are the number one way fraud is exposed. Half of being successful in determining fraud is being there.

The Sales Return Scam

In the sales return scam, returned goods are never sent back to the inventory but instead are sold by a fraudster. With fictitious sales, the goods are brought back to the organization. In the sales return scam, the fraudster never returns the goods back to inventory.

Many merchandisers actually destroy return products. They assume that the products cannot be resold efficiently, and they do not want to discount the products, which might deflate the brand name. This is more common in the apparel industry where used clothes or shoes might not resell. An employee might see the return products as waste and think that he or she is not hurting anyone by taking the products marked for destruction.

Eight-hundred-pound friendly gorillas need to observe the inventory accounts and look for returned goods to ensure that they are properly accounted for. They need to segregate the returned goods from the normal inventory and make a determination of the whether the returns are not resellable. Also, a review of the sales returns and allowances should be performed for unusual postings and fluctuations. A periodic unannounced physical inventory inspection is necessary since the fraudster will likely have falsified accounting documents and have a planned explanation if questioned.

Outright Theft

In outright theft, a fraudster just takes an organization's assets. Any outright theft or stealing is the most difficult to prevent. The only solution is to put 800-pound friendly gorillas at the points where theft can occur. Using surveillance cameras and locks and securing areas with 800-pound friendly gorillas who are watching are the best safeguard of organizational assets.

The temptation always exists when people meet value in a company, and opportunity is often present. After all, my definition of luck is "opportunity meets preparedness." Managers who have keys to the shop, or warehouse personnel who have little oversight, might manipulate situations to access cash or merchandise, or they may find themselves in an opportunistic situation where they decide not to resist the temptation (when 800-pound friendly gorillas are not watching). When they can isolate themselves, it is always easier for people in the organization to commit fraud alone. Once they solicit a co-conspirator, the odds of them getting caught greatly increase.

Eight-hundred-pound friendly gorillas create redundancy and overlap in operations. This enables the organization to use the people in the process to maintain the control as one responsibility overlaps with another. This scenario makes it difficult for fraudsters to isolate themselves and get away with thefts.

Stealing Deposits

A fraudster steals the deposits before they are taken to the bank. The accounting records are then manipulated or the deposits are never recorded at all on an organization's books. Here you have a classic violation of the segregation of duties within the internal controls. The fraudster has the ability to take the physical asset and also has control over the accounting recording process. Make sure your 800-pound friendly gorillas identify conflicting responsibilities that may allow your people to steal organizational assets. If the organization does not think its people can and/or will steal, then that organization is exposed to fraud risk.

Stealing Cash on Hand

A fraudster steals cash on hand by taking petty cash or by other means. The fraudster manipulates the accounting records or doesn't attempt to cover up the theft at all. The fraudster prevents getting caught by making up bogus receipts and supports to cover his or her tracks. When cash is involved, 800-pound friendly gorillas need to monitor closely by having sound procedures and policies in place. Organizations should utilize receipt inspection and documentation verification to minimize their fraud risk involving unsuspecting cash accounts.

One of the least likely fraud schemes that a fraudster can get away with is when a local manager of a retail outlet fails to make a bank deposit drop. People, whether out of necessity or just plain greed, sometimes resort to stealing money. What do they say to cover up the theft? Someone robbed me? I lost it? Holes can be poked in both stories to uncover fraud.

I had a situation where a friend who managed an establishment called me very distraught. He had misplaced $20,000 cash. We retraced his steps and the money was nowhere to be found. Further investigation of his closing routine showed us that he was a predictable and easy target because his routine was the same every night.

A few months later, he was closing the store at night following his usual routine, but this time, he had an unsuspecting 800-pound friendly gorilla watching him closely (one of his employees). Sure enough, a trusted friend who was in the shop during the closing process caused a diversion, and a second trusted friend stole the cash. In order to prove that someone actually stole something, it is often necessary to catch the party in the act. In our case, we had an unsuspecting 800-pound friendly gorilla employee watching. The manager's credibility was restored, and his fraudster friends had to pay him back the $20,000 they had stolen. When dealing with cash, do not be predictable unless you have an 800-pound friendly gorilla watching.

Forging Checks

A forged check is a check on which the payer's signature is either forged or unauthorized. With a forged check, the bank pays the payee, who is most likely the fraudster. The fraudster may have altered the accounting records by posting the check in the name of a vendor, supplier, or service provider that an organization does business with. A counterfeit check, which could be thought of in terms of a counterfeit ID, is regarded as the equivalent of a forged check. An unauthorized signature is one that is not recognized by the financial institution. It could also be a violation of a multisignature policy.

Organizations must use multiple signatures on checks to prevent forgery. With electronic signatures, rubber-stamp signatures, and electronic checks, 800-pound friendly gorillas must be well positioned to ensure that these controls are not overridden to commit fraud.

The Outstanding Check Scam

In the outstanding check scam, a fraudster makes a check payable to him- or herself or to an accomplice, and it remains on the outstanding check list in the bank reconciliation in the name of a typical vendor, supplier, or service provider. The fraudster then increases the amount of a check that previously cleared by the amount of the fraudulent check. The most likely check the fraudster would increase would be that of a vendor or supplier with whom the organization spends a substantial amount of money. Exhibit 7.6 shows a bank reconciliation without fraud and bank reconciliation with an outstanding check scam.

EXHIBIT 7.6 Outstanding Check Scam (O/Checks)

Bank Reconciliation with No Fraud

Bank		Book	
Bank Balance	$ 1,000	Beginning Book Balance	$1,000
Less: O/Checks		Add: Cash Receipts	—
Check #1 (Legitimate Named Disbursement Outstanding)	100	Less: Cash Disbursement	100
Adjusted Bank Balance	$ 900	Ending Book Balance	$ 900

Bank Reconciliation with Fraud

Bank		Book	
Bank Balance	$ 1,000	Beginning Book Balance	$1,000
Less: O/Checks		Add: Cash Receipts	—
Check #1 Legitimate Vendor Check Outstanding	$100***	Less: Cash Disbursement	100
Add to Check #1 Legitimate $100	$100***	Less: Fraudster Check Cleared Bank	100

(Continued)

Bank Reconciliation with No Fraud			
Bank		**Book**	
Check #1 Legitimate Vendor Named	$ 200***		
(Disbursement Fraudulently Increases)			
Adjusted Bank Balance	$ 800	Ending Book Balance	$ 800

*** The fraudster voids check #1 (the vendor's outstanding check) to cover up the fraudster check that cleared and is not reflected on the books.

The Voided Check Scam

The voided check scam is generally the same concept as the outstanding check scam. However, in this situation, the check that was written to the fraudster is voided (destroyed), and the amounts are added to other vendors, suppliers, or service providers that do business with the organization. Exhibit 7.7 shows bank reconciliation without fraud and bank reconciliation with a voided check scam.

Theft through Sales Promotions

In theft through sales promotions, a fraudster sells items to him- or herself under a different name at a reduced price to gain the benefit of the promotion and then sells the item for full value at a later date. Sales promotions are supposed to benefit the customers. Organizations typically use sales promotions to generate traffic into their stores or to buy more products by making items available at cost or below cost. The 800-pound friendly gorillas need to monitor these special promotions so that the promotional items are given to existing customers and used to gain new ones. The organization needs to ensure that its establish sound promotion policies and procedures.

The organization should monitor sales to determine whether they increased as a result of the promotion, or if the promotion met the design objectives by the offering, which could be name recognition or other sales development objectives.

The Vendor or Creditor's "Finance Your Purchase" Scam

The fraudster runs up large bills for sellable goods and items or convinces a vendor or a creditor to finance the purchase with the intention of never paying him or her back. Vendors are no different than anyone extending credit.

EXHIBIT 7.7 Voided Check Scam

Bank		Book	
Bank Balance	$ 1,000	Beginning Book Balance	$ 1,000
Less: O/Checks		Add: Cash Receipts	—
Check #1 (Legitimate Named Disbursement Outstanding)	100	Less: Cash Disbursement	100
Adjusted Bank Balance	$ 900	Ending Book Balance	$ 900

Bank Reconciliation with Fraud

Bank Balance	$ 1,000	Beginning Book Balance	$ 1,000
Less: O/Checks		Add: Cash Receipts	—
Check #1 Legitimate Vendor Check Outstanding	(100)***	Less: Cash Disbursement	(100)
Add Check #1 Legitimate Vendor		Add Check #1 Legitimate Vendor	
Voided and Removed by the Fraudster	100***	Voided and Removed by the Fraudster	100
Less: Fraudster Check That Cleared	(100)***	Less: Fraudster Check That Cleared	(100)
Adjusted Bank Balance	$ 900	Ending Book Balance	$ 900

*** The fraudster had to void Check #1, vendor from outstanding check, to cover up the fraudster check that cleared and is not reflected on the books.

Vendors are classified as accounts payable or a current liability and have the expectation of being paid in typically in 30 days. Unpaid vendors provide the fraudster with a financing opportunity to sell the goods to unsuspecting good faith parties outside the organization.

A common tool that can be put in place with accounts receivable is what we call "cross receivable analysis." In this case, we examine a payable, but the analysis is the same whether we look at a receivable or a payable. The examiner should look at any payables after 60 days. The examiner takes the total of the payables owed beyond 60 days and determines what percentage of the payables that number represents. If it is high and the organization is still able to make purchases, a red flag should be raised. An example would be when a customer buys goods from a vendor and the corresponding accounts payable schedule reads: in the 0 to 30 day column, the organization owes a $1,000; in the

31 to 60 day column, the organization owes $2,000; in the column 61 days and over, the organization owes $8,000; for a total owed to the vendor of $11,000. This means that 80 percent of the accounts payable are over 60 days past due yet the vendor is still selling goods to the organization. This raises a red flag and the situation should be investigated because most vendors would have put the organization's account into collections and would not do any business with the organization until the account was current (paid up to date).

Be wary when working with troubled or failing organizations since the general consensus can be that the organization will go under, so the tone of its employees is often less than ethical.

 ## FRAUD CONTROL POINTS IN THE ORGANIZATIONAL PROCESS

There are control points throughout an organizational process where you can check the ins and outs of the work being done. The three main control points are as follows:

1. **Before reaching an organization**. This type of fraud would be outright theft with no recording. Received funds never make it to an organization.
2. **Within an organization.** The funds for goods and services are received by an organization and are recorded on its books but are manipulated to benefit a fraudster.
3. **When leaving an organization.** This includes fictitious sales.

To ensure proper control and oversight (the 800-pound friendly gorilla is watching), you can do the following:

Conduct background checks on new employees, existing employees, and customers. Check references and employment dates and make sure that any time gaps in a person's resume are accounted for. Look for any changes in behavior with new employees. Have employees with access to cash or other financial functions bonded by obtaining a fidelity bond, which is available through insurance brokers.

Review all bank and credit card statements that are being recorded by trusted high-level employees. These high-level people should open sealed statements (as well as other important mail) and review them before sending them to the accounting (bookkeeping) department to be reconciled. Make sure the original sales invoices and necessary documentation exist and have the proper authorizations.

Reconcile accounts receivables on a monthly basis. Require all exceptions to be cleared by the appropriate personnel. Ensure that the assigned personnel cannot override the controls. Watch the journal entries being made. Look for intercompany and related-party transactions. Concentrate on sales. Every customer account should be examined.

Verify and monitor changes made to customer names, addresses, and federal tax identification numbers. Check with agencies (such as the Better Business Bureau) and monitor their financial strength and condition as well. Frequent gifts and lunches with personnel in the organization and the customers should be monitored. Ensure that no related-party sales exist without proper disclosure.

Restrict authorization and access to the sales process. Maintain the appropriate trust level with employees to oversee the process. Who is monitored to ensure that trust is still viable? Make sure that password-protected computer files and the appropriate dollar limits on monetary authorizations are in place. Institute a regular change-password policy for computers and delete the passwords of former employees.

Insist that all employees who are working in the accounting, cash-handling, and value areas of an organization take their allotted vacation time. While they are on vacation, have their work reviewed. Have a policy to cross-train employees so they can perform one another's duties when necessary. Have job rotation days, when people switch roles for a week, preferably unannounced,

This is the 800-pound friendly gorilla approach.

 ## SUMMARY

Know who in the organization has the ability to access the cash and/or cash equivalents. Put the proper tests into your systems to see whether you have real fraud risk with the employees in key trusted areas regarding cash. You must think like a fraudster, if you are going to detect, deter, and prevent fraud from occurring in your organization, by showing your people that the 800-pound friendly gorilla is always watching.

An organization must treat each dollar as material. Just as a little crack in the windshield of a car keeps growing unless it is attended to, little abuses

In contrast to the shark, the mosquito bite
may not be noticed.

EXHIBIT 7.8 Small Frauds Can Magnify

will grow into big ones if left unaddressed. Remember the mosquito bite. It may be so small you don't even notice it, but it can cause a lot of damage (see Exhibit 7.8).

 ## ONE-MINUTE FRAUD MYSTERY ANALYSIS

Did you establish where the greed exists in this chapter's one-minute fraud mystery? Remember, you are the fact finder and need to think divergently. Here are some of my thoughts on this chapter's mystery, based on my experience in the field:

- **Allegation.** The rent money appears to be skimmed. There is also a possible write-off of rents to cover up the potential fraud. We need to review their accounting process and procedures.
- **Probable cause.** There are two tenants stating the same fact: There were no deposits for Joint or Good, and there seems to be higher than normal write-offs of rent.
- **Action.** Further questioning is necessary. The approach you should take is a cautious one. While you want to treat Golf, Currency, and Sprint as people of interest, you need to use the 800-pound friendly gorilla approach when investigating them. You need to understand the level of socialization and relationships that exist among these parties. Who has a clear understanding of the organizational business process? Who is the potential ring leader? Who else may be involved (tenants)? Is the relationship limited to this transaction or is it ongoing? College brought the problem to light, is he credible? Look into his background. Do not assume that the victims are not involved. Rule them out only by using the proper due diligence. Examine where the greed exists that enables the fraudster to start the justification for the rationalization to commit fraud. Are there external influences? Look for lifestyle changes. Look for conflicts of interest. Know your answers before you ask critical questions by having a well-thought-out and planned approach.
- **Preparation.** Review the level of accounting prepared by outside accounts as well as the available accounting records, which appear to be computerized.
- **People of interest.** Peter College, even though he has no knowledge, since he has entrusted the responsibility to his property operations manager, Darin Golf. Johnny Civil was hired by the owner for the litigation, and the documentation is public record and available for review. Deb Joint and Charlie Good both paid cash, but can they produce the accounts showing where the cash came from? You need to establish if the paying of cash was normal and customary. Helen Sprint, on the surface, appears to be responsible for the accounting function, but does she touch the cash in the preparation of the deposit tickets? Jane Currency provided the receipt for the cash to the tenants, and she does touch the cash that is deposited. Golf received the funds directly; that transmission is the responsibility of Currency and Sprint. Golf also communicates with the tenants and Civil.
- **People-with-knowledge interview plan.** Joint, Good, Sprint, Currency, and Golf.
- **Documentary evidence.** Review the bank statements and reconciliations, cash deposit tickets, rent billing invoices, tenant receivable aging

(how long a tenant has not paid), and legal collection letter file with pending and settled collection matters

- **Formulate opinion.** The fraud appears to be a skimming of revenue and covering up of the skimming by writing off rents as being uncollectible. Golf has access to the funds and could cover up fraud by having control over the reporting function. To substantiate this claim, get proof from the tenants that the cash was paid. Golf's best defense is that he did not receive any funds. Review the accounting records and make sure the deposits were not made, and identify other situations in which the rents may have been written off. Make sure to rule out Currency and Sprint as potential accomplices. Observe any lifestyle or behavioral changes that Golf may display.

800-Pound Friendly Gorilla Suggestions for Yankee Property Management

With 320 rental units, Yankee Property Management is responsible for collecting a lot of rent revenue at this property. Who is watching the collection of these funds? With the owner removed from the process, the situation is rife for fraud if the wrong people are in the right positions with access to the organization's value. Yankee Property Management needs something to protect its interests. It needs to develop an 800-pound friendly gorilla to oversee cash transactions and the rest of the organization's operations. Here are some actions that could have reduced the risk of fraud:

- Set up a lockbox (such as a post office box) where the rents can be deposited into the bank directly.
- Monitor the responsibilities given to people with access to the value.
- Make sure the appropriate people are bonded so that any misappropriated funds are covered by insurance.
- Establish a greater segregation of duties. In this case, Golf, the property operations manager, can receive funds and also determine whether the rents are written off. College's signature should be required before allowing any write-offs on the accounting records.
- Have Golf or any collector of rents be the person issuing signed rent receipts.
- Establish one person (and a designated third party in case that person is out or on vacation) to receive funds and make deposits. The person should make the deposit and record the transaction but not be allowed to reconcile the tenant receivable accounts or the bank reconciliations.

■ Have a third party (an accountant or auditor) send confirmations to the tenants to verify unpaid balances and to the attorney to verify all collection matters that were open and closed during the accounting period.

A Simple Picture

Where does the greed exist in Exhibit 7.9?

Frauds involving cash can be very difficult to catch; they often require you to catch the perpetrators in the act. Make sure you are careful with the trust you bestow on the people in your organization's process. No matter how small the inappropriate behavior is, the proper action is necessary in order to detect, deter, and prevent fraud.

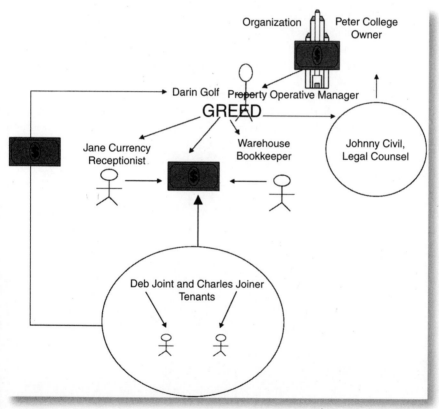

EXHIBIT 7.9 Yankee Property Management Company Drawing

This simple picture shows that Darin Golf is at the center of greed and his and others' access to the organizational value (cash). Who in your organization have you put in Darin Golf–type positions? This simple drawing follows the money and leads you to the fraud risk.

NOTES

1. Jim McElhatton, "Feds Use Video Surveillance to Catch Fraud for Workers' Comp," *Washington Post*, December 7, 2011, http://www.washingtontimes .com/news/2011/dec/7/feds-use-video-surveillance-to-catch-fraud-for-wor/?page=all.
2. Leonard G. Weld, Peter M. Bergevin, and Lorraine Magrath, "Anatomy of a Financial Fraud," *CPA Journal*, October 4, 2004, http://www.nysscpa.org/cpa-journal/2004/1004/essentials/p44.htm
3. Craig Schneider, "Did Auditor, Regulators Ignore HealthSouth Warning?" CFO.com, May 23, 2003, http://www.cfo.com/article.cfm/3009398?f=related Did Auditor, Regulators Ignore HealthSouth Warning?
4. Walter Pavlo Jr. and Neil Weinberg, *Stolen without a Gun: Confessions from Inside History's Biggest Accounting Fraud—the Collapse of MCI WorldCom* (Etikka Books, September 1, 2007).
5. Neil Weinberg, "Ring of Thieves," *Forbes*, June 10, 2002, http://www.forbes .com/forbes/2002/0610/064_print.html.
6. Internal Revenue Service, Topic 453: Bad Debt Deduction, http://www.irs.gov/ taxtopics/tc453.html.

CHAPTER EIGHT

Final Thoughts

Handy Tips and Quick Checklists for Reference

Fraud and falsehood only dread examination. Truth
invites it.

—Samuel Johnson

HAVE CHOSEN TO CLOSE THIS book with a handy reference guide that can aid you in your efforts to detect, deter, and prevent fraud. Keep in mind that nothing presented here is exhaustive, since fraud is a complex and ever-changing field. Still, the following resources should prove useful to you and help you as you become a better fraud detector.

POP: FINDING THE NEXT POTENTIAL FRAUD KERNEL IN YOUR ORGANIZATION

People have perspectives. Are the expectations and **perspectives** of the potential fraudster aligned with your organizations? People are classified within an organization by occupation (title). Is the potential fraudster in the right **occupation** to commit fraud? People get put in positions of trust based on occupation and title. Does the fraudster's **position** in an organization give him or her the ability to commit fraud?

From the CEO down to the mail room clerk, there are people who have the perspective, occupation, and position (POP) to commit fraud (see Exhibit 8.1).

People at the top are certainly in a position to commit fraud. Organizations are expected to deliver targeted earnings numbers, which of course puts a lot of pressure on a CEO, whether or not the expectations are attainable. This gives the CEO a perspective from which to commit fraud. A CEO by nature has the

EXHIBIT 8.1 Perspective, Occupation, and Position (POP)

Copyright © 2012 James Lee

occupation to commit fraud and is well positioned (being in a power position) to manipulate the earnings to meet the expectations.

But even people who are not part of an organization can commit fraud within it. Imagine that your organization uses a third-party cleaning service (occupation). The employees of this cleaning service are normally in your building when everyone has gone. They have the opportunity to look at files and documents that are not locked up. They take out your garbage and can find discarded unshredded files and obtain confidential information. All of these things create the opportunities to begin the fraudster development of the perspective needed to commit fraud. Even though they are outside your organization, they have access to your organizational value (the position) and have the opportunity to commit fraud.

A cursory application of principles (rules), models, checklists, or computer-generated analyses—without consideration of the limitations, assumptions, and conditions associated with them—often creates a false sense that fraud has been eliminated. However, one must not assume that fraud deterrents will stop all fraud. It is important to always remain proactive and focus on understanding the people inside and outside your organization's perspectives, occupations, and positions so you can see who has access to organizational value. If you pay attention to your people's POP, you can avoid fraud.

QUICK REFERENCES ON THE FUNDAMENTALS OF FRAUD

Exhibit 8.2 offers a broad overview of potential enablers, detractors, and areas of deflection in your organization. As you develop an understanding of these categories, you will be able to add to them, since each one will vary with different facts and circumstances.

Who are the enablers and detractors in your organization? Where are the areas of deflection in your organization?

Exhibit 8.3 offers a simple reference guide that defines some fundamental fraud requirements from the perspective of fraud management, the internal audit, and forensic accounting. It shows the different approaches each discipline takes in regard to fraud.

Exhibit 8.4 offers an accessible reference guide to aspects of fraud. It is by no means exhaustive.

Exhibit 8.5 lists three things that need to be considered in order to detect, deter, and prevent fraud.

EXHIBIT 8.2 Enablers, Detractors, and Deflectors

EXHIBIT 8.3 Fraud Approaches

	Fundamental Fraud Requirements by Discipline		
Description	Fraud Management	Internal Audit	Forensic Accounting
Primary Focus	Prevent and detect fraud	Validate and improve processes	Investigate and identify accounting entries
Usable in Litigations	Yes	No	Yes
Timing	Ongoing	Incremental	As needed
Monitor Operating Results	Consider	Yes	Consider
Verify Financial Records	Yes	Yes	Yes
Evaluate Internal Controls	Yes	Yes	No
Determine Efficiency	No	Yes	No
Determine Effectiveness	Yes	Yes	No
Detect Fraud	Yes	Yes	Yes
Deter Fraud	Yes	No	No
Scope	Enterprise	As directed	Well defined
Population Size	All	Sample	All
Top-Shelf Benefits	Real-time; flexible	Efficiencies and effectiveness	Highly analytical
Draw Conclusion	Yes	No	Yes
Process Control Validation	Yes	Yes	No
Industry Measurement Standard	None (but there are generally recognized practices)	Existing but not required	Legal standard
Limitations	A posteriori fraud	Unknown elements	Excessive or underreported information
Motivation	Yes	No	Yes

Exhibit 8.6 shows a National Business Ethics (NBE) survey indicating various misconduct observed by employees in organizations.

Exhibit 8.7 shows an NBE survey indicating various misconduct reported by employees in organizations. Compare these findings with those in Exhibit 8.6. (The findings in Exhibit 8.7 are the percentages of the observations in Exhibit in 8.6. For example, in Exhibit 8.6, in 2011, 12 percent observed someone falsifying time reports or hours works. In Exhibit 8.7, for the same line item, 61 percent of those who observed the falsifying reported it.)

EXHIBIT 8.4 Aspects of Fraud

Method of Financial Statement Fraud	Motivations
Inflating revenue	To influence stock prices
False or forged sales	To meet external forecasts
Recognition of incomplete sales	To increase value of firm by inflating stock prices
Misclassifying sales	To make new strategy succeed
Early recognition of rebates from suppliers	Loyalty to the organization
Deleting expenses from the books	Personal gain
Creating secret reserves through restructuring charges	Success of initial public offering
Incorrect valuation of stock	
Underproviding for depreciation	
Who Discovers Fraud?	**Potential Outcomes**
Tips	**Perpetrators**
New management	Prosecuted by the SEC/SFO
Existing management	Case investigated by SEC/SFO
Public interest leads to internal fraud	Perpetrators receive prison sentences
investigations	Company disciplines staff members involved
Auditors	Perpetrators receive monetary penalties
Failed rights issue	**Company**
SEC notice discrepancy between press release and filed accounts	New management employed as a result of fraud
	Company taken over as a direct result of the fraud
	Company bankrupt as a result of to fraud
	Company no longer in existence

Method of Financial Statement Fraud	Motivations
Organizational Factors	Company closed but re-formed under new name
Conflicts of Interest	**Auditors**
Weak internal control	Auditors/company for concealing fraud
Culture of meeting targets	Auditors are held responsible for the fraud and fined
Too much power held by one person	**Shareholders**
Weak audit committee	Sue company, auditors, and perpetrators
Weak board of directors	for loss of investment

GAAP VERSUS FAGAAPA: A SUMMARY

I have found that when asked, most people in the accounting industry cannot recite the generally accepted accounting principles. It is therefore not likely that other people in the organizational process will be able to, either. Understanding and applying these core principles is critical when proactively addressing fraud, since maintaining them will help to detect, deter, and prevent fraud.

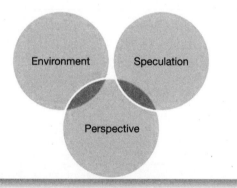

EXHIBIT 8.5 The Three Rings of the Fraudster

1. **Environment.** Maintain an organizational environment that creates the proper ethical and moral spirit inside and outside your organization.
2. **Speculation.** Manage the speculations that create organizational value and ensure that they are realistic and attainable.
3. **Perspective.** Understand the perspectives of the people inside and outside the organization who have access to its value by having open, effective, and transparent communication.

EXHIBIT 8.6 NBE Survey: Misconduct Observed

Types of Misconduct Observed by Employees						
Behavior	2000	2003	2005	2007	2009	2011
Observed misconduct overall	51%	45%	52%	55%	49%	45%
Misuse of company time	n/a	n/a	n/a	n/a	n/a	33%
Abusive behavior	24%	22%	20%	21%	22%	21%
Lying to employees	n/a	n/a	n/a	20%	19%	20%
Violation of company Internet use policies	n/a	n/a	n/a	n/a	n/a	16%
Discrimination	16%	14%	12%	13%	14%	15%
Conflicts of interest	n/a	n/a	18%	23%	16%	15%
Inappropriate social networking	n/a	n/a	n/a	n/a	n/a	14%
Health or safety violations	n/a	n/a	17%	15%	11%	13%
Lying to outside stakeholders	n/a	n/a	n/a	15%	12%	12%
Stealing	13%	13%	12%	11%	9%	12%
Falsifying time reports or hours worked	20%	22%	16%	17%	n/a	12%
Employee benefit violations	n/a	n/a	n/a	n/a	11%	12%
Sexual harassment	13%	14%	10%	10%	7%	11%
Employee privacy breach	n/a	n/a	n/a	n/a	10%	11%
Substance abuse	n/a	n/a	n/a	n/a	7%	11%
Poor product quality	n/a	n/a	10%	10%	9%	10%
Improper hiring practice	n/a	n/a	n/a	10%	10%	10%
Misuse of company's confidential information	n/a	n/a	6%	6%	6%	7%
Environmental violations	11%	n/a	n/a	7%	4%	7%
Customer privacy breach	n/a	n/a	n/a	n/a	6%	7%
Improper contracts	n/a	n/a	n/a	n/a	3%	6%
Contract violations	n/a	n/a	n/a	n/a	3%	6%
Accepting kickbacks or bribes	n/a	n/a	n/a	n/a	4%	5%
Offering potential clients bribes or improper payments	n/a	n/a	n/a	n/a	n/a	5%
Misuse of competitors' information	n/a	n/a	5%	4%	2%	5%
Misrepresentating financial records	n/a	6%	4%	5%	4%	5%
Falsifying expense reports	n/a	n/a	n/a	n/a	n/a	5%
Software piracy	n/a	n/a	n/a	n/a	n/a	5%
Offering public officials bribes or improper payments	n/a	n/a	n/a	n/a	n/a	4%
Anticompetitive practices	n/a	n/a	n/a	n/a	2%	6%
Insider trading	n/a	n/a	n/a	n/a	1%	4%
Illegal political comtributions	n/a	n/a	n/a	n/a	1%	4%

Source: 2011 National Business Ethics Survey (Ethical Resource Center)

EXHIBIT 8.7 NBE Survey: Misconduct Reported

Likely Employee Reporting Rates for Specific Misconduct, 2011	
Reported stealing or theft	69%
Reported offering improper payments or bribes to public officials	68%
Reported improper use of competitors' inside information	66%
Reported falsifying expense reports	66%
Reported trading securities based on inside information	65%
Reported making improper political contributions to officials	65%
Reported delivery of goods or services that fail to meet specifications	63%
Reported abusive behavior or behavior that creates a hostile work environment	62%
Reported falsifying and/or manipulating financial reporting information	62%
Reported entering contracts that lack proper terms, conditions, or approvals	62%
Reported offering improper payments or bribes to potential or exisiting clients	61%
Reported violation of environmental regulations	61%
Reported falsifying time reports or hours worked	61%
Reported violations of health or safety regulations	59%
Reported breaching customer or consumer privacy	59%
Reported abusing substances, such as drugs or alcohol, at work	58%
Reported violating contract terms with customer or suppliers	58%
Reported engaging in anticompetitive practices, e.g., market rigging	57%
Reported sexual harassment	55%
Reported behavior that places employee's interest over company's interests—a conflict or interest	55%
Reported misuse of company's confidential information	54%
Reported violating employee wage, overtime, or benefit rules	54%
Reported accepting inappropriate gifts or kickbacks from suppliers or vendors	52%
Reported software piracy	52%
Reported combined inappropriate gifts, kickbacks from suppliers or vendors, improper payments, bribes to public officials, or improper payments to potential or existing clients	51%
Reported discriminating against employees	50%
Reported breaching employee privacy	49%
Reported improper use of social networking	49%
Reported combined lying to customers, vendors, and the public or to employees	48%
Reported improper hiring practices	47%

(Continued)

EXHIBIT 8.7 *(Continued)*

Likely Employee Reporting Rates for Specific Misconduct, 2011	
Reported lying to customers, vendors, or the public	47%
Reported lying to employees	47%
Reported wasting, mismanaging, or abusing the company's resources	47%
Reported violating company policies related to Internet use	43%
Reported conducting personal business on company time	34%

Source: 2011 National Business Ethics Survey (Ethical Resource Center)

Chapter 2 listed the FAGAAPA as it correlates to GAAP. I am summarizing those principles again here; refer to Chapter 2 for a more in-depth analysis. By using these assumptions, you and your organization will be better poised to detect, deter, and prevent fraud.

- **Assumption 1:** Reliance on people principle (FAGAAPA) versus economic entity assumption (GAAP)

  Business transactions are to be kept separate from the business owner's personal transactions. Individual business-entity transactions are to be kept separate from one another as well.

- **Assumption 2:** Show me the money principle (FAGAAPA) versus monetary unit assumption (GAAP)

  Economic activity is measured in U.S. dollars.

- **Assumption 3:** Whatever time works for you principle (FAGAAPA) versus time period assumption (GAAP)

  Financial positions and activities, even the most difficult and ongoing business activities, can be reported in relatively short periods (e.g., monthly, quarterly, semiannually, and annually).

- **Assumption 4:** Unfair value principle (FAGAAPA) versus historical cost principle (GAAP)

  Goods and services are to be recorded at their original or historical cost.

- **Assumption 5**: Leap of good faith principle (FAGAAPA) versus full disclosure principle (GAAP)

  Information that could affect the decisions of an investor, a lender, or another user of the financial statement, based on the presented financial statement, should be disclosed in the notes or other supplemental information with that financial document.

- **Assumption 6:** Going under for sure (FAGAAPA) versus going concern principle (GAAP)

  An organization will continue to function without the threat of liquidation for the foreseeable future, usually for at least 12 months or the normal organizational operating cycle.
- **Assumption 7:** Matching game principle (FAGAAPA) versus matching principle (GAAP)

  Companies are required to use the accrual method of accounting. Expenses are matched with revenues in the period in which they are earned or incurred, regardless of whether cash has been exchanged.
- **Assumption 8:** Whatever I need principle (FAGAAPA) versus revenue recognition principle (GAAP)

  This is the accrual basis of accounting, which states that revenues are recognized when they are earned (i.e., when a product has been sold or a service has been performed, regardless of when the money is actually received); the realized or realizable expenses are recorded when incurred (when the goods or services are received) whether or not they were actually paid.
- **Assumption 9:** Tone at the top principle (FAGAAPA) versus materiality principle (GAAP)

  This is the magnitude of an omission or misstatement of accounting information that, in light of the surrounding circumstances, makes it probable that the judgment of a reasonable person relying on the information would have been changed or influenced by the omission or misstatement.
- **Assumption 10:** Write down, write off, rip off principle (FAGAAPA) versus conservatism principle (GAAP)

  This directs companies to choose an alternative that will result in less net income and/or a lower asset amount. The accountant is charged with "breaking a tie" if a regulation does not direct an accountant to be conservative.

Remember each of these assumptions when learning about fraud and have the 800-pound friendly gorillas apply them to deter, detect, and prevent fraud.

 ## FIVE CATEGORIES OF FRAUD

These assumptions can be applied to the following five categories of fraud:

1. **Misstatement of revenue:** Principles and assumptions 1, 2, 3, 5, 7, 8, 9, and 10 are violated.

2. **Misstatement of expenses:** Principles and assumptions 1, 2, 3, 4, 5, 7, 9, and 10 are violated.
3. **Misstatement of assets:** Principles and assumptions 1, 2, 3, 4, 5, 7, 8, 9, and 10 are violated.
4. **Inadequate disclosure:** All of the principles and assumptions are violated.
5. **Misappropriation of assets:** All of the principle and assumptions are violated.

Five Categories of Fraud	FAGAAPA Assumptions									
	1	2	3	4	5	6	7	8	9	10
Misstatement of revenue	✓	✓	✓		✓		✓	✓	✓	✓
Misstatement of expense	✓	✓	✓	✓	✓		✓		✓	✓
Misstatement of assets	✓	✓	✓	✓	✓		✓	✓	✓	✓
Inadequate disclosure	✓	✓	✓	✓	✓	✓	✓	✓	✓	✓
Misappropriation of assets	✓	✓	✓	✓	✓	✓	✓	✓	✓	✓

Misstatement of Revenues

Revenue manipulation is one of the most common schemes employed by fraudsters when they commit financial statement fraud. In this scheme, a fraudster manipulates the different types of revenue. Clearly identifying the different types of revenue that exist in an organizational process can help you to identify the potential risk of revenue misstatement.

Here are some examples of the types of revenue that can be manipulated (which may or may not be applicable to your organization):

- Product sales revenue (e.g., sales of software, byproducts, and scrap)
- Service revenue (e.g., service contract revenue)
- Long-term contract revenue (e.g., construction projects and government contracts)
- Licensing revenue (e.g., licenses for software, intellectual property, and merchandise)
- Internet portal fees or click revenue
- Royalties (e.g., oil, gas, and mineral royalties; patent royalties)
- Rental and lease income
- Trading revenue (e.g., revenue from trading commodities and financial instruments)

- Fee income (e.g., fees for retail shelf, vendor exclusivity, club membership, and franchise)
- Commissions (e.g., sales agency commissions, which may be improperly inflated to show the full value of the agency transaction instead of just the commission fee)
- Rebates (e.g., for volume purchase, which should reduce the cost of purchases)
- Barter revenue (e.g., Internet advertising)

Advanced or Deferred Recording

Advanced or deferred recording by a fraudster can intentionally recognize revenue before it is allowed to be recognized or defer it to a later time than the principles allow. You need people in your organization with the knowledge or experience of the overall control environment, conditions, and circumstances of your organization's revenue streams to determine whether the following eight fraudulent actions could be committed by a fraudster:

1. **Recording revenue before all terms of sale are completed.** *Terms of sale* includes delivery, installation, debugging, extensive modifications, customer testing, and customer acceptance.
2. **Improper billing and holding transactions.** The customer is billed for the sale before the delivery of the goods, which are held by the seller, who is not complying with all of the requirements for recording the bill and holding the transactions as sales.
3. **Conditional sales, or right of return granted**. Transactions are recorded as sales even though they involve unresolved contingencies, or the terms of sale are amended by side agreements that give a customer the right to return the goods.
4. **Consignment sales.** The evidence indicates that the customer's obligation to pay for the product is contingent on resale to another (third) party.
5. **Improper matching of revenue streams**. Revenue streams are recognized without matching them with their associated costs or with the period to which they apply.
6. **Improper sales cutoff.** Sales that are made just before or after the period end are not recorded in the correct period.
7. **Improper use of the percentage-of-completion accounting method.** This accounting method for long-term contracts is intentionally manipulated to misstate revenue and profit.
8. **Shipments not requested by the customer.** Sales are improperly recorded for items that have not been ordered by the customer.

Fictitious Revenues

There are different ways that a fraudster can intentionally record fictitious revenues. You need people in your organization with the knowledge or experience of the overall control environment, conditions, and circumstances of your organization's revenue streams to determine whether the following fraudulent actions could be committed by a fraudster:

- Bogus sales (sales to fictitious customers or inflated or unauthorized sales to real customers)
- Non–arm's length transactions (sales to affiliates and undisclosed related parties)
- Misclassified gains (manipulation of gains between ordinary and extraordinary items)
- Unrecorded discounts and allowances
- Unrecorded sales returns

Misstatement of Expenses

There are different ways that fraudsters can intentionally understate or overstate liabilities and their related expenses. You need people in your organization with knowledge or experience of the overall control environment, conditions, and circumstances of your organization's expenses to determine whether the following fraudulent actions could be committed by a fraudster:

- Understating or overstating recorded liabilities and their related expenses.
- Intentionally failing to record some liabilities (including contingent liabilities that are required by accounting standards to be recorded) and their related expenses.
- Recording revenue instead of a liability for deferred or unearned revenue when payment has been received for goods or services that have not been provided by the seller or for payments received for customer deposits, client funds, advances, loans, or other nonrevenue cash flows.

Misstatement of Assets

In financial statement frauds, assets are usually overstated rather than understated. However, assets may be understated as part of a scheme to understate reported earnings (e.g., when earning targets have already been met, to reduce taxable income, or to boost earnings in future periods). You can overstate assets in three ways:

1. Overstating existing assets
2. Recording fictitious assets or assets not owned
3. Capitalizing items that should be listed as expenses

The fraudster often uses multiple schemes to overstate assets. Assets may be overstated by manipulating the processing of transactions within the accounting system or by creating unusual transactions, such as large journal entries that increase income and overstate net assets. Any account may be changed by such journal entries—they do not have to make sense.

Existing assets are the assets most often misstated initially, because financial statement frauds usually start out small. Frauds tend to grow quickly in size, making it difficult to conceal a large fraud among existing assets only. So large fictitious assets or assets not owned may be required to continue the cover-up.

Particular assets may be selected for misstatement because they are easier to conceal. The ease of concealing a misstatement is determined by the size of the asset, the complexity of the determination of the asset's value, the judgment involved in determining the asset's value, or the relative difficulty of auditing the asset.

Ways in Which Fraudsters Intentionally Misstate Assets

These are a few of the basic ways in which assets can be intentionally misstated by fraudsters:

- Manipulating the quantity of the asset.
- Manipulating the pricing of the asset.
- Manipulating allowances (e.g., bad debts or excess and obsolete inventory allowances).
- Manipulating or avoiding write-downs for permanent diminution in value.
- Improperly writing up assets to the claimed appraisal or market values.
- Recording real assets that are not owned by the company.
- Recording fictitious assets.
- Improperly capitalizing expense items (or expensing capital additions).

Common Schemes for Misstating Assets

There are several common schemes by which a fraudster can misstate assets. You need people in your organization with knowledge or experience of the overall control environment, conditions, and circumstances of your organization's assets to determine whether the following misstatement schemes could be committed by a fraudster:

Cash
- Manipulating bank reconciliations.
- Failing to disclose that cash balances are pledged as collateral for loans.
- Failing to disclose that cash balances are controlled by others.
- Creating fictitious cash balances.

Investments and Marketable Securities
- Manipulating the pricing of the asset.
- Manipulating or avoiding write-downs for permanent diminution in value.
- Improperly writing up assets to the claimed appraisal or market values.
- Recording real assets that are not owned by the company.
- Recording fictitious assets.

Accounts Receivable
- Recognizing revenue prematurely or late.
- Manipulating allowance for bad debts.
- Creating fictitious accounts receivables.

Inventory
- Manipulating allowances for excess and obsolete inventory.
- Manipulating write-downs to lower cost or market value.
- Manipulating physical inventory counts.
- Manipulating inventory pricing.
- Manipulating inventory compilation.
- Creating fictitious inventory.
- Manipulating costs capitalized into inventory.

Fixed Asset
- Improperly capitalizing expenses as fixed assets.
- Creating fictitious fixed assets.
- Improperly writing up fixed assets to the claimed appraisal or market values.

Loans or Notes Receivable
- Manipulating allowance for loan losses.
- Creating fictitious loans or notes receivables.

Patents (and Other Intellectual Property)
  Improperly writing up assets to the claimed appraisal or market values.
- Recording real assets that are not owned by the company.
- Recording fictitious assets.
- Improperly capitalizing expense items (or expensing capital items).

Oil, Gas, and Mineral Reserves
  Improperly writing up assets to the claimed appraisal or market values.
- Recording real assets that are not owned by the company.
- Recording fictitious assets.

Inadequate Disclosures

There are various areas where fraudsters can intentionally withhold or provide inadequate financial information to commit financial statement fraud. You need people in your organization with knowledge or experience of the overall control environment, conditions, and circumstances of your organization's disclosures to determine whether the following fraudulent actions could be committed by a fraudster:

- **Liabilities.** Failing to disclose commitments, contingent liabilities, loan covenants, loan defaults, and other key facts that may give rise to liabilities and affect a company's financial condition.
- **Significant events.** Failing to disclose significant events affecting a company, thus making financial statements misleading.
- **Related-party transactions.** Failing to disclose transactions between one party and a second party that is under the control or significant influence of the first party or of a common third party. Although not necessarily fraudulent, transactions with undisclosed related parties are likely to be fraudulent.
- **Legal and regulatory compliance violations.** Failing to disclose violations of laws and regulations that may have a significant adverse effect on a company's financial position or on its ability to continue to operate.

- **Significant changes in accounting policies and estimates.** Failing to disclose significant changes in accounting policies and estimates, which renders financial statements misleading.
- **False statements.** Making false or misleading statements, orally or in writing, that may mislead people about an organization's financial condition or prospects.

Misappropriation of Assets

Based on your knowledge or prior experience of the client's overall control environment, conditions, or circumstances, consider whether a fraudster could commit material embezzlement in your organization. In material embezzlement, a substantial amount of money (or another asset) is stolen and the theft is concealed by misstating the financial statements in a way that is material to the company as a whole. It is extremely rare for embezzlement to be material to a large public company.

WHY AUDITORS AND ACCOUNTANTS FAIL TO DETECT FRAUD

Auditors and accountants often fail to detect fraud for the following 10 reasons:

1. They are fooled by fraudsters.
2. They lack professional skepticism.
3. They are too trusting of an organization's employees, executives, and managers.
4. They do not pay attention to the red flags that may indicate fraud.
5. They do not know what fraud looks like.
6. They base the current numbers on past or other relevant information instead of actual documentary evidence.
7. They accept clients' explaining away the findings they have uncovered.
8. They accept explanations for fraud symptoms without verifying the facts.
9. They put too much emphasis on evidence obtained through inquiry rather than the documents needed as support.
10. Their only responsibility is to provide reasonable assurance, not 100 percent accuracy.

RED FLAGS FOR POTENTIAL FRAUD

Look for the following 16 red flags to detect, deter, and prevent fraud:

1. Fraudsters appear to have total control and do it all.
2. Fraudsters do not take vacations.
3. Fraudsters complain about others in the process (e.g., employees and vendors).
4. Fraudsters exhibit morale and attendance changes.
5. Fraudsters exhibit lifestyle, habit, and behavioral changes.
6. Fraudsters operate on a crisis basis.
7. Fraudsters cannot explain variances in numbers.
8. Fraudsters will have missing and altered documents.
9. Fraudsters will make duplicate payments or not maintain the original documentation.
10. Fraudsters will use management overrides.
11. Fraudsters will not reconcile.
12. Fraudsters will not fully investigate.
13. Fraudsters circumvent approval processes.
14. Fraudsters have inappropriate relationships with vendors and suppliers.
15. Fraudsters process transactions outside the normal organizational channels.
16. Fraudsters maintain adversarial attitudes toward control functions.

Exhibit 8.8 is a fraud scheme guide that offers a general overview of some of the fraud risks your organization may face.

USING THE ACCRUALS-TO-ASSETS RATIO

As organizations grow and the dynamics of financial reporting change, a useful tool for the fraud investigator is to analyze key ratios from year to year to identify unusual fluctuations and findings. I frequently use the accruals-to-assets ratio to identify excessive accruals. An accrual can sometimes inflate earnings without increasing an organization's cash. This ratio identifies increases or decreases in accruals and is a key tool for fraud detection.

The accruals-to-assets ratio is described by author Steven M. Bragg in this way:

EXHIBIT 8.8 Fraud Scheme Guide

The fraud schemes in this guide is meant to inform and assist in the consideration of fraud risk in your organization. This guide is neither comprehensive nor authoritative; there may be other fraud schemes not included in this guide to consider. Every fraud scheme listed here may not be applicable in all circumstances.

We believe that fraud is possible wherever people and anything of value meet.

GENERAL EMPLOYEE SCHEMES	
Skimming of Cash or Cash Larceny	• Diversion of funds intended for entity
	• Lapping of receivables
	• Theft of incoming checks
	• Theft of cash in registers
	• Theft from daily deposits
	• Check fraud (altering, forgery, & endorsements)
Purchasing Fraud	• Fictitious vendor
	• False invoicing
	• Overbilling
	• Personal use of company accounts
	• Product substitution
	• Rigged bidding (competitive bidding process)
Sales / Inventory	• Shorting receiving reports
	• Fraudulent write-offs of inventory to scrap
	• Theft with concealment (making inventory adjustment)
	• Fraudulent shipping documentation or orders
Payroll	• Ghost employees
	• Falsified hours worked or rate per hour
	• Fictitious expense reimbursements

BALANCE SHEET SCHEMES	
Cash	• Recording fictitious cash receipts to reduce fictitious accounts receivables associated with fictitious sales
Accounts Receivable	• Crediting and rebilling aged receivables to refresh the aging of accounts
	• Failing to establish appropriate reserves for bad debt and associated expenses
Inventory	• Overstating inventory quantities and unit costs
	• Failing to recognize obsolete inventory

Fixed Assets	• Depreciating fixed assets with unreasonable methods and assumptions
	• Recording assets when no title or ownership rights exist
	• Overstating the value of assets
Payables / Liabilities	• Failure to record known liabilities (accounts payable)
	• Failing to record contingent liabilities
	• Failing to record customer prepayments as a liability
INCOME STATEMENT SCHEMES	
Revenue	• Recognizing revenue from sales billed but not delivered
	• Booking revenue for goods on consignment
	• Recording fictitious revenue
	• Recognizing revenue when disputes or claims exist
	• Deferring revenue that should be recognized in the courrent period
Expenses	• Capitalizing expenses that have no future benefits
	• Recording journal entries to reduce expenses or cost of goods sold
	• Recording fictitious vendor discounts
	• Accelerating expenses

Calculate the change in working capital from a predetermined earlier reporting period. Then subtract from this amount the net change in cash and depreciation over the same period. Then divide the remainder by the change in total assets. There should be no excessive usage of accruals if the ratio results in the same figure over several periods, whereas it may indicate more aggressive accounting practices if the ratio increases over time. The formula is: (Change in working capital–Change in cash–Change in depreciation) / Change in total assets.[1]

The accruals-to assets ratio allows you to see if the proportion of accruals to assets varies over time. If this number indicates that the proportion is increasing, it can alert you to fraud, because fraudsters use accruals to create the necessary diversion to remain undetected. An increase in accruals is a red flag; it does not mean that there is definitely a fraud present, but further investigation is warranted. An accrual may be justifiable if an organization's size has increased. It is critical to support your conclusions with the proper evidences for a judge and jury to ultimately decide if fraud has occurred.

 ## A SIMPLE FRAUD RISK PLAN

This section contains a basic plan of action for detecting fraud in your organization. Here you can find a beginning foundation for your organization's fraud forces. Keep in mind that every organization is different and that circumstances often require different actions. Use this list as a guide, but also consider your organization and its specific circumstances in order to develop the most effective ways to detect, deter, and prevent fraud. Put the 800-pound friendly gorilla to work and improve controls by implementing continuous auditing and monitoring over your organizational process.

The basic plan of action consists of the following steps:

■ Always be strengthening your controls over the transaction authorization process. Use continuous unannounced (unpredictable) auditing and monitoring tests to validate the effectiveness of the controls you have in place. An organization needs to use simple repetitive analysis by setting up the necessary algorithms to run against large volumes of data to identify the signs of potential fraud, such as abnormalities that occur over time. Using computers can drastically improve the overall cost benefit, efficiency, consistency, and quality of your fraud detection risk plan. Running the created algorithms against data so you get periodic notification when an anomaly occurs in the data helps you to create the impression that someone is monitoring the organization's process. This is critical in deterring, detecting, and preventing fraud. This not only assists in mitigating fraud but also provides the users of the financial communication with more accurate and reliable findings, since not all abnormalities are fraud related. The findings often lead to greater efficiencies in the organizational process, since you are working with more accurate information.

The 800-pound friendly gorilla can run the created algorithms every night by going through all of those transactions to develop timely notifications of trends, patterns, and exceptions to the reporting that can be provided to management. For example, this algorithm could run specific tests against all employee expense transactions as they occur to ensure they are in accordance with controls and in line with the history.

- Make sure the 800-pound friendly gorilla has communicated the monitoring activities that are in place throughout the organization.
- Communicate the fraud prevention program throughout the organization. An inch-by-inch fraud prevention communication is equal to inch-by-inch fraud detection. Everyone inside and outside an organization should know that there are systems in place that will alert someone to potential fraud or a breach of controls. You accomplish this by communicating that every transaction run through your systems is monitored and that you have more significant, preventative approaches to fraud.

The sooner you identify the issue and document it, the better the outcome will be. An organization needs to have the necessary reports with recommendations on how to enhance the existing controls or make the necessary changes to reduce the risk of fraud. Remember the example of the mosquito from earlier in this book, and do not take even the smallest potential fraud lightly.

Perform full tests of transactional data to see if there is the potential for fraud around the value created in the organization.

Fraudulent transactions do not occur randomly; therefore, complete testing should be performed. While some fraudulent transactions may fall within the boundaries of sample type testing, others may not. Many smaller inconsistencies may be missed and add up over time, resulting in very large instances of fraud, if left unattended.

Make sure weaknesses in the controls are fixed immediately.

- Identify overlapping responsibilities and, when necessary, increase the segregation of duties. Make sure the people in your organization cannot initiate, approve, and also receive the goods from transactions.
- Continually expand the fraud risk plan and enhance it over time to account for changes in the organization.

Update databases by staying on top of trends in fraud. Make sure your profiles of key people are updated annually. Know the most common fraud schemes and those that pose the greatest risks to your organizational process. Keep the investigations of the 800-pound friendly gorilla on the move and unpredictable. Use analytics (algorithms) to find out where controls are not working. Maintain trusted people who oversee the findings and safeguard the organizational value. Investigate suspicious patterns and watch for the red flags of fraud that you have learned or that emerge from the fraud detection tests and continuous auditing and monitoring you have put in place.

■ Compile and maintain a database of the types of fraud that have occurred in the past in your or another organization and see whether your organization is still exposed to these types of fraud risks. In doing this evaluation, you need to look at the people in your organization from top to bottom and see whether your organization's value is exposed—and if so, where. Emphasize the areas that have the potential to cause the greatest reduction in organizational value.

While fraud can exist in an organization in many different ways, my experience has led me to determine four main areas of concern, which are listed in Exhibit 8.9.

The simple receipt of money can expose an organization to fraud risk. Organizations no longer just receive cash or checks; they also receive wire transfers, credit memos from banks, services and goods (bartering), letters of credit, and so on. Anywhere there is a receipt of money, the organization's value is exposed, and 800-pound friendly gorillas should be in position.

Another fraud risk to an organization is the receipt of goods and services. Did the organization receive the goods? Was the quality of the goods received sufficient? Were there services performed? Where goods and services came from is another place to position 800-pound friendly gorillas.

Payroll is yet another area that could expose an organization to fraud risks. Are people working the time they are paid for? Is the person who is getting paid a real employee or a fictitious one (a person who is added to the payroll system but does not actually work for the organization)? Are there proper controls on

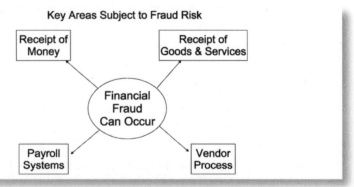

EXHIBIT 8.9 Key Areas Subject to Fraud Risk

items such as employee expense reimbursement, workers' compensation, disability, and the like? Payroll is an area in which a lot of people have control over the value, and their actions can access and take away organizational value. Make sure you have well-positioned 800-pound friendly gorillas in this area to detect any wrongdoing.

Finally, the vendor process is another significant fraud risk to an organization. Did the organization pay the correct amount for goods received or services rendered? Are there conflicts of interest? Did the organization receive what it paid for? This area requires 800-pound friendly gorillas well positioned both inside and outside the organization because it is vulnerable to conflicts of interest.

CONCLUSION

By now, my hope is that you have recognized that the 800-pound friendly gorilla is not intended to be just one person in your organization. It is a spirit that is created by involving all the people in the organization by setting the proper ethical tone. While it is wishful thinking that everyone will be ethical, it should be the mission of your organization to get as close to 100 percent as it can. This is a work in progress and does not happen overnight.

The 800-pound friendly gorillas treat people who commit fraud the same way as people who do not. This is to gain the proper perspective when investigating fraud. People will not speak and open up to an aggressive 800-pound gorilla. The 800-pound friendly gorilla takes a more diplomatic approach and wants to understand why and what causes someone to commit fraud.

The cost of fraud to an organization goes well beyond dollars and cents. Fraud ruins reputations, lives, and even the most successful organizations. Fraud is a significant business risk to an organization and requires your immediate attention. Having a well-designed fraud detection system, based on the transactional data analysis of operational systems, can significantly reduce the chance of fraud occurring within an organization. However, nothing replaces a correct ethical spirit from top to bottom in an organization. Here are some final things to consider when developing your organization's fraud prevention plan:

- Ratings can be useful, but what good is a rating if it is falsified or inaccurate? Ratings can be manipulated by fraudsters. This is why using only one component to judge something is a bad idea.

- Organizations need to consider perception. Throughout the book we have discussed the importance of outrage and a willingness to fight fraud. The way that people look at fraud and the organization they work for affects the organization's susceptibility to fraud. If the people believe in their organization and want to combat fraud, that is a big step toward preventing fraud. If the people do not have any interest in the well-being of their organization, it makes the organization more conducive to fraud.

    An article on the increasing problem of corporate corruption says that currently, "nearly three in four Americans believe that corruption has increased over the last three years. We should be alarmed that corporate wrongdoing has come to be seen as such a routine occurrence."[2]

    This applies to fraud in an organization. If employees think of fraud as something that is inevitable or commonplace, this is the wrong attitude. Employees should be aware of or even expect fraud, but organizations should establish a zero-tolerance policy. We have discussed how looking the other way or assuming that fraud will not happen can be problematic. An attitude of "it will happen anyway" is likely to perpetuate apathy and prevent the necessary outrage and motivation needed to combat fraud.

- Organizations need to consider their ethics and work to create an environment in which people are encouraged to do the right thing. One of the best fraud deterrents is having the right people on staff—people an organization can trust.

- Organizations need to consider trust. The aforementioned article also states that "capitalism cannot function without trust."[3] If an organization cannot trust its employees, then it cannot function effectively. There should be trust in an organization, but organizations also need to think about the oversight, communication, and power assigned to specific responsibilities.

    Even a trustworthy staff and environment needs oversight. People need to be monitored by the 800-pound friendly gorilla, and that gorilla needs to establish an open and communicative environment. If there is a lack of communication in an organization or the employees do not feel they have a voice or that they matter, this is likely to make it more difficult for organizations to establish trust and, in turn, prevent fraud.

    Finally, even a trustworthy and communicative environment needs a limit on power. No one in an organization should be given too much power. As Lord Acton said, "Absolute power corrupts absolutely."

Begin your 800-pound friendly gorilla spirited journey so that you can detect, deter, and prevent fraud within your organization.

. . .

Thanks for taking this journey through the topic of fraud. Remember, fraud is a people problem first and foremost. Know your people, follow the cash, create an ethical tone from the top to the bottom of your organization, and monitor your organizational processes, including accounting and checks and balances, and you will be successful at detecting, deterring, and preventing fraud.

 ## NOTES

1. Steven M. Bragg, *Business Ratios and Formulas* (Hoboken, NJ: John Wiley & Sons, 2006), p. 104.
2. Eduardo Porter, "The Spreading Scourge of Corporate Corruption," *New York Times*, July 10, 2012, http://www.nytimes.com/2012/07/11/business/economy/the-spreading-scourge-of-corporate-corruption.html.
3. Ibid.

Afterword

A S OF THE FINAL WRITING of this book, Superstorm Sandy hit the East Coast and caused severe damage. In addition to the unprecedented damage, the storm also brought the potential for massive fraud. Hopefully, people affected by Superstorm Sandy have learned from past frauds associated with Hurricane Katrina and other similar catastrophic events to safeguard themselves from potential fraudsters. Here are some fraud examples and indicators (motivations) that may be present during the aftermath of a natural disaster:

- People are desperate. This makes them vulnerable due to the immediate needs (for example, shelter, food, clothing) created by the natural disaster.
- The economy is already distressed (no jobs). High unemployment and a sluggish economy create a ripe environment for scams.
- People are very charitable. Avoid bogus charitable websites, and do not give cash gifts (use credit cards or checks instead). Watch out for phony or fictitious charities that have similar names to well-established and well-known charities. Make sure the funds you contribute are going directly to those affected.
- There is lots of value (money) available in the form of federal aid and insurance claims. Government agencies, such as FEMA, and insurance companies are subject to potential false claims.
- Contractor fraud can include overstated pricing by dishonest repairmen. Watch for contractors who take your money and then vanish without completing the work you hired them for. Make sure any contractor you use is licensed and bonded.
- Damaged vehicles and boats can lead to towing/hauling fraud when salvage companies falsely disclose that vehicles and boats were damaged in a natural disaster. Someone needs to track vehicle and boat identification numbers and inspect physical damage.

- Vendor fraud occurs due to claims of shortages (such as gas) and the overwhelming demand that drives prices up. Look for price gouging.
- Looting and theft are common.
- Beware of postdisaster scams.

What other potential frauds can you think of that give these unscrupulous people access to value? Be proactive and create an awareness of the types of fraud that can be present during a natural disaster. Let's hope that the people at the top set the proper ethical tone and place 800-pound friendly gorillas in key positions in their organizations to ensure that those who have been affected by natural disasters have their self-interests preserved and not the self-interests of greedy individuals who are trying to take advantage of vulnerable people.

My heart and prayers go out to all of those affected by Superstorm Sandy. We, the people of the United States, will continue to rise from tragic events. It's what we do!

Bibliography

Ariely, Dan. *Predictably Irrational: The Hidden Forces That Shape Our Decisions.* New York: HarperCollins, 2008.

————. *The Upside of Irrationality: The Unexpected Benefits of Defying Logic at Work and at Home.* New York: HarperCollins, 2010.

Capaldi, Nicholas, and Miles Smit. *The Art of Deception: An Introduction to Critical Thinking.* Amherst, MA: Prometheus Books, 2007.

Cardozza, Dick. "Spotting Those Elusive Liars." *Fraud Magazine* 27, no. 3 (2012), http://www.fraud-magazine.com/article.aspx?id=4294972760.

Cohan, William D. *House of Cards: A Tale of Hubris and Wretched Excess on Wall Street.* New York: Anchor Books, 2010.

Cohen, Jeffrey A. *Intangible Assets: Valuation and Economic Benefit.* Hoboken, NJ: John Wiley & Sons, 2005.

Covey, Stephen M. R., and Rebecca R. Merrill. *The Speed of Trust: The One Thing That Changes Everything.* New York: Free Press, 2008.

Crumbley, D. Larry, Lester E. Heitger, and G. Stevenson Smith. *Forensic and Investigative Accounting,* 5th ed. Chicago: CCH, 2011.

Downing, Douglas, and Jeffrey Clark. *Business Statistics.* Hauppauge, NY: Barron's, 2005.

Einstein, Albert, and Sonja Bargmann. *Ideas and Opinions.* New York: Crown Publishers, 1982.

"Embracing Ethics and Morality." *The CPA Journal* 82, no. 1 (2012): 16–21.

"Enron 10 Years Later." *The CPA Journal* 82, no. 5 (2012): 16–25.

Fishman, Jay E., Shannon P. Pratt, and William J. Morrison. *Standards of Value: Theory and Applications.* Hoboken, NJ: John Wiley & Sons, 2007.

Godin, Seth. *Free Prize Inside: How to Make a Purple Cow.* New York: Penguin, 2007.

Green, Stuart P. *Lying, Cheating, and Stealing: A Moral Theory of White-Collar Crime.* New York: Oxford University Press, 2006.

Hawkins, David R. *Power vs. Force: The Hidden Determinants of Human Behavior.* Carlsbad, CA: Hay House, Inc., 1995.

Hitchner, James R. *Financial Valuation: Applications and Models.* Hoboken, NJ: John Wiley & Sons, 2006.

Jackson, Cecil W. *Business Fairy Tales: Grim Realities of Fictitious Financial Reporting.* Mason, OH: Thomson, 2006.

Keirsey, David. *Please Understand Me II: Temperament, Character, Intelligence.* Del Mar, CA: Prometheus Nemesis Books, 1998.

Kohn, Mark. *How They Stash the Cash.* San Clemente, CA: Sourced Media Books, 2012.

McCann, David. "Power from the People." *CFO Journal* 27, no. 9 (2011), http://www.cfo.com/article.cfm/14604427.

Mulford, Charles W., and Eugene E. Comiskey. *The Financial Numbers Game: Detecting Creative Accounting Practices.* Hoboken, NJ: John Wiley & Sons, 2002.

Osterwalder, Alexander, and Yves Pigneur. *Business Model Generation: A Handbook for Visionaries, Game Changers, and Challengers.* Hoboken, NJ: John Wiley & Sons, 2010.

Owen, David. *The Little Book of Frauds: From Enron to Madoff, 50 Economic Scandals That Shocked the World.* London: Elwin Street, 2010.

Pope, Thomas R., Kenneth E. Anderson, and John L. Kramer. *Prentice Hall's Federal Taxation 2011.* Upper Saddle River, NJ: Prentice Hall, 2011.

Pratt, Shannon P. *The Market Approach to Valuing Businesses.* Hoboken, NJ: John Wiley & Sons, 2005.

Pratt, Shannon P., and Roger J. Grabowski. *Cost of Capital: Applications and Examples.* Hoboken, NJ: John Wiley & Sons, 2008.

Pratt, Shannon P., and Alina V. Niculita. *Valuing a Business: The Analysis and Appraisal of Closely Held Companies.* New York: McGraw-Hill, 2008.

Pratt, Shannon P., Robert F. Reilly, and Robert P. Schweihs. *Valuing Small Businesses & Professional Practices.* New York: McGraw-Hill, n.d.

Sachs, Jeffrey D. *The Price of Civilization: Reawakening American Virtue and Properity.* New York: Random House, 2011.

Schilit, Howard M., and Jeremy Perler. *Financial Shenanigans: How to Detect Accounting Gimmicks & Fraud in Financial Reports.* New York: McGraw-Hill, 2010.

Sharma, Ruby, Michael H. Sherrod, Richard Corgel, and Steven J. Kuzma. *The Guide to Investigating Business Fraud.* Durham, NC: American Institute of Certified Public Accountants, 2009.

Silverthorne, Sandy, and John Warner. *Mind-Boggling One-Minute Mysteries and Brain Teasers*. Eugene, OR: Harvest House, 2010.

Singleton, Tommie W., and Aaron J. Singleton. *Fraud Auditing and Forensic Accounting*. Hoboken, NJ: John Wiley & Sons, 2010.

Smith, Stanley, Tom Bullimore, Derrick Niederman, Hy Conrad, and Tatjana Mai-Wyss. *Classic Whodunits*. New York: Sterling, 2008.

"Smooth Operation." *Journal of Accountancy* 213, no. 3 (2012).

Spiceland, J. David, James F. Sepe, and Mark W. Nelson. *Intermediate Accounting*. 2 vols. New York: McGraw-Hill/Irwin, 2009.

Sun Tzu. *The Illustrated Art of War*. Boston: Shambhala, 1988.

Trugman, Gary R. *Essentials of Valuing a Closely Held Business*. New York: Linda Prentice Cohen, 2009.

2010 Ibbotson Stocks, Bonds, Bills, and Inflation Valuation Yearbook. Chicago: Morningstar, 2010.

Weber, Kenneth. *Five-Minute Mysteries 37 Challenging Cases of Murder and Mayhem for You to Solve*. Philadelphia, PA: Running Press Kids, n.d.

Wells, Joseph T. *Fraud Casebook: Lessons from the Bad Side of Business*. Hoboken, NJ: John Wiley & Sons, 2007.

Weygandt, Jerry J., Paul D. Kimmel, and Donald E. Kieso. *Accounting Principles*. 2 vols. Hoboken, NJ: John Wiley & Sons, 2009.

———. *Managerial Accounting: Tools for Business Decision Making*. Hoboken, NJ: John Wiley & Sons, 2010.

About the Author

JOSEPH R. PETRUCELLI IS THE founding partner of PP&D Accounting Services Inc., where he provides various types of forensic accounting, tax, and consulting services. Included in these services is testifying at trials as a qualified expert, which he has done for numerous cases. He also formed Fraud Forces, Inc., where he provides fraud training and prevention, detection, and investigative services for professionals. He is a licensed certified public accountant in the states of New York and New Jersey as well as a forensic certified public accountant, a certified valuation analyst, a certified financial forensic analyst, a public school accountant, and a certified fraud examiner. He is also certified in financial forensics.

Mr. Petrucelli held a New Jersey banking license and now holds a loan solicitor license in New York and New Jersey. He is a recognized Housing and Urban Development direct endorsed underwriter and was a New Jersey real estate commissioner. (Before serving on the Real Estate Commission, he held a New Jersey Realtor license.) He has also served as an appointed federal receiver for Judge Mary L. Cooper in New Jersey in federal court and for Superior Court Judge Maureen Sogluizzo in Hudson County, New Jersey.

Mr. Petrucelli has been an adjunct professor at the College of Staten Island since 2008. He has taught accounting and taxation courses and has served as an academic adviser. Recently, he assisted in developing a forensic accounting graduate class for the College of Staten Island. He was also part of the development team for the fraud risk management and detection certification curriculum for the Consultants Training Institute, a division of the National Association of Certified Valuation Analysts.

Mr. Petrucelli graduated from Kean College in Union, New Jersey, with a BS in Economics and a concentration in accounting. He is currently a member of the Money Laundering Task Force created by the New York State Society of CPAs. He has also served as a trustee on the Edison Chamber of Commerce.

Currently, Mr. Petrucelli is a member of the Edison Finance Committee in New Jersey, where he assists council members with the municipal budget. He presents and is developing continuing education and outreach courses for various organizations. He has worked with many nonprofits and other organizations. Joseph Menza, the mayor of Hillside, New Jersey, appointed Mr. Petrucelli as his special financial adviser. Mr. Petrucelli has also been appointed as the New Jersey State Fraternal Order of Police (FOP) labor council forensic accountant and has represented many FOPs and Police Benevolent Associations throughout the state of New Jersey as a testifying forensic accountant expert at the local, county, and state levels.

Mr. Petrucelli is an avid guitar player, a former Division III college soccer all-American, and the father of two. He has been happily married for more than 25 years. One of his favorite sayings is, "The more opportunities we explore, the more chances we have for success."

About the Website

TO MAINTAIN THE SPIRIT OF this book—keeping fraud awareness alive—my website, www.joepetrucelli.com, will have a specific secured area that will be made available to the purchasers of this book. The password for this area is 800BeFriendly.

This section of the website will include information that was not included in the book, detailed case studies that will continue to be developed, and a research database of articles and information on frauds that relate to the material found in this book.

The site will also maintain a fraud awareness hotline, so we can continue to educate people on what fraud looks like, continue to learn from past frauds, and prevent fraud in the future.

Index